AN UGLY WORD

AN UGLY WORD

RETHINKING RACE IN ITALY
AND THE UNITED STATES

Ann Morning and Marcello Maneri

Russell Sage Foundation   NEW YORK

LIBRARY OF CONGRESS CATALOGING-IN-PUBLICATION DATA
Names: Morning, Ann Juanita, 1968- author. | Maneri, Marcello, author.
Title: An ugly word : rethinking race in Italy and the United States / by Ann Morning and Marcello Maneri.
Other titles: Rethinking race in Italy and the United States
Description: New York, NY : Russell Sage Foundation, [2021] | Includes bibliographical references and index. | Summary: "Scholars as well as politicians have often assumed that there is a significant gap between the ways that Americans and Europeans think of race. In the U.S., the thinking goes, the notion of race is associated with physical characteristics, while in Western Europe it has disappeared and its legacy of racism targets cultural incompatibilities. We gather empirical evidence to test this assumption, interviewing young Italians and Americans broadly about what we call 'descent-based groups.' Sidestepping the usual language of 'ethnicity' and 'race,' which can be unnecessarily narrow, poorly defined, or simply offensive to some, we cast a wide net in asking our respondents to tell us how they perceive the distinctions between groups as diverse as Chinese, Muslims, whites, or Roma. In response to the claim that there is a significant gap between the ways that Americans and Europeans think of descent-based difference, a clear rebuttal emerges from our data. While ways of speaking about group difference vary considerably across the Atlantic, our interviews with young people in Italy and the United States show that underlying beliefs about it do not. To be sure, they are not identical, and there are many intriguing and meaningful distinctions to which we draw attention—for example, in the ways that race is understood to be 'constructed.' But the extensive overlap between American and Italian understandings of human difference cannot be ignored. Nor can they be usefully described as pursuing separate, biological versus cultural tracks. These findings lead us to propose a new approach for characterizing concepts of difference that takes into account their multiple dimensions. Specifically, we break down such concepts into six key components: the traits that are believed to define descent-based groups, the range or set of groups that are associated with particular concepts of difference, the presence (or absence) of hierarchy among them, the mechanisms that are believed to give rise to such groups, and the permanence and determinism (or consequences) ascribed to defining group traits. Within this framework, we identify four principal types of concepts of descent-based difference in Italy, with counterparts in the U.S.: biological essentialism, psychological (or 'temperamental') essentialism, cultural primordialism, and a notion of acquired culture. This method of decomposing concepts of descent-based group difference also helps us pinpoint where such conceptualization varies most between the U.S. and Italy: in the fixity and consequences that are attributed to biological and to cultural traits"—Provided by publisher.°
Identifiers: LCCN 2021050210 (print) | LCCN 2021050211 (ebook) | ISBN 9780871546784 (paperback) | ISBN 9781610449137 (ebook)
Subjects: LCSH: Race awareness—Italy. | Race awareness—United States. | Italy—Race relations. | United States—Race relations.
Classification: LCC DG455 .M675 2021 (print) | LCC DG455 (ebook) | DDC 305.800945—dc23/eng/20220119
LC record available at https://lccn.loc.gov/2021050210
LC ebook record available at https://lccn.loc.gov/2021050211

RUSSELL SAGE FOUNDATION
112 East 64th Street, New York, New York 10065
10 9 8 7 6 5 4 3 2 1

CONTENTS

ILLUSTRATIONS

Figures

Table

Figures

Table

ABOUT THE AUTHORS

ANN MORNING is associate professor of sociology, New York University.

MARCELLO MANERI is associate professor of sociology, University of Milan–Bicocca.

ACKNOWLEDGMENTS

THE FIRST place to start is with the young people who generously contributed their time, thoughts, and words to our attempt to understand how they saw and made sense of difference. Interviewed as college-age students, they are now mostly in their thirties. Who knows whether they ever wonder what happened with those researchers who came to their campus to ask them weird questions about things like ethnicity and race? Whether this book ultimately finds its way into their hands or not, it is theirs as much as ours, so our deepest thanks go to the students in Italy and the United States—158 in all—who sat down to talk with us.

This book is also a product of the proverbial village, both professional and personal. It was born from a Fulbright scholarship that allowed Ann Morning to spend the 2008–2009 academic year at the University of Milan–Bicocca, where Marcello Maneri teaches, and their work was supported along the way by a 2011 Research Challenge Fund award from New York University and by affiliated faculty research funding provided by NYU Abu Dhabi in 2012. The transition from data collection to analysis took place at the Russell Sage Foundation, a dream haven for academic work where Morning was in residence as a 2014–2015 Visiting Scholar, and at NYU, which graciously hosted Maneri that year. To all of these dedicated research institutions, we are immensely grateful.

Many groups and individuals made meaningful contributions to our project over the years. Chief among the former is Morning's writing circle, now going on fifteen years (we think—nobody remembers anymore exactly when we started). Its members, who have included Catherine Lee,

Alondra Nelson, Wendy Roth, and Torsten Voigt, read and commented on drafts of every single chapter. Another wonderful source of feedback was Morning's spring 2019 graduate class "'Race' in Translation: Concepts of Difference in Comparative Perspective"; its participants provided terrific input on multiple chapters, and we thank every one of them: James Barbosa, Alyssa Mattocks, Allison Motz, Edna Otuomagie, Laure Rousset, Safa Salim, Robert Simmons, Xinyi Zhang, and visiting scholar Dina Bader, as well as fellow instructor Jacob Boersema. Finally, we have had the good fortune to discuss our research in multiple venues, including the following universities (in reverse chronological order): University of Trento, Federal University of Minas Gerais, State University of Rio de Janeiro, University of Pennsylvania, American University of Paris, Rutgers University, Sorbonne University, New York University, Harvard University, Paris Institute of Political Studies, University of Hamburg, University of Padua, New York University Florence, University of Warwick, University of California–Santa Barbara, University of North Carolina–Chapel Hill, University of California–Berkeley, City University of New York, Stanford University, University of Connecticut, Princeton University, Columbia University, and University of Milan–Bicocca. We also had the opportunity to present our work at the European Parliament and at the Russell Sage Foundation, as well as at the annual meetings of the American Sociological Association, the Council for European Studies, the Eastern Sociological Society, and the Society for the Advancement of Socio-Economics.

These settings and others opened up countless exchanges that were of real benefit to our work, and we thank all those interlocutors for their time and keen insights. Unfortunately, there were too many for us to recognize here, but we would like to extend special thanks to the following scholars with whom we had the chance to engage at greater length: Laure Bereni, Mathilde Cohen, Bruno Cousin, Crystal Fleming, Annalisa Frisina, Tanya Golash-Boza, Camilla Hawthorne, Constanza Hermanin, Michèle Lamont, Marco Martiniello, Mathias Möschel, Ekédi Mpondo-Dika, Sabrina Onana, Angelica Pesarini, Giovanni Picker, Daniel Sabbagh, Patrick Simon, Anna Skarpelis, Stan Thangaraj, Guido Tintori, and Andreas Wimmer, as well as outstanding discussants Gaia Giuliani, Sunmin Kim, and Tommaso Vitale.

The execution of this project depended on the assistance of many people, to all of whom we are most grateful. Gaia Sartori Pallotta was in charge of outreach to vocational schools in Milan, and Monica Colombo and

Elisabetta Camussi kindly allowed us to hold pilot interviews with their students. Roberta Marzorati and Daniela Cherubini skillfully conducted interviews in the vocational schools, while Gabriella Sarracino interviewed undergraduates in Naples. Claudia Paci transcribed interview recordings with accuracy and intelligence, as did the incomparable Elena Skall, who provided insightful commentary to boot. Translator Clare O'Sullivan and editor Karin Horler offered invaluable assistance in transforming Maneri's Italian prose into American academic English.

During this book's many years of gestation, we benefited from the unflagging support of our editor at Russell Sage, Suzanne Nichols. Exacting yet patient, she kept the faith despite missed deadlines and interminable drafts. Thank you, thank you, thank you, Suzanne! We are also indebted to two anonymous referees and to Mary Waters for constructive criticism that was so spot-on that not only did it improve the manuscript immeasurably, but its value and perspicacity were so immediately apparent that they almost made up for the pain of revision. To all three referees, we say thank you from the bottom of our hearts for helping us uncover the book that was hidden within an overburdened original draft.

Turning now to our individual acknowledgments, Ann Morning would like to thank her NYU colleagues in the Department of Sociology, the Faculty of Arts and Science Deans' Office, the Office of the Provost, NYU Abu Dhabi, and at 19 Washington Square North, NYU Abu Dhabi's home in New York, for the countless ways in which they have supported her completion of this book. Once she started to list all the people who had in one way or another offered advice, camaraderie, resources, it seemed like half the office was involved, so she hopes that they will accept this blanket thanks, which is no less heartfelt for being anonymous. Finishing up this book also coincided with the global Covid-19 pandemic, which gave rise to regular gatherings online of friends who cheered her on, each group with an acronym its participants will recognize: LC51 (Gina Detmer, Laurie Geck, Dahlia Lithwick, Chloe Martin, and Suzanne Yelen); WSV MNO (Clare Aronow, Sue de Beer, Fabienne Doucet, Cynthia Miller-Idriss, Janelle Scott, Georgia Silvera Seamans, and Alyssa Sharkey); and AW/BGC (Rina Agarwala, May Al-Dabbagh, Gayatri Gopinath, and Natasha Iskander). The pandemic also made Ann especially grateful for the encouragement she received in person over the years from friends like Afia Ali, Sara Benjamin, Carl Haacke, Susan John, Julie Jones, Susanne Quadflieg, Zadie Smith,

Miri Song, Jyoti Thottam, and last but far from least, Niobe Way. To her daughters Gaia and Sofia as well as her father John, Ann expresses her deepest love and gratitude; this book spanned the first and the ninth decades of their lives, respectively, and yet they never lost interest in it.

Finally, Marcello Maneri, who shrinks from putting his personal life on professional display, wishes simply to thank the many colleagues, friends, and family who continued to ask us eagerly about the forthcoming publication of our book in defiance of all evidence to the contrary.

We dedicate this book to the pursuit of intercultural comprehension.

Thinking and Talking about Difference

> All citizens have the same social dignity and are equal before the law, without distinction of sex, race, language, religion, political opinion, personal and social conditions.[1]
>
> —ARTICLE 3, Constitution of the Italian Republic, 1947

> We can't [accept all immigrants] because we can't all fit, so we have to make choices. We have to decide whether our ethnicity, whether our white race, whether our society should continue to exist or should be wiped out. Here it's not a question of being xenophobic or racist, but of being logical or rational. It's a choice.
>
> —ATTILIO FONTANA, candidate who would be elected president
> of Italy's Lombardy region in 2018, quoted in *La Stampa*[2]

WHEN ATTILIO Fontana, a regional candidate for Italy's xenophobic League Party, made his impassioned plea for the survival of *la nostra razza bianca* (our white race) in January 2018, it sent shock waves through the country's political and media circles. Speaking explicitly of "race" was an inadmissible act, and one for which he quickly apologized, reformulating his political plank in much more palatable language. "I meant to say," he backtracked, "that we have to reorganize a different welcome reception, [one] that respects our history and our society."[3] He also sought absolution by arguing that the Italian Constitution should be rewritten, "because it's the first to say that races exist."[4] The public conversation that ensued leaned heavily in favor of Fontana's proposed revision as politicians across the ideological spectrum lined up behind it.[5] The reasoning seemed obvious, even impeccable, because, as one professor had written, "Races don't exist. All the research of the last decades by biologists and geneticists converges on this point."[6] Moreover, the idea of race had amply proved its perils in the past, as Liliana Segre, a senator and Holocaust survivor, reminded her compatriots.[7]

Less attention was paid to whether something like race might still exist in Italy as a social reality, if not a biological fact. Despite a horrific rampage a few weeks after Fontana's comments, in which a twenty-eight-year-old man opened fire on six Africans encountered randomly on the streets of Macerata, former prime minister Silvio Berlusconi supported the removal of the word "race" from the constitution by suggesting that it was unnecessary.[8] "Italians are not racist, we're hospitable," he maintained. "There isn't a general climate of hatred, just some crazy people."[9] Questions of what everyday Italians actually believed about racial, national, or other differences—or what measures beyond rewriting the constitution might be called for—got relatively short shrift. Senator Segre's call for a massive project that would educate young people—"class by class, head by head"—about historic persecution was largely overshadowed by the clamor to simply erase "race" from the law of the land.[10] As one of the few sites where "race" is overtly referenced in Italy's official state business, the constitution was a symbolic lightning rod. And perhaps ironically, the favored solution seemed to be to combat racism by removing a constitutional clause that outlawed it. Or is the very mention of "race" so inextricably entwined with racism in Italy that the word, everywhere and always, is necessarily a bearer of it?

Despite the considerable attention—not to mention the social media "likes"—that Fontana's proposal received, the idea of removing the word "race" from Italy's constitution was hardly a new one. Instead, it was part of a broader European move to eject the term from political life. After a 2012 presidential campaign promise by François Hollande, the French National Assembly voted to eliminate "race" from that nation's laws in 2013 and eventually voted in 2018 to remove it from the constitution.[11] "In eliminating the legal category of race," stated the first bill's author, a member of the Left Front coalition, "the Assembly has helped our country move forward on ideological and educational levels."[12]

Although similar debates had taken place elsewhere in Europe, it was the French case that inspired the first call in Italy for a purge of its constitution and official documents.[13] Beginning with the biologists Olga Rickards and Gianfranco Bondi's 2014 "Appeal for the Abolition of the Term 'Race,'" which urged Italy's political establishment to follow France's lead, academics promoted the measure well before Attilio Fontana seized on it.[14] In 2016, the Italian Anthropological Association joined forces with the Italian Institute of Anthropology to request that the nation's political leadership replace "the term 'race' in the Italian Constitution and in all of the Republic's official acts"—without however specifying an alternative. In subsequent years, other groups of academics militated for the same.[15]

Among sociologists, the question of when to use "race" has sparked some of the fiercest controversies to have animated our journals in recent years. Disagreement over whether the concept of race is a useful tool for analyzing social inequalities across the globe has provoked particularly acrimonious debate between scholars from Western Europe and North America. To some European observers, U.S. researchers indiscriminately apply a racial framework to their studies of society, or they impose a particularly American version of race that is inappropriate elsewhere in the world.[16] U.S. scholars retort in turn that their critics deny or obscure the workings of a powerful mechanism of inequality that did not originate in, and is not limited to, North America.[17] The frequent framing of the dispute as one between national scholarly communities has lent it a bellicose air, rife with accusations of American "incursions" into a Europe that is besieged by U.S. academic culture and political correctness.[18]

Because the "resistance to American hegemony," in Loïc Wacquant's words, is often led by French scholars, the battle takes on a "clash of the Titans" quality as two nations with similarly high-flown and self-aggrandizing universalist pretentions square off against each other.[19] Using each other as foils, each camp defines itself against the other, which is depicted as the epitome of misguided and morally flawed reasoning. Even though the question of whether or how to use race for social-scientific analysis can be examined without acrimony in other geographic regions, it has become a matter of morality, and not just methodology, in the transatlantic arena.[20] At issue is the question of who is complicit with racism, and whose strategy— color-conscious versus color-cautious (or "color-obsessed" versus "color-blind" to their respective detractors)—is better for fighting it.

Clearly, the debates about the place of "race" that academics and politicians have joined mix both factual and ethical concerns; indeed, they interweave a series of distinct questions. How should the term "race" be used in public discourse? How should the concept of race be defined and applied to the analysis of social life, if at all? Should race play a role in public policy (including law), and if so, how? Amid these intertwined normative controversies over "what should be done," a basic empirical question often goes unaddressed: How do everyday people actually think and talk about race? Ideally, our speech norms, research agendas, and governance tools would take into account on-the-ground realities. Yet much of the cross-Atlantic conflict over the appropriate uses of race has proceeded without a solid grounding in comparative knowledge of what Europeans and Americans believe or say about race. In response, this book aims to bring to light the neglected buried layer of the widespread ideas that underlie the ethical dilemmas that have been so vociferously argued.

Points of Departure: From the "New Racism" to the Conceptualization of Descent-Based Difference

An important starting point for comparing U.S. to European notions of difference is Martin Barker's 1981 book *The New Racism: Conservatives and the New Ideology of the Tribe*, which analyzed political debates over immigration in the United Kingdom of the late 1970s and early 1980s.[21] Barker discerned in these debates an emerging discourse about race that seemed to break with the past. This discourse discarded long-standing notions of biological difference between races ("old racism") in favor of arguments about insuperable cultural distinctions ("new racism"), and it abandoned overt claims of group inferiority or superiority but championed a "natural" desire for segregation.

Not only did other academics in the United Kingdom find the idea of a "new racism" compelling, but so did scholars in France and the United States.[22] Michel Wieviorka concluded that "the new racism described by Martin Barker ... is very close to what we can observe in France," and Étienne Balibar expanded on "neo-racism," describing it as "a racism whose dominant theme is not biological heredity but the insurmountability of cultural differences, a racism which, at first sight, does not postulate the superiority of certain groups or peoples in relation to others but 'only' the harmfulness of abolishing frontiers, the incompatibility of life-styles and traditions."[23] Similarly, sociologists, political scientists, and psychologists in the United States developed myriad theories of new racism, including Samuel Gaertner and John Dovidio's "aversive" form, Janet Ward Schofield's "colorblind perspective," David Sears's "symbolic racism," the "laissez-faire racism" of Lawrence Bobo and his colleagues, and Eduardo Bonilla-Silva's "racism without racists."[24]

As the idea of a "new racism" expanded across national borders, it gradually acquired a subtle comparative claim: that the new cultural racism was found in Western Europe, while the United States remained mired in old biological racism.[25] Balibar, for example, attributes "tendentially biologistic ideologies" to "the Anglo-Saxon countries, where they continue the traditions of Social Darwinism and eugenics," and he notes that France seems to pursue "pure culturalism."[26] Riva Kastoryano also juxtaposes the centrality of (ostensibly physical) race notions to group boundaries in the United States with the salience of religious (that is, cultural) divisions in France.[27] Moreover, comparative interview studies by Philomena Essed and Michèle Lamont lend empirical support to these arguments. Essed discerns a more "racial" racism in the United States and a more "cultural" form in the Netherlands; similarly, Lamont finds that French workers "provide mostly cultural explanations for ethnoracial differences that stress cultural incompatibility," while "American workers offered a multicausal explanation of black inferiority that pointed to nature, history, psychology, and culture." Perhaps most strikingly, Lamont finds that "the genetic and biological explanations found in the United States are simply absent in France."[28]

The hypothesized contrast between European and North American understandings of race has not been subjected to systematic or targeted investigation, however, so questions about its accuracy remain. As Lamont herself has written, "While some social scientists have noted the prevalence of cultural arguments over biological arguments in the French rhetoric of racism . . . this has yet to be established by a detailed and empirically grounded analysis of the range of types of arguments used in French vocabularies of exclusion."[29] Fatima El-Tayeb, for one, contests the assumption that "a complicated, culture-based rather than biological notion of 'race' is somehow specific to Europe as opposed to the United States," and Bonilla-Silva sees such a cultural perspective as present in Western nations across the board.[30] Conversely, it is worth exploring whether the enduring vitality of the biological model of race in the United States truly has no counterpart in Europe.[31] It was precisely the scarcity of individual-level evidence for the claimed U.S.-European divergence that inspired us to design an empirical, comparative project focused on it.

Importantly, however, we reformulate the working hypothesis of different types of racism in two major ways. First and foremost, we contend that the varieties of racisms that Barker described fundamentally reflect distinct understandings of human difference. To speak of new "cultural" racism versus old "biological" racism is to speak of competing ideas about the root or form of racial distinction. So rather than investigate the totality of racism—by which we understand systemic beliefs, practices, and institutions that give rise to and reinforce racial stratification—we hone in on its underlying beliefs about the nature of human difference.[32] These conceptualizations are complex; they are webs of ideas about which groups exist, how they are constituted, the traits shared by their members, and the ways in which we can ascertain an individual's membership in one.[33]

Our second innovation on the comparative "new racism" claim is, perhaps surprisingly, to pare back our reliance on race as a category of analysis.[34] We do so for several reasons. The first is pragmatic: the term "race" may not mean the same thing, have the same connotations, or be used in the same ways or to the same degree—if at all—in different settings.[35] As a result, race is an unreliable tool for cross-national comparisons; we could not presume, for example, that the Italian *razza* is a straightforward equivalent to "race" in the United States. The meaning of these words for native speakers is something we want to study, not something to assume.

Second, a narrow focus on race risks excluding closely related if not identical concepts that might be labeled differently from place to place, such as "ethnicity," "population," or "caste."[36] Comparative and historical research suggests a great deal of similarity and interrelatedness between such terms, and none of them have unique, clear-cut, or fixed meanings and boundaries.[37] Instead, concepts like race and ethnicity share a family resemblance, as each is a "categorical distinction that names or delimits sets of human beings who are construed to belong together naturally, as a collectivity or community, due to some source of heritable similarity."[38] Indeed, they share a common function, according to Rogers Brubaker, Mara Loveman, and Peter Stamatov:

> What cognitive perspectives suggest, in short, is that race, ethnicity, and nation are not things in the world but ways of seeing the world. They are ways of understanding and identifying oneself, making sense of one's problems

and predicaments, identifying one's interests, and orienting one's action. They are ways of recognizing, identifying, and classifying other people, of construing sameness and difference, and of "coding" and making sense of their actions. They are templates for representing and organizing social knowledge, frames for articulating social comparisons and explanations, and filters that shape what is noticed or unnoticed, relevant or irrelevant, remembered or forgotten.[39]

These parallels in the forms, uses, and consequences of racial, ethnic, and other discourse motivate Mara Loveman's call for a "comparative sociology of group-making," "deghettoizing the study of 'race' and approaching it as part of a larger field of issues related to processes and consequences of symbolic boundary construction, maintenance, and decline."[40] We also adopt this approach because it allows us to consider the wide range of groups that are socially salient in Western Europe and North America, regardless of whether they are locally known as "races," "ethnic groups," or something else. Such disparate communities as Roma, Eastern Europeans, Muslims, and *meridionali* (Southern Italians), on the one hand, and American Indians, Latinx, and African Americans, on the other, all have a place in our comparative analysis of concepts of difference.[41]

To avoid relying on assumption-laden ideas of race (or ethnicity) as analytical tools for this comparative study, we turned to the historian David Hollinger's notion of "communities of descent."[42] In other words, we aim to explore individuals' beliefs about the differences between groups that they understand, more or less explicitly, to be defined by shared ancestry. In short, *An Ugly Word* is a cross-national inquiry into the *conceptualization of descent-based difference*.[43] Kinship need not be prominent in such interpretations; for example, we need not see all whites as members of one big family for whites to figure as a descent-based group. But the idea of lineage must be there somewhere, as in the idea of whites as people descended from earlier inhabitants of Europe. This approach also borrows from Kanchan Chandra's equation of the criteria for ethnic membership with "descent-based attributes," or "the sum total of the attributes of our parents and ancestors (which we acquire as an inheritance through descent), our own genetic features (which we acquire through descent, even though they include features which may not have characterized our parents), and all those attributes which we can credibly portray as having been acquired through descent."[44] Chandra's attention to what "we can credibly portray" is a crucial reminder that our ideas of ancestry and its inheritance are always subjective.[45]

Given the analytical broadening we have sketched out, we will largely refer to "concepts of descent-based difference" in this book rather than "race" or "ethnicity"—with two important exceptions. We will use that language when we report on the ideas that others have expressed using it. Debates over constitutional texts, scholarly analyses of social stratification, and interviewees' comments, for example, may all hinge or be premised on the word "race," and in those cases, we will preserve its usage. We will even put it in quotation marks at times, either to make clear that it comes from *verbatim* text or speech or simply to underscore that a subjective belief or "category of practice" is in play.[46] The other instance in which we reference race will be to invoke it as an analytical category designating a narrow range of descent-based conceptualization: what we call the "classical (or traditional or Linnaean) Western race concept." Specifically, in analyses we use the term "race" to refer to an ideal-type of Linnaeus's eighteenth-century taxonomy of *Homo: africanus; americanus; asiaticus*, and *europaeus*.[47] In other words, we think it appropriate to use "race" analytically as a label for the family of European-origin concepts of descent-based difference that incorporate both a black-red-yellow-white symbolic color scheme and a clear hierarchy of groups whose bodies are imagined as the locus of their signature traits.[48] But as we will show, this basic template takes on additional features in different settings and thus morphs into distinctive conceptual variants.

Our Research—and Its Relevance

To bring empirical evidence to bear on transatlantic differences—and similarities—in the conceptualization of descent-based difference, we contrast the United States to Italy, for reasons we outline in the next section. More specifically, we pose two key research questions:

1. To what extent do culture and biology figure in Italian and American concepts of descent-based difference?
2. Do other characteristics distinguish Italian from American concepts of difference?

While the first inquiry addresses the "new racism" hypothesis of a U.S.-European divergence in understandings of difference, the second is a more open-ended exploration that allows for the possibility that a biology-versus-culture distinction may not be the best—or the only—way to describe and compare such concepts.

It was with these questions in mind that Ann Morning embarked on a Fulbright scholarship to visit the University of Milan–Bicocca during the 2008–2009 academic year, having learned the language and grown interested in the impact of immigration on Italy. Meeting Marcello Maneri at "Bicocca" gave her the opportunity to work with one of the few Italian scholars at the time with an interest in the Anglophone sociology of race, cultivated in the course of his research on depictions of *lo straniero* (the foreigner) in Italian media. Together we designed an interview-based project that would allow us to compare young Italians' thinking about human difference to the data that Morning had collected from fifty-two college students in the United States and would analyze in her 2011 book, *The Nature of Race*. The result was a series of 106 in-depth interviews conducted with Italian students from 2012 to 2013 in Milan, Bologna, and Naples, after pilot sessions in 2010. (See the appendices for detailed information on the sample selection and characteristics, interview methodology, and questionnaire.)

Although the focus on college-age students in Italy was dictated by the goal of comparing them to young adults in the United States, this constraint offered several advantages. Interviewing people roughly twenty to twenty-two years old allowed us to tap into the thinking of a generation whose impact on their nations' cultural lives and structural realities would be substantial for decades to come. Moreover, the future influence of college students in particular is likely to be pronounced, as higher education remains a privilege and is far from universal in both countries. Their views also open a window onto the messages about human difference that are being conveyed to young people in the early twenty-first century.

At the same time, however, we enlarged and broadened the Italian sample relative to the United States study in ways that allowed us to explore socio-demographic diversity in relation to beliefs about descent-based groups. While the American sample was drawn from four universities in the U.S. Northeast (which we dub "City University," "State University," "Ivy University," and "Pilot University"), in Italy we interviewed students in both the North (Milan and Bologna) and the South (Naples). We also included students in Italian vocational schools (31 of the 106 interviewees), adding diversity in the type, level, and prestige of the educational track to that sample.[49] Accordingly, we will make note of how or when these factors, absent in the U.S. sample, played a role in our Italian results. More broadly, we take care not to make sweeping national generalizations from our data; in both countries, our samples are small and far from representative of the larger population. Yet by comparing people of the same age in a similar stage of life, all pursuing formal education, we find the many pronounced differences in their perspectives to be instructive. And as we will show, their many similarities are no less telling.

Exploring concepts of descent-based difference means opening a window onto patterns of thought that have wide-ranging implications. Broadly speaking, notions of human diversity influence attitudes, practices, and policies. In the United States, for example, social psychologists have shown that racial conceptualization is associated with prejudice; it also shapes activities from genealogical DNA testing to census enumeration to health care.[50] And as our opening discussion of controversies over "race" language in European constitutions suggested, beliefs about difference also make themselves felt in law and public policy. Those debates underscore the importance of coming to empirical grips with how everyday people think about difference; without such knowledge, disagreements about appropriate, desirable, or promising measures governing the uses of race in public discourse or policy cannot be resolved. In short, concepts of difference are significant because they shape all kinds of social phenomena and projects that we think matter.

Although the conceptualization of difference is thus worthy of attention even in domestic contexts alone, it is a topic that, like so many other sociological domains, stands to benefit enormously from cross-national comparisons. It is difficult, for example, to fully capture the particularities of the American "one-drop rule"—the folk belief whereby a single "drop of black blood" makes a person a full member of the "black race"—without contrasting it to the *castas* racial taxonomies of colonial Latin America or the conventions for classifying "mixed-race" people elsewhere in the world.[51] Comparative research offers an unparalleled tool for unearthing the deeply buried worldviews that color our social analyses; simply put, it is difficult to realize just what it is we take for granted until we are confronted with another setting where our assumptions are absent.[52]

Transatlantic comparisons, like the Italy–United States contrast we explore, offer an especially fruitful line of analysis given the many commonalities between industrialized nations on either side of the ocean. Although today's heated scholarly debates over race may obscure their common ground, it is hard to overstate just how much the United States and Western Europe share when it comes to the historic roots of belief about racial difference. How could it be otherwise when the nascent United States was a cultural heir to—and eager participant in—eighteenth-century European intellectuals' construction of a racial hierarchy, not to mention a major site for the European imperial project of white supremacy?[53] Consider Howard Winant's 2001 book title, *The World Is a Ghetto*. At first glance, it might seem an unacceptable "projection of North American raciology on the rest of the world," indiscriminately locating what is often considered a U.S. phenomenon all across the globe.[54] Yet "ghetto," of course, is of European—Italian—origin, both as a word and an institution. And it symbolizes the way in which, distinct as North American and Western European societies are today, their ideas of race have grown from shared roots. As a result, we are like a family whose members operate on the same fundamental premises without realizing it because they are in thrall to their differences. The fiery conflicts in our scholarly journals, then, are akin to a family squabble—which does not necessarily make them any more tractable and indeed may make them less so.

Moving beyond this academic impasse is especially urgent, however, as the United States and Western Europe face strikingly similar changes in the makeup of their populations. For one thing, Europe is becoming more like the United States as large-scale, multigenerational communities of immigrant descent emerge there.[55] Such native-born populations cannot be dismissed as cultural outsiders as easily as their immigrant ancestors were, nor as neatly segregated or disadvantaged in socioeconomic and legal terms, and their phenotypic characteristics may be given more or less weight—all of which are likely to have consequences for everyday concepts of difference. This multigenerational layering coincides, moreover, with the "browning"—and aging—of North America and Western Europe. In the British demographer David Coleman's scenario of the "third demographic transition," "the ancestry of some national populations is being radically and permanently altered by high levels of immigration of persons from remote geographic origins or with distinctive ethnic and racial ancestry, in combination with persistent sub-replacement fertility and accelerated levels of emigration of the domestic population."[56] Coleman also captures the anxiety that these processes provoke for many when he writes that they "are changing the composition of national populations and thereby the culture, physical appearance, social experiences, and self-perceived identity of the inhabitants of European nations."[57] Such "demodystopia" or "demographobia" has left a deep imprint on both U.S. and European politics, raising the question of how these fears feed—and are fed by—notions of descent-based difference.[58]

For another thing, the United States is becoming more like the immigration destinations of Western Europe in terms of the primacy of voluntary migration as a motor of diversification. Historically, much of the ethnoracial heterogeneity in the United States has been produced through involuntary processes of colonization, slavery, rape, and imperial conquest, which together produced particular notions and expressions of "racial" difference. For example, as blackness gradually came to be equated with perpetual servitude, beliefs about the innate and permanent inferiority of Afro-descent people provided a crucial ideological justification for their enslavement.[59] Such rationales about essential differences were less necessary for people whom white Americans regarded as foreign—like American Indians or Asians—and who could be expelled from the nation with little loss of slave labor. Instead, these ostensibly inferior racial groups could be marked simply as culturally aberrant.[60] Today, however, it is voluntary migration that drives the further diversification of the United States, as in Europe, raising the question of how this transformation is affecting Americans' concepts of difference. Equally important, how will evolving understandings of human difference shape the social, political, and policy treatment of an expanding array of descent-based groups, both the newly arrived and the deeply rooted?

To sum up, several notable demographic processes under way augur a transatlantic convergence that is likely to invite further cross-national comparisons of concepts of group difference.[61] Such inquiries will benefit scholars and policymakers on both shores. As demography follows similar paths on either side of the ocean, policies on a range of issues—not just immigration but also naturalization, education, employment, welfare, criminal justice, antidiscrimination, and so forth—will come under similar pressures.[62] By considering similarly dynamic contexts that lead to diverse outcomes, comparative research on the conceptualization of difference can shed new light on some of the beliefs that are most closely intertwined with such societal developments.

To fully grasp the implications of evolving beliefs about descent-based difference for public attitudes, behaviors, and policies, however, and to benefit from cross-national comparisons, it is crucial to get our social scientific analyses right. For that reason, *An Ugly Word* ultimately aims to push beyond simple descriptions of descent-based concepts as either "biological" or "cultural." Our U.S.-Italy comparison provides a methodological model for the comparative study of the conceptualization of difference, and it culminates in a theoretical framework that is intended as a toolbox for an updated version of what Pierre van den Berghe called "the comparative sociology of race and ethnicity."[63] In this way, we hope to contribute to a language and set of metrics that can facilitate the exchange of ideas and data between scholars who hail from or focus on different areas of the world and who have had difficulty coming to a shared understanding and treatment of concepts like "race" and "ethnicity." Doing so requires the development of a comparative sociology capable of identifying similar understandings of difference across settings without, however, being misled by "false friends" or apparent likenesses—in terminology or ideas—that may be no more than surface deep. Likewise, this scholarly program must not sidestep, but rather embrace, the challenges of discourse and thought that are not easily "translated" or applicable abroad. Without an empirical, comparative sociology of the conceptualization of difference, researchers will be unable to resolve their disagreements about where in the world particular understandings of difference play a meaningful role.

Either way, cross-national comparisons of notions of group difference will become only more frequent with time. For one thing, they will be easier to undertake, as technologies that diffuse news, information, and opinion make the world a smaller place. Already, commentary on right-wing nationalism links the United States to India and Hungary, and alarm over white supremacism is stoked by events from Norway to New Zealand. For another, activists, politicians, and others will be more easily inspired by their counterparts elsewhere, making comparison inevitable. The American Black Lives Matter movement has sparked protest and reflection around the globe.[64] And Russian-style "memory laws" that aim to "guide public interpretation of the past" have taken root in the United States, where one state legislature after another has banned the teaching of (what they take to be) critical race theory.[65]

These phenomena are all grounded in beliefs about human difference—about groups, their characteristics, and their place in society—and regardless of how similar or dissimilar these ideas are, they are caught up in a single global conversation, as multifaceted and wide-ranging as that may be.

Italy and the Study of Difference in the Heart of Europe

Having explained why we study concepts of descent-based difference, and why we do so through U.S.-European comparison, another important question remains: Why select Italy as a site for comparison? The "old racism" versus "new racism" claim has juxtaposed the United States and Western Europe more generally, so why do we choose *il bel paese* (the beautiful country) specifically to represent the latter?[66] Italy has many relevant similarities with its Western European neighbors, as well as meaningful particularities, that together make it a productive site for exploring the comparative claim embedded in "new racism" literature.

First and foremost, Italy's population now includes significant numbers of immigrants. As figure I.1 shows, in 2019 the foreign-born made up 10.4 percent of its total population of over 60 million, putting Italy in the company of France (12.8 percent), the United Kingdom (13.7 percent), and the European Union average of 13.8 percent.[67] Perhaps even more salient for our purposes, immigration is a high-profile political issue and media topic in Italy, as it is elsewhere in Western Europe.[68] Another indicator of the centrality of immigration in Italian society as elsewhere on the continent is the prominence of nationalist, xenophobic political parties like La Lega (the League, formerly the Northern League), with its slogan *prima gli italiani* (Italians first). And not surprisingly, public opinion surveys suggest that Italians are as concerned about immigration as their neighbors. In a 2018 Pew Research Center survey, 54 percent agreed with the statement "Immigrants today are a burden on our country because they take our jobs and social benefits," compared to 74 percent in Greece and 37 percent in Spain.[69]

Equally relevant is Italy's embeddedness within Europe. It is a founding member of the European Union and the home of the Roman civilization of antiquity that many see as an illustrious primogenitor of the West. It is also effectively the seat of the Catholic Church, whose cultural power is unparalleled in European history, as a visit to churches, schools, and museums in any town will confirm—even in the Protestant regions defined by their rebellion against

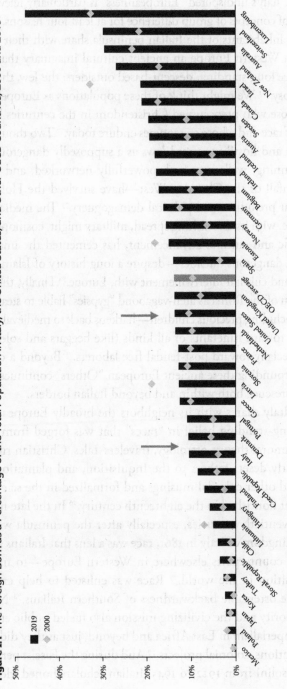

Figure I.1 The Foreign-Born as a Percentage of the Total Population in Italy, the United States, and Other OECD Countries, 2000 and 2019

Source: OECD 2020, figure 1.12.

Catholicism. Italy's undisputed "Europeanness" is particularly relevant for an exploration of concepts of group difference for at least four reasons.[70]

First, the inhabitants of the Italian peninsula share with their neighbors elsewhere in Western Europe an ancient cultural imaginary that is populated by three long-standing, descent-based outsiders: the Jew, the Muslim, and the "gypsy."[71] We might think of these populations as Europe's "ancient others"—those who preoccupied Christendom in the centuries before the invention of race and whose stereotypes endure today.[72] Two thousand years of suspicion and hostility toward Jews as a supposedly dangerous internal enemy—cunning, well organized, powerfully networked, and dedicated to the downfall of the Christian West—have survived the Holocaust, in both popular prejudices and political demagoguery.[73] The medieval legacy of Islam's rise, with its astonishing spread, military might, cosmopolitanism, and scientific and cultural advancement, has cemented the image of the Muslim as a dangerous outsider—despite a long history of Islamic embeddedness in, and cultural intertwinement with, Europe.[74] Finally, the modern-day depiction of the Roma as arch-vagabond "gypsies" liable to steal anything of value—including precious children—harkens back to medieval European antagonism toward itinerants of all kinds (like beggars and soldiers), and perhaps especially toward post-feudal free laborers.[75] Beyond a doubt, the imagery surrounding these ancient European "Others" continues to have a significant presence both within and beyond Italian borders.

Second, Italy shares with its neighbors the broadly European cultural legacy of long-standing belief in "races" that was forged from a hodge-podge of humoral theory, astrology, travelers' tales, Christian rumination from the early desert fathers to the Inquisition, and plantation owners' accounts and other colonial musings and formalized in the scientific taxonomies that flourished in the eighteenth century.[76] In the late nineteenth and early twentieth centuries, especially after the peninsula was unified under the Kingdom of Italy in 1861, race was a lens that Italians applied—as did their counterparts elsewhere in Western Europe—to make sense of their position in the world.[77] Race was enlisted to help explain, for example, the ostensible backwardness of Southern Italians.[78] Notions of racial superiority and the civilizing mission also fueled public enthusiasm for Italy's imperialism in East Africa and beyond, just as they did for other European nations' colonial projects.[79] And during the Fascist period under Benito Mussolini from 1922 to 1945, Italian scholars honed ideas of race that were institutionalized in anti-Semitic and other "racial laws," both at home and in the colonies. As a wartime Axis power (at first), Italy's theories about "Nordic," "Mediterranean," and other races also fed the German Nazis' genocidal machine.[80] Without making a priori assumptions about exactly how this sustained historical engagement with race colors the present, there is no doubt that it must be reckoned with.

The third way in which Italy's "Europeanness" is meaningful is through its shared conviction that equality and democracy are integral—and perhaps even unique—to the culture of the West. This is apparent in the broad juxtaposition of Western tolerance against Muslim intolerance that is popular today in European commentary on religion, gender roles, and terrorism, but which harkens back to much older anxieties about the fate of Christendom in the face of Islam's medieval flourishing.[81] This long-standing contrast has hardened today into the imagery of "Fortress Europe," the symbolism of the European Union, and the abject figure that Italians call *l'extracomunitario*—"the one from outside the community"—to signify non-Europeans.[82]

Finally, particularly relevant for the study of concepts of difference is a striking cultural thread that Italy shares with several of its Western European neighbors: namely, a national self-image as an especially inclusive society. Like French faith in the color-blindness of their universal republicanism or Dutch self-regard for their supposed tolerance, the phrase *italiani brava gente* (Italians [as] good people) colors Italians' understanding of historical episodes that might call into question the belief in their intrinsic aversion to racism.[83] *Italiani brava gente* can equally denote Italians as "good" colonizers and as the people who helped Jews during World War II, unlike the vilified Germans.[84] Of course, such national imaginaries as tolerant societies are not limited to Europe; witness the messianic (and ironic) self-proclamation of the United States as the "land of liberty." What is important here is that Italy's membership in a larger Western European cultural community— and its participation in the ongoing construction of Europe—makes it a very productive site for investigating the "new racism" that scholars have attributed to the region.

To be sure, no single nation is perfectly typical or representative of the larger Western European ensemble. But many of the ways in which Italy diverges from the broader continental experience make it an unusually strategic site for examining concepts of difference. Modern Italy's relatively late experimentation with overseas colonization, for example, never rivaled that of the Portuguese, the Spanish, the Dutch, the English, or the French. Its short-lived and small empire did not translate into a broad reservoir of former colonial subjects, and so large-scale immigration arrived only toward the end of the twentieth century in Italy and was much more varied in its geographic composition.[85] Italian colonialism was also unusual for its turn-of-the century timing alongside mass emigration to the Americas, a coincidence that led to Italians simultaneously imposing and undergoing racialization, at home and abroad. Indeed, Italians' stigmatization as an undesirable, inferior race in the United States made the whitening offered by the subjugation of Africans all the more urgent.[86] Empire promised the racial uplift that would address Italy's anxieties about being held back by its primitive South, fears that would echo when Southerners moved in large numbers to the post–World War II North.

The rise of immigration toward the end of the twentieth century has put Italy in an earlier phase as a receiving country: its population includes fewer (and younger) second- and later-generation members of immigrant descent than is the case for the European countries that have been major destinations for newcomers since the 1950s. Italy's contemporary immigration is also deeply shaped by its long Mediterranean coastline and proximity to North Africa—a frontline position that situates it differently than most of its European Union partners with respect to large-scale migrant inflows. Together, these political, demographic, economic, social, and geographic features distinguish Italy from many of its neighbors, yet make it a promising place to explore the conceptualization of difference. In a context where multiple forms of descent-based exclusion have crystallized over time, the heterogeneous origins of Italy's population offer myriad directions for exploring the interplay of beliefs about similarity and difference and for comparing them to those found in the demographic mosaic that is the United States.

Ideas of Difference in Italy and the United States

In response to the claim that there is a significant gap between how Americans think about descent-based difference and how Europeans think of it, a clear rebuttal emerges from our data. While ways of *speaking* about group difference vary considerably across the Atlantic, we argue, our interviews with young people in Italy and the United States show that underlying *beliefs* about it do not. To be sure, they are not identical, and there are many intriguing and meaningful distinctions to which we will draw attention— for example, in how race is understood to be "constructed," or in the varying degrees to which biological difference is linked to physiognomy versus genetics. But the extensive overlap between American and Italian understandings of human difference cannot be ignored. Nor can those understandings be usefully described as pursuing separate, biological versus cultural tracks.

Accordingly, this book puts forth a second theoretical and methodological argument about how to analyze and compare concepts of difference that is built on our primary empirical contention that American and Italian views are more similar than dissimilar. Finding that the labels of "cultural" and "biological" are too blunt and too limited to capture the subtleties of descent-based thought that we encountered, we propose a new approach that takes into account multiple dimensions of the conceptualization of difference. Specifically, we propose a framework for breaking down such concepts into six key components and taking the measure of each. More-over, it is essential to flesh out concepts of difference by scrutinizing ideas about a wide range of descent-based groups; their local labeling as "races," "ethnicities," or something else is no guide to beliefs about their nature. Only in this way will we have the fuller and more precise understanding of the notions about difference that underpin entrenched inequalities and are at the heart of controversies in both the political and academic spheres.

To substantiate these two central arguments, *An Ugly Word* is organized around a core of three empirical chapters. These are preceded by a review in chapter 1 of the existing literature on the rhetorical and analytical uses of race in the United States, Italy, and Western Europe more broadly. Although we are ultimately interested in Italian and American beliefs about descent-based difference in general, the relevant scholarship has focused on race in particular. Chapter 1, "Debating 'Race' in Europe and the United States," prepares us for the kinds of *discourse* around descent that we can expect to find on either side of the Atlantic; moreover, it reveals how little empirical research currently exists to make a similar comparison of underlying *concepts* of difference. In the absence of such work, this chapter explores norms and practices of racial speech and contrasts what we call "conscious" versus "skeptic" attitudes toward the use of race as an instrument of social analysis. Although opposing positions in both realms have often been attributed to Americans and Europeans, our investigation of the available literature reveals meaningful instances of convergence, foreshadowing the conceptual similarities to emerge from our interviews.

Chapter 2, "Italian Mental Maps of Difference," introduces readers unfamiliar with Italy to its contemporary landscape of descent-based differ-ence, as described by our young interviewees in Naples, Milan, and Bologna. Borrowing Lamont's open-ended approach to tracing "mental maps," this chapter reports the students' criteria for *italianità* (Italianness), eliciting which descent-based groups were salient to them and the distinctions they perceived between them.[87] By employing a "likability thermometer" to gauge the respondents' evaluations, both quantitative and qualitative, of groups like "Southerners" or "Moroccans," the chapter offers further insight into the kinds of differences that, in their view, demarcated one group from another. In keeping with the "new racism" hypothesis, at first glance cul-ture, not biology or "race," appeared to predominate in Italian students' minds as the basis of group difference, albeit in an unstable manner that could quickly shade from rigid to malleable, essence to acquired trait. What ultimately emerges from close attention to the ways in which they catego-rized, described, and privileged various descent-based groups, however, is the clear imprint of a centuries-old Linnaean race taxonomy that draws on convictions about biological as well as temperamental difference—and that obscures structural mechanisms of inequality.

Chapter 3, "'Race' Talk," relays American and Italian responses to direct questions about the meaning of the word "race." A constant refrain from the Italians was a characterization of the term as *una brutta parola*—an ugly word. Yet neither their recoil from the word nor their prior preference for cultural boundary-marking prevented them from articulating biologically grounded understandings of racial difference much like those espoused by their counter-parts in the United States. This finding, along with the American respondents' enthusiastic application of a "culture" lens to their definitions of race, rejects the hypothesis that European concepts of difference stand in stark contrast to those in the United States, or that the comparison can be cast as a culture-versus-biology divide. Instead, we conclude that both sets of interviewees were united in turning away from social accounts of race that highlight its con-structed nature and its role in structuring group outcomes.

Our last empirical chapter, "Difference in Play: Sport and Descent," turns to the playing field to offer a final refutation of the "new racism" claim. When asked to reflect on African- and European-descent athletes' overrepresentation in various sports, our Italian and American interviewees' explanatory accounts were virtually indistinguishable. Both samples converged heavily on a "black biological exceptionalism" that attributed the outcomes of African-descent competitors to their physiognomy, while white and Asian athletes' successes were chalked up to their dedication to certain culturally valued sports.[88] In short, both American and Italian interviewees drew on notions of cultural and biological difference, and they did so in identical ways, even coming up with the same evolutionary "back stories" to account for the present-day landscape of athletic representation. These commentaries frequently conflicted, however, with what respondents had said about race earlier in our conversations, and so we take advantage of the disjuncture to consider why certain questions elicited certain depictions of descent-based difference. The result is a reflection on the interplay between rhetoric and conceptualization as they are shaped, respectively, by speech norms and long-standing stereotypes.

We begin the book's conclusion, "Rethinking Race: A New Model of Descent-Based Difference," with a summary of findings that support our reply to the book's primary research question. Rather than revealing conceptualizations of descent-based difference to be based in distinct spheres—cultural versus biological—our findings show considerable similarity between our U.S. and Italian interviewees' beliefs. In response to our second research question about how to better grasp the features that actually do distinguish European from American ideas, we argue that more precise tools are needed, and to that end we present a new model for decomposing, describing, and comparing concepts of difference. Specifically, we suggest that any such concept can be broken down into six constituent elements: (1) its imagined defining trait(s) or basis for difference, such as genes or folkways; (2) the scope of descent-based groups to which a given concept is applied; (3) the hierarchy (if any) among these groups; (4) the ostensible mechanism for the acquisition of group traits, for instance, socialization or biological inheritance; (5) the perceived fixity or fluidity of the resultant trait(s); and (6) the extent to which these traits are believed to determine other outcomes, such as interpersonal relationships or criminal behavior. After providing methodological guidance for implementing this model, we illustrate its use by applying its more detailed set of measures to the Italian and U.S. cases. As part of this exercise, we describe four concepts of descent-based difference as having emerged most strongly from our interviews: biological essentialism, psychological (or temperamental) essentialism, cultural primordialism, and cultural acquisition. Finally, the conclusion returns to the implications of this research for the political controversies around "race" with which we began this book. We also show how our research might offer a way out of the current academic impasse over the place of "race," in which U.S. and European scholars have had difficulty understanding and thus learning from each other. Greater insight into the beliefs about descent groups that profoundly shape attitudes, practices, and policies of exclusion and inclusion would be of real value on both sides of the Atlantic.

Contributing to Global Conversations and Ongoing Debates

An Ugly Word engages and contributes to several areas of scholarship that touch on beliefs about human difference and their heterogeneity across geographic space. It clearly builds on and extends Morning's idea of "racial conceptualization" by locating it in the broader category of "concepts of descent-based difference" and by widening the scope beyond the United States. Although her monograph *The Nature of Race* already contained the seeds of our current project, the present volume has pushed us to rethink and refine the ideas that were originally developed in an American context; this is the payoff of comparative sociology. Accordingly, we envision the present work as adding to a growing literature that explores "race" and "ethnic" thinking beyond the usual suspects of U.S., South African, and Brazilian society.[89] In other words, we hope to contribute to a comparative sociology of the conceptualization of descent-based difference.

Our work complements the structural orientation often characterizing sociological comparisons of Western Europe to North America that touch on descent-based difference. By "structure" we mean societal features like political and legal institutions, economic organization, and demographic composition, as opposed to the "culture" that inheres in widespread beliefs, norms, values, and symbolically meaningful traditions and behaviors. The structural approach is particularly noticeable in the literature tracing the integration and assimilation of immigrants and their second-generation offspring on both sides of the Atlantic.[90] At times cultural beliefs figure indirectly in this kind of work, through references to the prejudices under-pinning discrimination.[91] But even when the content of stereotypes is noted, as in Nancy Foner's exploration of Islamophobia as a barrier to immigrant and second-generation inclusion in Europe and the United States, it is not the primary object of detailed scrutiny.[92]

In contrast, our in-depth interviews with white, Italian-born students explore the cultural world that members of the first and second genera-tions must navigate, with special attention to the educational realm that previous research has highlighted.[93] This approach offers two additional advantages. First, it supplements what has often been an abstract focus on political and media discourse when we compare the national framing of difference to our empirical data on individuals' everyday expression, which echoes discourse from the public arena.[94] Second, we bring into the conversation an understudied case that has drawn less international attention than European nations with larger colonial footprints or longer histories of large-scale immigration—Italy. The existing transatlantic second-generation surveys that have been such a productive source of sociological analysis do not include Italian samples, mirroring a broader neglect of the *bel paese* in U.S. social science.[95] For this reason, we think it especially valu-able to draw on the growing research by Italian and other scholars who are taking up the question of the place of "race" in Italy, often by interrogating Italian colonial memory.[96]

Finally, it is our hope that our binational cooperation will allow us to make an especially valuable contribution to debates about the comparative study of descent-based difference that have proved to be so contentious. As we discussed at the beginning of this chapter, the understandable concern that researchers' national frames influence and even limit their analyses has sown a great deal of mistrust and even derision. It is not surprising then that Maurice Crul and John Mollenkopf warn against simply "transplanting American theoretical frameworks to the European context," or that Jens Schneider and his colleagues note that "transatlantic comparison teaches us something new about how research perspectives are embedded in the idiosyncrasies of their respective societies."[97] Although Adrian Favell attri-butes successful transatlantic comparisons to "the few European scholars who have put in serious time on both sides of the ocean," we have as models multinational collaborations like those of the Canadian Michèle Lamont with the French Laurent Thévenot, the American Nancy Foner with the

French Patrick Simon, and especially the Dutch Maurice Crul with the American John Mollenkopf; Crul and Mollenkopf paired up experts on either side of the Atlantic to undertake comparisons of North America and Western Europe in varied domains such as employment or education.[98]

Like our predecessors, we have tried hard to avoid the pitfalls of intellectual ethnocentrism by confronting our assumptions and habits of thought at every step of the way. As Lamont and Thévenot explain, "talking things through" is paramount: "Abstract differences became very concrete as researchers deeply committed to them . . . attempted to make their colleagues understand the inner logic of their thinking."[99] For us, this process began in earnest with the design of an interview questionnaire that we knew could not simply be a translation into Italian of the English one that Morning had used in *The Nature of Race*. Not surprisingly, the interviews themselves proved to be marvelously thought-provoking experiences for both of us, ones that we enjoyed rehashing directly afterwards to exchange our initial thoughts, reactions, and questions. The interests and preoccupations of the different national audiences to whom we have presented our work—in the United States, Italy, France, and elsewhere—have also given us invaluable food for thought. Our hope is that this challenging work of blending and balancing our divergent national approaches has produced a book that identifies what is taken for granted by our academic conationals and helps far-flung research communities—particularly those around the Atlantic—understand each other better. Another way to put it is that we have aspired to write a book that makes sense, is persuasive, and resonates for both European and American audiences simultaneously. A comparable measure of success, however, might be the degree to which we provoke skepticism, indignation, or offense equally on all sides.

Our ambitions may be complicated—yet well served—by the fact that ours is not just a cross-national team, but also one composed of individuals who are differently racialized. The contrast between our racial identities, whether embraced or held at arm's length, and between our daily treatment as a white man and a woman of color has enriched our work and given it special salience. Maneri was brought up in a middle-class residential development outside Milan where Northern Italianness was the norm, Southerners were stigmatized, whiteness was inconceivable, and people of color were virtually nonexistent. Class, generation, gender, and region of origin were all recognizable social cleavages; race—deemed by Italians a foreign problem—was not. Yet sensitivity to descent-based exclusion marked Maneri's family, which was headed by a father frequently teased for his Sicilian birthplace (despite his Milanese upbringing and dialect) and by a Colombian-born mother of Italian origin who regularly objected to anti-Southern prejudice even though she was not a target of it. Morning, on the other hand, grew up in New York City's Harlem, the daughter of light-skinned African American professionals consumed with what was then called "racial progress." One of her earliest memories is of being asked by a babysitter, "What race are you?" Since then, she has learned that the answer depends on where she is. From being black at home, she has gone on to be considered *métisse* (mixed) as a student in France and *blanca* (white) as a U.S. Foreign Service Officer in Honduras. To strangers in Italy, she is not viewed as African American but rather taken to be Brazilian, Caribbean, or Hawaiian, at least by those who speculate openly. And on the streets of her native New York City, she is often read as Latina.

Our respective racializations have not only shaped our outlooks and the ways in which others interact with us but also, in so doing, fueled a sustained dialogue that forms the backdrop of this book. This has been true from the earliest days of our project planning over coffee at the University of Milan–Bicocca, where Morning was startled to find that the sugar packets were decorated with a blackface logo—and even more stupefied to learn that none of her Italian sociologist colleagues had even noticed it. What the advertising image reflected and its impact on busy professors and students rushing through their morning *espresso* were some of the first questions among a decade's worth to follow that we have posed to each other and tried to reason through together. Such everyday incidents have provided fruitful terrain for an ongoing conversation about how our compatriots see, create, think about, and discuss difference.

CHAPTER 1

Debating "Race" in Europe and the United States

An automobile engine can be turned off, in neutral, or going at 5000 rpm. But even when off it is a coordinated whole; the elements are tuned and linked to each other and, with appropriate maintenance, ready to enter into motion when the car is ignited. The system of racist thought that is part of our society's culture is like this motor: built, fine-tuned and not always moving or pushed to maximum speed. Its hum can be almost imperceptible, like that of a good engine in neutral. At the right time it can, in a moment of crisis, take off. In any case, in different ways and measures, it consumes information, materials, lives.

—PAOLA TABET, *La pelle giusta* (The right skin) (1997, v)

IN 1990, the anthropologist Paola Tabet began collecting essays from Italian schoolchildren on themes like "If I Were an Indian" or "My Life in an African Country." Over the following years, her initiative enrolled countless primary school teachers who, through word of mouth, enlisted others to assign their pupils these exercises in social imagination and mail the resulting compositions to Tabet. By 1997, she had amassed over seven thousand essays written by children ages seven to thirteen in every corner of the country. By far the most powerful reflections she received—the most vivid and emotionally charged—were the assignments on the topic "If My Parents Were Black."

The book that Tabet published in 1997 on this research, *La pelle giusta* (The right skin), identifies a striking range of feelings that the young writers so forcefully expressed: fear, disgust, shame, rejection, denial, violence, paternalism, and desire for resolution. In contrast to the essays on "If My Parents Were American," in which schoolchildren imagined pleasure and material comfort, the prospect of parents becoming black was highly distressing to many. "If my parents were black," wrote a second-grader, "I don't know if I want them in my house because they scare me, and at night I can't sleep because they scare me, they scare me so much."[1] A third-grader in Ferrara imagined, "If my parents were black I wouldn't hug them, I wouldn't cuddle with them. . . . If my parents were black I wouldn't have them sit on my bed or on my sister's, because there are the sheets that are white, I wouldn't have them sit on the couch even."[2] And a first-grader in Florence simply stated, "If my parents were black I would throw them out of the house because they're too ugly. If I were black I would kill myself."[3]

At first glance, the dramatic scenarios envisioned by Italian children may seem to offer above all a primer on racial stereotypes. But Tabet's aim was more far-reaching: her object of analysis was instead the broader "racist ideology" or "system of racist thought" in Italy—the finely tuned motor that, even when dormant, is always present and ready to spring into action. "'Race,' that scientifically imaginary but socially real and fatal category," she writes, "is at the bottom of the solutions and formal choices, at the bottom of the emotions and representations of these children."[4] In their writing she found what she considers "the fundamental elements of the ideology of 'race'"—the classification of humans into discrete and hierarchical categories, based on biological traits real or presumed, and the attribution of psychological and cultural consequences to these physical traits.[5] Tabet illustrated the latter with the essay of a Sardinian third-grader who imagined that upon dousing his black parents with warm milk, they would become white and thus able to speak Italian.[6]

Tabet's findings may seem to lay to rest the question of whether race exists as a meaningful concept in Italy. But her young subjects' words also complicate any straightforward conclusion about a global race notion. In particular, they reveal that taxonomies of imagined human groups are so infinitely malleable as to call into question the centrality or necessity of biological distinction that Tabet underscored. For "blacks" turn out to be not a collective of human beings with dark skin or ancestral roots in Africa, but rather a motley assortment of people the children associated with poverty, foreignness, and powerlessness. In the words of a Calabrian fourth-grader:

> I wouldn't ever want to be the child of negroes because no one accepts them and they're inferior. The life of negroes is really terrible because, just looking at them, they're poor.[7] I wouldn't know how to define a negro, but I've never liked negro skin and never will. Negroes are born in South America, Iraq, Morocco, Albania etc. . . . Negroes aren't accepted at school, and they throw them out, and I wouldn't want to be outside by myself. . . . Negroes are born from three races of black, yellow, and white skin.[8]

As Tabet notes, such notions of blackness should not be dismissed as erroneous or fanciful interpretations of children with little knowledge of the world. Instead, she argues, "the children's essays are . . . not wrong, but rather they mirror and respect a specific social classification, a projection of the power relations between social groups, when they make 'negroes' of Albanians, Tunisians, Moroccans or Yugoslavs."[9] Her observation raises the question: What analytic notion of race would capture and include this variation?

La pelle giusta throws into relief the semantics, conceptual content, and analytical utility of race. Can the ideas expressed by her young writers—fundamentally notions about differences between types of human beings—be profitably described using the terminology of "race"? Are ideas of race at work when Eastern Europeans and sub-Saharan Africans are lumped together? If so, what is the definition of "race" that makes its analytical application appropriate here? And if not, is there another concept of difference at work that we should name and use as an analytic tool? There often seems to be an implicit consensus on both sides of the Atlantic that discourse about blacks is racial, but does that hold true for ideas about Asians or Roma or Jews or Muslims? In short, under what circumstances do we employ the language of race and find it suitable?

The question of how people employ terms like "race" takes on special importance in the virtual absence of empirical scholarship on how they conceive of descent-based difference. Even in the United States, where race and ethnicity have been fixtures of academic sociology for a century, social scientists have not seriously explored their underlying conceptual landscape. As a result, we know little of how everyday people understand the differences—cultural, biological, or other—that ostensibly distinguish the descent-based categories with which they live.[10] What Americans think "races" are exactly has been overlooked—or taken for granted. In continental Europe, where race and ethnicity are not fundamental topics of academic research and teaching the way they are in the United States and the United Kingdom, scholarship theorizing the conceptualization of descent-based difference is even thinner. Although there is no shortage of work on stereotypes of descent-based groups or by premier theorists of racism or alterity, there is little in the way of systematic empirical investigation of just how Western Europeans think about descent-based categories and the types of difference that supposedly demarcate them.[11]

In the absence of data on individuals' notions of difference, there are no ready answers to this book's central comparative questions regarding the beliefs that hold sway in Europe as opposed to the United States. Accordingly, this chapter turns instead to scholarship on two adjacent domains that have been taken as evidence of a transatlantic rift in the conceptualization of difference. Both concern the uses of "race," either as a discursive term or as an analytic tool; we investigate the literature on them in an attempt to take the measure, even if only indirectly, of the ways of talking and thinking about descent-based difference that predominate in Europe and the United States. In the first realm, researchers have pointed to a marked distinction in linguistic practices and norms regarding discussion of "race," where the dangers or benefits of speaking about race are at issue. The second body of work highlights differences between European and American academics on the relevance of race for understanding society. Although our literature review outlines differences in speaking and reasoning about descent-based groups between the two settings, we ultimately conclude by underscoring meaningful commonalities across the Atlantic.

Linguistic Norms and Practices

The depiction of Western Europeans as taking a more cultural perspective on group differences and of Americans as viewing them in a more biologized fashion may be colored in no small part by the speech practices and norms that prevail on either side of the Atlantic. In particular, the greater deployment of the word "race" in the United States seems to have led many to assume that physical difference—traditionally at the heart of classic racial taxonomy—is more salient for Americans than for Europeans.

A closer look at how Americans and Europeans use racial language, however, complicates the picture.

The Avoidance of Public "Race" Speech in Western Europe

When it comes to discourse in the public sphere, continental Europe is a world away from the "hyperracial" talk—overt, quotidian, and even casual—that is on display throughout the United States.[12] The ubiquity of racial classification in official or medical matters and the prominence of the word "race" in journalism, academia, and law has little parallel across the Atlantic. Like most countries worldwide, continental Western European nations do not register individuals' race on their censuses, and even in the United Kingdom, which does classify its inhabitants as white, Asian, black, or mixed, it is "ethnicity" that is officially requested.[13] Individuals are not asked to indicate their race when applying for schools or filling out medical forms, and newspapers do not often report on "racial" differentials in employment rates or access to medical care.

Even in the legal landscape concerned with antidiscrimination, "race" figures little in Europe. Although some national constitutions (like Italy's) prohibit race-based discrimination, there have been multiple attempts to excise the term from those and other laws, and concern about its mention has been expressed even by bodies like the European Commission on Racism and Intolerance.[14] For example, the 2000 European Racial Equality Directive (RED) includes this disclaimer: "The European Union rejects theories which attempt to determine the existence of separate human races. The use of the term 'racial origin' in this Directive does not imply an acceptance of such theories."[15] Michele Grigolo, Costanza Hermanin, and Mathias Möschel argue that such "racial skepticism" characterizes "the continental European approach" in general, and they locate it at the root of European reluctance to employ the word "race" in official business. "The view that races do not exist at all," they posit, leads to racial skeptics' desire to "simply eliminate race from political and normative discourse."[16]

Avoidance of racial language is not limited to official documents but is also evident in public speech practices in Europe. As Grigolo and his colleagues put it, "Any discourse about race in a normative, epistemological or ontological sense is still, to a large extent, a taboo."[17] Anna Skarpelis calls this "bracketing race," echoing Anna Curcio and Miguel Mellino's idea of it as a "foreclosed"—and "ghostly"—subject in Italy.[18] Cristina Lombardi-Diop also sees race in Italy as "often unnamed and ultimately silenced."[19]

It is, however, in France—"the archetype of a colourblind society"—that social scientists have most closely traced the contours of European prohibitions on racial discourse.[20] For example, Mathilde Cohen's observations of French courtrooms and interviews with judges, prosecutors, and other legal workers revealed strong proscriptions against the mention of race or ethnicity. Identifying as a minority was considered an unacceptable departure from magisterial impartiality, and it was nearly impossible to discuss the lack of racial or ethnic diversity in the judiciary because "race and ethnicity were unspeakable in the sense that they were declared inexistent and, therefore, inappropriate to discuss."[21] In a less elite occupation, François Bonnet has found equally strong speech norms concerning race and ethnicity among security personnel working in a mall and a train station in France. Like the judges, they embraced "colourmute" talk and were sensitive to any deviations from it.[22] The evidence from very distinct sectors of French society of a strong preference for "race"-free public speech illustrates Skarpelis's observation that this semantic absence is produced across myriad sites, including "the law, the bureaucracy, social science scholarship, political and popular rhetoric and narratives, historical representation and collective memory, architecture, and the arts."[23]

The practice of sidestepping race (or ethnicity) in Western European discourse is rooted in not just one speech norm but several. One is the "racial skepticism" we have already seen, where the moral injunction is to be truthful, to remain faithful to the reality that there is no such thing as human races. Another anti-"race talk" norm is grounded in concerns about privacy and the potential for state abuses of administrative data to the detriment of vulnerable populations.[24] The most powerful of these norms, however, is rooted in the fear that racial discourse will "perpetuate the idea of the existence of biological races and, by extension, racism."[25] Michael Banton sums up this view nicely when he quotes a former mentor, Cedric Dover, as having asserted that "the most fundamental cause of racism . . . is the use of the loaded word race."[26]

As many have noted, this anxiety about the consequences of racial terminology on the continent is rooted in the Holocaust, which David Theo Goldberg has characterized as "the defining event—the turning-point, perhaps—of race and racially inscribed histories. . . . The Holocaust signals the horrors of racial invocation and racist summation."[27] In Italy, a further layer of "semantic refusal" is added by the contemporary rejection of the anti-Semitic language and laws that flourished under Fascism.[28] Overall, the moral repugnance of "race" discussion in Western Europe renders the word "unmentionable, unspeakable" for many, and ultimately "an embarrassment."[29]

Where "Race" Can Be Spoken

Yet "race" speech retains an unmistakable hold in certain contexts in Western Europe. Evidence suggests that adherence to public color-blindness is uneven across national settings, and it may not extend to private discussion or to all public domains. For example, there is a "discussion in Britain about 'race' and 'race relations' [that] is not to be found in other European societies," according to John Solomos and John Wrench.[30] In a comparison of France, the Netherlands, and Italy, François Bonnet and Clotilde Caillault find marked differences in the way police officers speak about ethnoracial minorities. In interviews, French officers were very uncomfortable with the explicit mention of ethnic categories, while Dutch and Italian police were not. However, both Dutch and French officers were anxious not to be labeled as racist, whereas "Italian respondents [were] virtually indifferent to a possible accusation of racism."[31]

Bonnet and Caillault's findings also lend support to the claim that ethno-racial labeling is accepted in Europe when used toward repressive ends. So does Cohen's observation that race is noted in courtroom files on people of color but is not considered mentionable when the fairness or inclusiveness of France's overwhelmingly white judiciary is being challenged. Noting that French courts have upheld policies of racial segregation in prisons, even when segregation is tied to unequal living conditions, Möschel charges that

> race is only selectively silenced. When race (or ethnic origin) is to be used in an anti-subordination and anti-discrimination mode the legal arguments of unity, indivisibility and equality are being deployed to thwart attempts at promoting justice. On the contrary, in the repressive mode, e.g. in prisons, by police or the secret services, race and ethnicity withstand legal challenge. Hence, far from establishing a symmetrical vision of colour-blindness, the French legal system asymmetrically recognizes race and ethnicity in ways which ultimately benefit the white majority.[32]

In a similar vein, Hermanin traces the unfolding of state targeting and expulsion of Roma people—even when citizens—in Italy and France despite general qualms about official ethnoracial classification.[33] Möschel also sees "bias and hypocrisy" when it comes to European debates about anti-white racism: "The slowness and reluctance of institutions, public actors, and the media to call something racism when it involves the victimisation of people of colour is not equalled by slowness and reluctance to frame things in terms of race and racism when the victim belongs to the White/Christian majority."[34]

Ethnoracial classification flourished, moreover, in Europe's colonial territories—the ultimate in repressive societies—and so the modern-day continuation of such colonial relationships has repercussions for the uses of racial terminology today.[35] In her interviews with French judges, Cohen found a striking exception to the racial "rule of silence" among those who had served in courts in overseas France, including regions, territories, and collectivities such as Guadeloupe, Réunion, and Saint Martin. Heirs to French colonial law, "which deviated from universalistic principles . . . by instituting a specific regime based on racial inequality and oppression," these magistrates were familiar with settings where race was openly discussed. But while they connected racial categories to overseas France—and had for the first time experienced themselves as raced in those settings— once back in metropolitan France they were "unwilling to apply racial lens, or as Fassin (2014, 236) put it, to 'repatriate whiteness.'"[36]

In contrast, some Europeans of color have embraced the language of "race" as a means of recognizing and grappling with their experiences. Consider, for example, the following developments in France: the 2005 founding of the Representative Council of Black Associations, which broke taboos by embracing the label "black" and pushing for an accurate count of the black population in France; the movement to acknowledge and come to terms with the colonial and slave past; Le Monde magazine's 2014 cover story on the black elite; and searching documentaries by Isabelle Boni-Claverie (Too Black to Be French?, 2015) and Rokhaya Diallo (From Paris to Ferguson: Guilty of Being Black (Not Yo Mama's Movement, 2016).[37] These developments in France have parallels elsewhere in Western Europe—such as the "Black Pete Is Racism" movement in the Netherlands or new recognition of black Germans—where "race" or racial labels are explicitly mentioned in the pursuit of social justice.

Perhaps the biggest challenge to depicting continental Europe as a "race"-free zone, however, comes from ample evidence that overt race talk and categorization live on in more informal or private conversation. Bonnet finds that French security officers' adherence to nonracial speech norms in interviews does not prevent them from actively using racial categories in their work (for example, in the hiring or deployment of guards), much as Cohen reports having heard racial references in French courtrooms, where people of color are disproportionately processed, despite judges' hostility to discussing the ethnoracial makeup of their profession.[38] And when Patrick Simon and Martin Clément asked French survey-takers to identify themselves in ethnic and even racial categories and then inquired about their reactions to the exercise, the researchers discovered that their respondents registered much less discomfort than expected. That only about 12 percent reported being very uncomfortable with such self-identification suggests that ethnoracial classification is about as sensitive for French respondents as income reporting.[39]

The slippery slope from racial labels to racial epithets reveals another area in which European race talk flourishes. Despite the presumption that Italians have no vocabulary for discussing race, everyday Italian slurs illustrate the opposite.[40] *Vu' cumprà* (Wanna buy?), for example, is a label largely applied to sub-Saharan Africans that mocks Senegalese peddlers' imperfect Italian—heavily inflected with also stigmatized Southern Italian dialect—and yokes them to their marginal socioeconomic position.[41] *Marocchini* (Moroccans) has been "used as a sort of racial shorthand by Italians to signify all immigrants of color."[42] Similarly, Annamaria Rivera notes how in professional soccer, players of all stripes come to be *negrizzati*; Colombian, Brazilian, North African, Italian-French, Belgian-Moroccan, Albanian, Neapolitan, and Sicilian athletes can all find themselves the object of anti-black epithets.[43] The sports stadium is just one of several arenas in Italy—like advertising, film, television, and politics—where explicit race talk and imagery can be found, likely mirroring a certain acceptance in private.[44]

To account for the uneven impact of prohibitions on everyday race speech, Bonnet concludes that they vary by the type of social interaction in question; they "are not about what can be said (in the abstract), but about to whom it is said." As a result, even racial epithets can be normalized. "When an interview begins as a conversation between strangers," he maintains, "slurs are offensive. A few minutes later, when the interview interaction is redefined as a casual chat among acquaintances, the slurs may lose their offensiveness for the participants."[45] David Sulmont and Juan Carlos Callirgos's comments on the variegated uses of racial language in Peru are also applicable even though they are not observations on Europe:

> While Peruvians are taught the "official truths" that we are all equal before law and that racism is to be reviled, individuals acquire, through subtle but efficient methods, the ability to classify and discriminate racially, and to reproduce historically constructed and emotionally loaded racial prejudices. Since Peruvians learn that racism instilled in them should be rejected, the manifestations of racism are usually covert, disguised, or appear in conflict situations, for example, when composure is lost, and in insults.[46]

Like the finding that implicit bias may be most consequential in split-second decisions over which individuals exercise less conscious control, Sulmont and Callirgos suggest that public exhortations to eschew race talk are not enough to make it disappear from the emotional language of daily life.[47]

Revisiting the United States versus Europe Contrast: Converging Speech Norms?

The evident limits of the continental European taboo on "race" language call into question the idea that speech norms and practices are markedly different on either side of the Atlantic. Upon closer inspection, some important discursive similarities are apparent and indeed may be growing.

For one thing, we would be remiss if we overlooked how familiar Americans are with color-blind speech as both practice and norm, despite domestic variation in both.[48] Even though Americans apparently have fewer reservations about explicitly mentioning "race," direct discussion of it remains sensitive, particularly in public social settings, including at school or work.[49] It comes as no surprise, then, that the semantic strategies that Cohen and Bonnet encountered in France parallel linguistic findings in the United States. Bonilla-Silva argues that the post–civil rights era in the United States has come to be characterized by a particular style—that is, "peculiar *linguistic manners and rhetorical strategies* (or *racetalk*)"—that he calls "the language of color blindness."[50] Chief among its hallmarks is the avoidance of overtly racial rhetoric, a semantic device noted by other observers; in other words, Americans are no strangers to the self-censorship of "race" talk.[51] Indeed, in a different national contrast, John Hartigan notes that, "while the 'national conversation on race' in the United States may stand in stark contrast to the still common Mexican insistence that 'race' is a foreign, distorting optic when applied to that country's public discourse, Americans are deeply ensnared by 'color-blind racism' that obscures the important, ongoing operations of racial domination."[52] Not surprisingly, a popular reaction to the Black Lives Matter movement in the United States has been to assert that "All Lives Matter."

An even more striking transatlantic convergence has been the rise of political initiatives in the United States that mirror France's efforts to rein in educators' discussion of race. In 2017, Minister of National Education Jean-Michel Blanquer announced that he would sue a French teachers' union that was planning a series of workshops for its members that would discuss *racisme d'Etat* ("state" or institutional racism); he also contended that the words *racisé* (raced, or racialized) and *blanchité* (whiteness) disseminated racism.[53] In 2020, Blanquer denounced the "ravage" of France's university system by "Islamo-leftists," paving the way for Minister of Higher Education Frédérique Vidal to call for an investigation of their impact on social scientific research in 2021. By "Islamo-leftism," the ministers meant scholarship exploring race, gender, intersectionality, and postcolonialism, which they—along with President Emmanuel Macron—saw as a dangerous import from U.S. and British academia that fueled divisiveness in their country.[54]

In the meantime, conservative politicians in the United States were busy trying to stamp out what they saw as "critical race theory." In September 2020, President Donald Trump issued an executive order banning the federal government and its contractors from offering diversity training that took aim at gender and racial bias.[55] And in the very last days of his administration, Trump's 1776 Commission released a report calling for "patriotic education" that the president hoped would counter "decades of left-wing indoctrination in our schools," particularly their teaching on slavery and systemic racism. Like his French counterpart, the U.S. president saw in the nation's universities in particular "hotbeds of anti-Americanism, libel, and censorship that combine to generate in students and in the broader culture at the very least disdain and at worst outright hatred for this country."[56] Since the end of the Trump presidency, the Republican Party has continued the agenda of blocking teaching on white privilege or oppression, usually by legislative attempts to ban the use of the "1619 Project"; published in the

New York Times, this work is an exploration of slavery and its aftermath in the four hundred years since the arrival of the first African slaves in British North America.[57] It comes as no surprise, then, that GOP senator Mitch McConnell dismissed President Joseph Biden's proposal to support school initiatives on systemic racism as "divisive nonsense."[58]

These cases make clear that attempts to shape public discourse on race—whether in North America or Western Europe—are not rooted solely in norms of antiracism, respect for individuals' privacy, or adherence to scientific truth. More fundamentally, they are anchored in what Michael Omi and Howard Winant call "racial projects," which harness the "interpretation, representation, or explanation of racial dynamics" to "effort[s] to reorganize and redistribute resources along particular racial lines."[59] In the United States, Biden's educational agenda is intended to lend special support to U.S. racial minorities "who have been historically underserved, marginalized and adversely affected by persistent poverty and inequality."[60] Conversely, Trump followers see the need to protect white Americans through "memory laws"; hence the promotion of "Anglo-Saxon political traditions" and the exculpatory attempts to prohibit teaching that "individuals, by virtue of sex, race, ethnicity, religion, color, or national origin, are inherently responsible for actions committed in the past by other members of the same sex, race, ethnicity, religion, color, or national origin."[61] Similarly, the French watchdog group Observatoire du décolonialisme et des idéologies identitaires (Observatory of Decolonialism and Identitarian Ideologies) shares the government's preoccupation with "Islamo-leftist" scholarship, fearing that it will "deconstruct all the 'privileges' of white culture wherever it is expressed in society: the Republic and all its institutions, starting with school."[62]

In a nation like the United States, where race is a highly institutionalized feature of governance, public color-blindness can probably go only so far. To be sure, animosity toward affirmative action has prompted several states to ban consideration of race in sectors like public employment and college admissions. But the long and unbroken history of federal use of overt racial classification makes it impossible—or at least highly aspirational—for Americans to avoid the language of "race." Doing away with explicit references to race might seem more feasible in Europe. In addition, Europeans' relatively recent and immediate experience of the Holocaust gives a powerful moral impetus to the push to erase "race" from their vocabulary. In contrast, the history of colonialism and slavery that the United States shares with Western European nations seems to be perceived as too temporally or geographically removed to have the same galvanizing force, on either side of the Atlantic. Yet in both regions the outlines of similar racial projects can be discerned, manifested in a comparable range of attitudes toward "race" speech, whether public or private. This leads us to ask what similarities or differences emerge between the United States and Western Europe when we move from the question of whether race should be discussed in the classroom and other spaces to the matter of how race should figure—or not—in our scientific analyses of the social world.

The Perceived Societal Relevance of "Race"

Might perceptions of the analytic utility of race—of its relevance for understanding the workings of society—offer another avenue for comparing how Americans and Western Europeans understand descent-based difference? In this section, we first explore what might be called the "race-conscious" (or "realist" to its proponents) position—more solidly grounded in the United States than in Europe—that either race structures contemporary society or it is a useful tool for making sense of the social world.[63] We then take up the "race-skeptic" (or perhaps "cautious" to its adherents) view— apparently more widespread in Europe than in the United States—that either race is not a factor in producing social outcomes or it is of limited use in explaining such results.

Racial Consciousness: The Social Existence and Utility of Race

In the American imagination, racial difference looms large. Despite many unifying social characteristics—such as a shared national language in English, a largely Judeo-Christian religious tradition, and widespread embrace of the individualist, market-based American Dream—Americans see racial groups as markedly distinct, and "a large number of white Americans have become comfortable with as much racial inequality and segregation as a putatively nondiscriminatory polity and free market economy can produce."[64] In such a race-steeped society, it is not hard to imagine how race might be at work, whether one takes the laissez-faire view that minority groups are responsible for their own socioeconomic shortcomings; subscribes to the supremacist view that nonwhites are inherently incapable of attaining an equal footing with whites; or believes that society's characteristics have a hand in inequalities. Polls estimating that more than 80 percent of Americans believe that racial discrimination exists in the United States today provide further indication that race is widely associated with social outcomes there.[65] With such a high degree of consensus on the relevance of race, regardless of the mechanisms imagined to be at work, it comes as no surprise that it holds a prominent place in American social science.[66] Race-focused books, journals, conferences, textbooks, courses, and so on, are standard fare in the U.S. academy.

While this is not the case in Western Europe beyond Great Britain, race is undoubtedly gaining new prominence as a meaningful subject of scholarly inquiry there. In France, for example, monographs like Didier Fassin and Éric Fassin's *From the Social Question to the Racial Question? Representing French Society*, Emmanuelle Saada's *Empire's Children: Race, Filiation, and Citizenship in the French Colonies*, and the historian Pap Ndiaye's *The Black Condition: Essay on a French Minority* have succeeded earlier work on racism and have been followed by important contributions by Magali Bessone, Jean-Frédéric Schaub, Sarah Mazouz, and others.[67] Italian scholars have also transitioned from earlier studies of racism (and colonialism) to a growing openness to research on race, despite resistance from "the many different voices of the whole Italian anti-racist movement."[68] The last decade has seen a flourishing of Italian academic writing on race, including: *White and Black: History of Italians' Racial Identity* by Gaia Giuliani and Cristina Lombardi-Diop; *Speaking of Race: The Language of Color between Italy and the United States* by Tatiana Petrovich Njegosh and Anna Scacchi; *Racial Cities: Governance and the Segregation of Romani People in Urban Europe* by Giovanni Picker; *The Black Mediterranean: Bodies, Borders, and Citizenship* by Danewid and her colleagues; and *Contesting Race and Citizenship: Diasporic Politics in Italy and the Black Mediterranean* by Camilla Hawthorne.[69] Finally, networks of European scholars of race have been formed through institutions like the Black Europe Summer School in Amsterdam; the Global Race Project run by the French National Institute of Demographic Studies; and the University of Padua's Interdisciplinary Research Group on Race and Racisms (InteRGRace).

"Race consciousness" in Europe is grounded in the recognition that Western racial classification is the legacy of continental intellectuals like François Bernier (1620–1688), Carl Linnaeus (1707–1778), and Johann Friedrich Blumenbach

(1752–1840) and was formed in large part before the founding of the United States. "To reference race as native to contemporary European thought," Fatima El-Tayeb writes, "violates the powerful narrative of Europe as a colorblind continent, largely untouched by the devastating ideology it exported all over the world."

> This narrative, framing the continent as a space free of "race" (and by impli-
> cation, racism), is not only central to the way Europeans perceive them-
> selves, but has also gained near-global acceptance. Despite the geographical
> and intellectual origin of the very concept of race in Europe, not to mention
> the explicitly race-based policies that characterized both its fascist regimes
> and its colonial empires, the continent often is marginal at best in discourses
> on race or racism, in particular with regard to contemporary configurations
> that are often closely identified with the United States.[70]

Philomena Essed similarly rejects the "Dutch myth that racism is a structural problem in the United States but not in the Netherlands. Few manifestations of racism are unique to the United States. This is consistent
with the fact that anti-Black racism is ideologically rooted in the same
Euro-American value system and in the same historical relations between
Europeans and Americans."[71]

Making the empirical case that race continues to shape social structure
and culture in contemporary Western Europe is hampered, however, by the
general dearth of racial or ethnic statistics there.[72] In the absence of census or
other official data detailing socioeconomic differentials, claims about racial
or ethnic boundaries in Western Europe are often buttressed by survey
reports—and to a lesser extent, by qualitative studies—of prejudice and
discrimination.[73] Based on the 2007 TIES (The Integration of the European
Second Generation) survey, which collected data from more than ten thousand respondents in fifteen European cities, Foner and Simon reported that
"in France and the Netherlands, for example, Afro-Caribbeans and sub-
Saharan Africans perceive discrimination against them as based in good
part on color."[74] Similarly, substantial numbers of people of sub-Saharan or
North African descent reported in the "Trajectories and Origins" survey of
nearly twenty-two thousand inhabitants of metropolitan France that they
had been the target of racist insults or attitudes, including in public settings like schools, universities, government offices, and police stations, with
the figure reaching as high as 55 percent among some sub-Saharan origin

groups.[75] In Italy, research has pointed to prejudice in political and media discourse as well as individual and institutional discrimination against Roma and immigrants.[76] In sum, work like this has tried to empirically document, analyze, and make visible what Goldberg identified as European "generalizabilities," including "the extended and untouchable exclusions, denigrations, and alienations at once racially presupposed, expressed, and reproduced"—for example, in education, employment, housing, media, and police profiling—as well as "the informal insults that circulate so readily. Raceless racisms, everyday and every way."[77]

The proponents of "race consciousness" take issue with "race skepticism," then, because they are persuaded that it misrepresents social fact.[78] Alana Lentin, for example, charges that "by not naming race because, in essence, it would be racist to do so, influential thinkers . . . were in fact denying both the significance of racism . . . and the persistence of the racism embedded in institutions that did not change simply because the word 'race' could no longer be uttered."[79] There are several ways in which such scholars see the societal role of race as being misrecognized if not outright ignored. First and foremost, many have argued that there is a "reduction of the racial to the Jewish question," which not only overlooks the non-Jewish victims of the Holocaust—like those targeted as Roma, sexual minorities, disabled, or communist—but also obscures other forms of race thinking, past and present.[80] Europe's colonial past is thus freed from any connection to race, and indeed, colonialism is seen as irrelevant to Europe, having "taken place elsewhere."[81] Limiting the scope of race's role to World War II also removes it from contemporary life. As a result, racist discourse today can be treated as simply a vestige of the past, and the racism of the present can go unexamined unless it refers explicitly to the ideal-type of Nazism.[82] The end result, the race-conscious argue, is the "denial," "silencing," "bracketing," or rendering invisible of a major social force in modern Europe. Indeed, this invisibility is what allows race to persist, they contend.[83]

Worse, according to a race-conscious perspective, color-blind speech and social science not only obscure racism but actually facilitate it. Such practices allow racism to flourish free from scrutiny, and they rob policy-makers, officials, academics, activists, and everyday people of an important set of analytical, legal, and communicative tools for combatting racism.[84] What is needed instead, they assert, is a transparent engagement with the social fact of race—for example, by allowing for the collection of statistical data on individuals' self-reported racial identification. In this vein, the demographer Patrick Simon writes: "For the first time in their history, European societies are confronted [by] racial diversity [in] the populations they have portrayed as inferior for centuries. Is colourblindness an appropriate intellectual and policy frame to achieve equality and cohesion with this new diversity?"[85] Another concrete realm where color-blindness impedes attempts to address racial discrimination is hate crime prosecution, according to Möschel:

> The difficulties of police, judges and institutions to recognise and sanction racially motivated crimes have a number of facets that require deeper reflection and analysis. First, it vastly reduces the phenomenon of racism and the existence of racists, thus making European societies and their statistics on racist crimes look much better than they actually are. Second, in light of the current situation our construction of a racist is extremely narrow and limited to the most evident and outrageous cases. And even in those cases, sometimes one can only wonder what else must be done in order to qualify the crime as racially motivated. This legal construction mirrors and reinforces the social view, which allows racist sentiments and acts while at the same time rejecting any affiliation with racism. Racism and racists in mainland Europe remain limited to openly anti-Semitic statements and acts perpetrated by right wing neo-Nazis, or to the occasional case where a judge finds things have gone too far. Third, given those extremely narrow boundaries within which racism is recognised, anti-racist NGOs are prevented from intervening in the trial thus leaving the victims or their families even more isolated. Fourth, it sends the message to those perpetrating racially motivated crimes that they will go free or at least that the racial motivation will not be recognised as such. Last but not least, the case law sends out a message to those individuals and groups most victimised by racist attacks that the law and the institutions are not with them, are not protecting them in the same way as they do with people who are not prone to that type of attack.[86]

In this context where "race is not, or really is no longer," Goldberg finds that "Europe begins to exemplify what happens when no category is available to name a set of experiences that are linked in their production or at least inflection, historically and symbolically, experientially and politically, to racial arrangements and engagements." What we are left with, he suggests, is "a compelling case study in the frustrations, delimitations, and injustices of political racelessness."[87]

Racial Skepticism: The Nonexistence or Selective Relevance of "Race"

Not all societies are quick to perceive race or other forms of descent-based difference as existent or active in shaping social outcomes within their borders. Hartigan describes the Mexican insistence that "discrimination is not a problem in their country," and the notion of Brazil as a "racial democracy" is well known to researchers.[88] This attitude may circulate among laypeople, among social scientists, or among both. Moreover, the fact that racial classification is so rarely used on national censuses worldwide suggests that it is not a widespread tool for producing social knowledge.[89]

For making sense of society in the Western European context specifically, we discern four interrelated planks to the "skeptic" position that race is not a useful and accurate tool (or "category of analysis").[90] First is an idea that we have seen previously: that race is an intrinsically erroneous idea—a "fallacy" or "myth," in the words of Ashley Montagu—and thus worthless as a guide to the social world.[91] Second is the concern that outcomes that may appear at first glance to be driven by race are actually produced by other social forces. Third is the belief that while race played a role in Europe in the past, it no longer does so. Finally, we explore the argument that "race" is a concept too freighted with assumptions rooted in the American experience to do justice to European (and other) realities.

The idea that race is not "real," encouraged by post–World War II efforts to denounce or defang the race concept, grounds an important strand of race skepticism in Western Europe.[92] For it raises the question: If race does not exist, why and how should we use it to explain the social world around us? This question is especially pertinent where the constructivist message that race can be socially real without being biologically so has not been as widely diffused.[93] A simplistic version of this skepticism is the stance that "races, at least officially, do not exist. Hence neither does racism."[94] However, some scholars have elaborated a more nuanced approach, one in which racism can exist without "race."[95] In this vein, skeptics of race depict it as a folk concept inadequate for rigorous analytical use. Robert Miles, for example, chastised those who have "employed uncritically the common-sense notion of 'race,' reified it and then attributed it with the status of a scientific concept. . . . Thus, perversely, social scientists have prolonged the life of an idea that should be consigned to the dustbin of analytically useless terms: 'There are no "races" and therefore no "race relations".'"[96] Wacquant adds that,

> with precious few exceptions, students of "race" have *accepted lay preconstructions* of the phenomenon. They have been content to tackle "race" in the manner in which it has been constituted as a "social problem" in reality itself. Worse yet: they have taken over as tools of analysis the reified products of the ethnoracial struggles of the past. In short, they have failed to establish a clear demarcation between folk and analytic understandings of "race."[97]

Although the simple idea that "race does not exist, end of story" is less subtle than the academic complaint that the race concept is too infused with lay notions to provide an analytical instrument, both are fundamentally assertions that race is too logically flawed to be of use in understanding society.

A second, related form of skepticism portrays race as something of a mirage, seemingly producing social outcomes that are instead the result of other factors like class or nativity. Instead of taking the strong position that race does not exist, this milder approach does not entirely disavow the existence of race as social fact, but questions its weight and centrality. This softer racial skepticism is exemplified by Andreas Wimmer's critique of the tendency he identifies "to see ethnicity, race, or nationhood wherever one looks," and especially "race-centrism."[98] Möschel characterizes this stance as asserting that "other categories such as gender and class, and not race, help explain the lines of subordination, marginalisation or discrimination in the European context." He attributes it, moreover, to "the strong Marxist and Socialist tradition on the Old Continent, which resulted in a class-based framework of analysis in social sciences in general."[99]

This camp of skeptics aims to demonstrate, however, that a wider array of axes of stratification than just class might be more relevant than race in specific contexts. In a study of Swiss neighborhoods, Wimmer argues that ethnicity (which encompasses race in his definition) is not the most significant boundary at work, although he acknowledges its existence; rather, a master category of the orderly versus the disorderly is uppermost in inhabitants' mental schema.[100] Similarly, in a critique of Richard Alba and Nancy Foner's *Strangers No More: Immigration and the Challenges of Integration in North America and Western Europe*, Favell contends that the impact of race cannot be simply assumed to always be operative and determinant; instead, a specific kind of research design is needed in order to bolster such an assertion—"one that was able to separate out from the 'race' variable(s) causing persistent discrimination or variations in outcome, other possible *explanans* such as: migrant-origin, nationality, citizenship (not always the same thing), non-migrant ethnicity (i.e. visible regional minority origin), or (non-immigrant) mobility histories and trajectories."[101] This call echoes Wimmer's advocacy of "a more systematic disentangling of ethnic and nonethnic processes to avoid an all-encompassing 'ethnic lens' of interpretation."[102] It is worth noting, moreover, that in the United States William Julius Wilson's *The Declining Significance of Race* attempted such a parsing out and was met with no little academic criticism for it.[103] But its adherents might characterize it instead as a clear-eyed, "not necessarily race" orientation, one that does not jump to conclusions about the salience of race worldwide and rather is what we dub "race-cautious."

The third main form of European race skepticism is one that we have already seen because it is often targeted by the race-conscious camp: the argument that while race may have played a role in the past, it is no longer operative at present. Möschel calls this "a common European narrative, whereby race has only played a marginal and exceptional role in each country's history and law, which disappeared and became discredited." The anomalous period in question is the Holocaust, which is seen as "the one and only time, in which domestic laws were explicitly racial"; this view allows the "framing [of] post-World War II Europe and its new institutions, new constitutions, and international human rights instruments as a radical break with the past, as a new era."[104] This location of race in the past also has an American counterpart in the "postracial" optimism that with emancipation, or the civil rights movement, or the Obama presidency, racism was definitively put to rest.[105]

The European association between race and the Holocaust—evident, for example, in the Italian term for the anti-Semitic measures introduced in 1938, *leggi razziali* (racial laws)—has specific repercussions, however, that go beyond historical periodization. For one thing, it identifies race so strongly with the overt policies of totalitarian states that "anything less, such as unconscious, indirect, and structural racism will not be perceived as 'real' racism."[106] For another, it establishes biological interpretations of human difference as *the* race concept, sidestepping the question of whether claims of cultural difference can be racist as well. Both of these ways of conceptualizing the workings of race also act to reduce its salience, because neither indirect racism nor cultural essentialism conjure it up. In short, race skepticism in Western Europe has been fed by the distancing judgment that race is irrelevant because it is *no longer* relevant—it is not now, not here, and not in its true form.

Finally, a fourth type of skepticism about the utility or relevance of the race concept in Western Europe revolves around the apprehension that it is freighted with implicit assumptions of American origin that are simply not applicable across the Atlantic. Ann Laura Stoler for one has noted "the well-worn claim that racism is an organic American problem, not a French one," and El-Tayeb discerns "the idea that U.S. cultural imperialism destroys organic, authentic, and formally unmitigated analytical concepts inherent to the affected regions by superimposing inorganic categories like race."[107] At first glance, this form of European racial skepticism may seem to be simply another kind of distancing move; akin to locating race in the historical past, this view depicts race as a social force operating elsewhere in geographic space. Racial thought thus becomes an intrusion—formerly imposed by the Nazis, now the U.S. cultural hegemon—or a faraway reality (for example, in South Africa or Brazil). This mechanism should be familiar to Americans, especially those in the North who see the South as the national home of racism.

Nevertheless, debate over the portability of race raises an important point about the cultural embeddedness of what passes for knowledge—and travels as such—that should come as no surprise to sociologists.[108] As Wacquant elaborates:

> Social scientists have not only accepted a preconstructed object; they have also elevated *one particular national preconstruction* of "race," that evolved by the United States in the twentieth century, as the basic yardstick by which to measure all instances of ethnoracial subordination and inequality. Like it or not, the sociology of "race" all over the world is dominated by U.S. scholarship. And since U.S. scholarship itself is suffused with U.S. folk conceptions of "race," the peculiar schema of racial division developed by one country during a small segment of its short history . . . has been universalized as the template through which analyses of "race" in all countries and epochs are to be conducted.[109]

It is difficult to argue that the American academy has not enjoyed globally disproportionate power and reach. (The same could be said of France.) More importantly, Wacquant attempts to identify features of the American race concept that bear the mark of its national origins, such as the notion that "'race' is a matter of 'physiology alone'"—in contrast, for example, to the ancestry- and status-based conceptions that Charles Wagley found.[110] The U.S. race concept has also been noted for its distinction between "race" and "ethnicity" and the "Herderian perspective" that "each ethnic group is supposed to be characterized by a specific culture, dense networks of solidarity, and shared identity."[111] This final form of race skepticism brings us back to the question that Paola Tabet's interviews with Italian schoolchildren raised: What kind of "race" idea, if any, might be better suited for understanding Western European societies?

Shared Ground between Race Consciousness and Skepticism?

Examining race-skeptic argumentation side by side with its race-conscious counterpart not only raises questions worthy of exploration but also reveals potential areas for conciliation. For one thing, the skeptics' caution that race may not always be the driver of social outcomes implies that in some instances it is, thus signaling some shared ground with race consciousness. For another, the skeptic argument that "race" is too loaded with American concerns suggests that it might be adapted for use in Europe—as the race-conscious would have it—rather than rejected altogether. In this connection, it is worth noting, for example, that Wacquant's goal is not to do away with all consideration of race but rather to propose a different approach to its study, namely through "an analytic of racial domination." His critique of prevailing approaches that "collapse the different dimensions and modalities of racial domination into a one-dimensional judgmental grid, obscuring crucial differences in the bases, forms, and implications of racial division," suggests that rather than giving up on any analysis of race, more rigorous attention is needed.[112]

At the same time, the race-conscious emphasis on the power of race as a social force need not be at odds with skeptics' attention to the role of factors like class or gender in shaping institutions as well as individual outcomes. They can all be closely entwined, as intersectionality theory maintains, and as research on Italy illustrates. Jeffrey Cole's Sicilian ethnography, for example, links race to class when he identifies three factors that "relegate immigrants to the margins of Italian society and problematize them as physically and culturally different from Italians": economic subordination, political discourse, and Western ethnocentrism.[113] In other words, attitudes toward immigrants are not just reactions to the politically instrumental rhetoric of "invasion" but are also colored by a mix of apprehension and repulsion toward perceived poverty, human bodies marked as irredeemably other and inferior, and cultural practices seen as strange and off-putting. The stereotype of the African vendor, for example, is alarming on many levels: he represents the "transient and poor, dependent on transactions with Italians but independent and unknown to any community," and so "these itinerant peddlers embody the marginal Other and recall the poverty and helplessness of the Third World."[114] Similarly, Kitty Calavita grounds "the racialization of immigrant difference" in the institutionalization of economic marginality:

> Immigrants' stigmata of poverty is [*sic*] every bit as conspicuous and consequential—as racialized—as somatic signs inscribed in bodies, and are at the heart of the social interpretation of those signs. . . . It should be pointed out that . . . while somatic distinctions may be neither necessary nor sufficient for racialization to occur—witness the racialization of Albanians in Italy—the *sine qua non* of immigrant racialization may be their status as members of the third world, their poverty, and their need.[115]

In Turin, the anthropologist Donald Carter's observations of the role of dress, dialect, and Italian-language mastery in Senegalese migrants' daily interactions with Italians also speak to the many levels—of "race," gender, culture, and class—on which reactions to newcomers are constructed.[116]

These multiple signifiers make themselves felt in everyday language, like the semantic dichotomy—not limited to Italy—between dark-skinned "immigrants," *extracomunitari*, or *clandestini* (undocumented) who flee poor nations; and light-skinned *stranieri* (foreigners) who elect to reside temporarily outside their wealthy home countries.[117] Moreover, it is this multiplicity of intertwined conditions that led some of Tabet's school-children to lump Latin Americans, North Africans, and Eastern Europeans all together as members of the same "negro" group. Unbeknownst to them, their perceptions reflected what Nicholas De Genova calls "a more expansive, if provisional, understanding of Blackness as a racialized sociopolitical category," one that "encompass[es] the full spectrum of social identities produced as specifically 'not-white.'"[118]

As was true of overlapping "race speech" norms and practices in Europe and the United States, there is no clear-cut dividing line in the common ground between "conscious" and "skeptic" views on the societal relevance of race. Caricatures of each as monolithic and extreme—as American "race obsession," on the one hand, and as European "race denial," on the other—are unwarranted. As we have seen, the ideological elements of both approaches can be found on either side of the Atlantic, cohabiting in the same societies, though to different degrees. Although many Western Europeans may be dubious about race as a tool, arguments about anti-white racism have been given a respectful hearing.[119] And though large numbers of Americans appear to be of the race-conscious opinion that racism exists in their country, they are hardly strangers to color-blindness or the optimistic view that race is a problem of the past. In short, American and Western European cultural tool kits for making sense of descent-based diversity have more elements in common than may usually be recognized, even if their preferred instruments are not always the same.

Conclusion: The Limits of Indirect Measures of Conceptualization

Competing ideas about race—regarding its place in discourse, analysis, and policy—revolve around questions of what is said and not said, what is heard and not heard, what is seen and not seen. For this reason, they resonate with the analogy to the automobile engine with which we opened the chapter. As Paola Tabet suggests, racial thought is not always in motion; it can be dormant, yet capable of roaring into action or sputtering to life. Even when running, its motor can hum along imperceptibly, unnoticed. In any circumstance, the race idea has not disappeared; its engine remains, a fine-tuned, "coordinated whole." What appears like silence, then, guarantees neither absence nor presence.

In this chapter, we turned to two bodies of comparative scholarship— one on racial speech, the other on social scientists' analytical uses of race— for clues to the underlying concepts of descent-based difference that have received little academic attention in their own right. Starting with the premise from "new racism" theory that U.S. and Western European behaviors would look very distinct in these two realms, we instead found notable similarities alongside the differences. These areas of convergence—in racial speech, project, and analysis—raise the real possibility that Europeans and Americans also share a great deal when it comes to their fundamental beliefs about descent-based difference.

This literature review also reveals, however, the limits to inferring concepts of difference from speech about, and even inquiry into, descent and its consequences. As Tabet writes of the motor of racial thought, its sounds are not enough for us to make out its contours or state. When it comes to public discourse about race and the norms around it, we can see racial projects at work in the exhortation to speak or not speak. What is much less apparent is the background conceptualization of race. One reason is that discursive practices encapsulate more than just concepts of difference; in addition to norms and understandings of society, they also embody diverse histories and attitudes toward the regulation of speech in general.[120] Another reason is simply the general reality that what people say—or profess to value—is not always a reliable indicator of how they think. Empirical research on both sides of the Atlantic makes clear that an individual's claim to be "color-blind" is no guarantee that color does not figure in their speech, actions, and presumably thought.[121] As Bonnet concluded, "A national colour-blind ideology does not translate into a world where racial cognitions have been erased from people's mind. Race is definitely a category of practice, a category most French people use in their making sense of the social world. A national colour-blind model does not prevent people from engaging into [sic] race-conscious practices."[122] Similarly, El-Tayeb contends that "a discourse of colorblindness that claims not to 'see' racialized difference" is no impediment to a coexisting "regime of continentwide recognized visual markers that construct nonwhiteness as non-Europeanness."[123]

Even more relevant to our investigation is that when we parse the literature on racial discourse or social scientific analysis, it becomes clear that neither is necessarily evidence of one concept of race versus another. Put differently, very diverse understandings of difference can result in the same rhetoric or analytical approach. The rejection of "race" language due to fears that it will either inflame racism or be used against people, for example, might accompany the view that racial classification is a human invention. Such qualms are also perfectly consistent, however, with the belief that human races are objective biological entities but social recognition of their "natural" differences could simply have undesirable outcomes (like conflict, hierarchy, or discrimination). Similar ambiguity surrounds academics' assessments of the societal importance of race. Either race skepticism or race consciousness could be anchored in a concept of difference that rejects "the existence of separate human races" (to quote the European Racial Equality Directive), and ostensibly biologically delineated ones in particular. But both could also be reconciled to an essentialist notion of race as biology, simply with different perceptions of the impact of inherited physical traits on individual and collective outcomes. In sum, our existing empirical knowledge of how race is invoked—whether by laypeople, politicians, academics, or others—is insufficient to make solid inferences about how people think about cultural, biological, or other forms of descent-based difference.

Instead, the scholarly literature we have reviewed points to two other conclusions. One is that we are in need of a more precise and complex method for characterizing concepts of difference, one that not only cuts through the welter of competing connotations that a term like "race" carries but also provides social scientists with tools to clear out areas of common ground and mutual understanding across national borders. The question we posed at the start of this chapter thus becomes: What analytic notion—whether labeled "race" or not—do we need to devise in order to comprehend the mental landscape of Tabet's Italian schoolchildren, with their understandings of Albanians, Moroccans, and Senegalese as all "negroes"? This is the challenge we set for ourselves in the concluding chapter.

In the meantime, the other lesson that we take away is simply that there is no substitute for empirical research focused on the conceptualization of descent-based difference. This is the enterprise on which we embark, accordingly, in the next chapter. Over the course of the three empirical chapters to come, we aim to get at just what concepts of difference—biological, cultural, or other—come to mind when Italians and Americans are asked to think about the descent-based groups that are most salient to them.

CHAPTER TWO

Italian Mental Maps of Difference

You can't say the n-word (*la parola negra*) in Italy, only think it. Soon you won't even be able to say "clandestine," you'll say "Your Excellency."

—MARIO BORGHEZIO, European Parliament member,
in a radio interview, April 30, 2013

THE APPOINTMENT of Italy's first black cabinet minister in 2013 unleashed a storm of political and media commentary. At its center was Cécile Kyenge, an ophthalmologist who had been born in the Democratic Republic of the Congo and moved to Italy at the age of nineteen. When Prime Minister Enrico Letta named her minister of integration, it was Kyenge's African heritage and appearance—rather than her professional credentials or policy agenda—that dominated public discourse. Dredging up a hoary trope, one Italian parliament member, Roberto Calderoli, likened Kyenge to an orangutan.[1] And the Europarliamentarian quoted in the epigraph, Mario Borghezio from the xenophobic Northern League party, claimed that "Africans are Africans, they belong to an ethnicity very different from ours that hasn't produced great geniuses."[2] For Borghezio, who hails from Kyenge's city of Modena, African inferiority tarred Letta's entire cabinet: "This is a bonga bonga government," he told the national newspaper *La Repubblica*. "They want to change the citizenship law with *ius soli* and Kyenge wants to impose her tribal traditions on us, those from the Congo. Is she [even] Italian?"

Tellingly, his list of grievances about the political changes that Kyenge supposedly represented included complaints about what could no longer be said about blacks or immigrants—yet his radio interview and the press coverage it garnered suggested just the opposite: plenty could in fact be said in the public sphere.

Equally telling was Cécile Kyenge's reception compared to that of another foreign-born member of Enrico Letta's cabinet. German-born Josefa Idem was not accused of belonging to a "very different" ethnicity or of imposing foreign customs. Her *italianità* (Italianness) was not questioned, though she hailed from a wartime enemy of the Italian nation—indeed, one whose atrocities against the Italian people are far from forgotten. The contrast with Idem suggests that pointing to foreign roots or "traditions" does little to explain the virulent caricaturization of Kyenge; although Borghezio invoked cultural difference, the imagery that he, Calderoli, and others dredged up borrowed unabashedly from a colonial archive of racial hierarchy.

To many Americans' ears, such raw commentary might be shocking, especially coming from politicians speaking on the record to journalists. To impugn blacks' intelligence or equate them with apes seems beyond the pale of contemporary norms for official public discourse. Yet these ideas are of course quite familiar to Americans, who are no less heirs to the Western European racial imaginary than Italians are. Long-standing notions of Africa as the antithesis of modernity, and of blacks as intellectually deficient, can be found everywhere in the United States, from popular culture to opinion surveys. Calderoli's "orangutan" insult made headlines across the Atlantic not because of its novelty in the United States, but because of its transgression of U.S. norms regarding race and speech at the time. We might ask, moreover, whether such norms have the same purchase today, after a sitting president repeatedly and openly insulted multiple communities of color by associating them with "rapists," "huts," and "shithole countries."[3]

This chapter is the first of three to present our empirical findings on the ways in which Italians and Americans speak—and think—about descent-based difference. Departing from the "new racism" hypothesis, we might expect a solidly cultural approach in Italy. Borghezio's remarks suggest, however, that culture can inform rhetoric while other bases of group difference—like the long-standing racial belief that blacks are biologically subhuman—can figure prominently in our unspoken notions of difference.

In this chapter, we focus on the interviews we conducted in Italy, where we posed a unique suite of questions on "Italianness," integration, group characteristics and likability that were quite revealing of the role that culture played in our respondents' "mental maps" of descent-based difference.[4] This exploration is also an opportunity to familiarize readers outside Italy with the country's demographic diversity. And it is a prelude to the following two empirical chapters, where we directly compare our U.S. and Italian subjects' reactions to a shared series of interview questions.

As we detail in appendix A on our interview data and methodology, our Italian sample was largely made up of university students in the northern cities of Milan and Bologna and in the southern city of Naples. Roughly one-third, however, were young people of the same age enrolled in less prestigious vocational institutes in the Milanese periphery, where they studied trades like graphic design, hospitality services, audiovisual technology, and fashion. Much more likely to have classmates and friends from immigrant backgrounds than were the relatively elite college undergraduates, these vocational students also tended to be more outspoken in drawing the line between Italians and "others." In this native-born, all-white sample, the class gradient captured by the university versus trade school distinction was one of the more important sources of variation in interviewees' ways of talking, if not thinking, about group difference.

Descent-Based Prejudice and Discrimination in Italy

Research on Italian attitudes and behaviors toward descent-based others provides a useful introduction to our findings on concepts of difference. Preceded by a brief description of contemporary migration to Italy, our summary of this research will also familiarize readers with the makeup of the country's foreign-born population. By examining political and media discourse on immigration as well as studies of descent-based prejudice and discrimination, we can begin to discern some of the ways in which culture, physical traits, socioeconomic status, and other attributes surface in Italian discourse on difference.

Immigration in Politics and Media

Toward the end of the twentieth century, Italy went from being a net sender of emigrants to becoming a net receiver of a sizable and heterogeneous inflow of immigrants. Foreigners began arriving in the 1960s to fill certain occupational niches: Tunisian fishermen and agricultural laborers found work in Sicily, and domestic workers came from Italy's former East African colonies as well as from the Philippines. Later they would be followed by Middle Easterners employed in factories in Reggio Emilia, Yugoslav construction workers, and Senegalese and Ghanaians working in the quarries, mills, and factories of Bergamo, Brescia, and the Veneto.[5] Since 2004, successive enlargements of the European Union to admit Eastern European members like Poland and Romania have reinforced inflows from that region. Economic immigration to Italy has also been intertwined with other sources of newcomers, like refugees, asylum-seekers, and others fleeing violence or persecution.[6] Since the mid-2010s in particular, large numbers of people have sought refuge in Europe by crossing the Mediterranean or entering on land from the southeast. Despite official efforts to rein in immigration, it is now an extensive feature of Italian society. At the start of 2019, the Istituto Nazionale di Statistica put the number of foreign residents of Italy at nearly 5.3 million, or 8.7 percent of the national population, with the top ten sending countries being (in descending order): Romania, Albania, Morocco, China, Ukraine, Philippines, India, Bangladesh, Moldova, and Egypt.[7] Moreover, taking into account the undocumented population, estimated at 533,000 at the start of 2018, would put the total foreign share at over 10 percent of Italy's inhabitants.[8]

Since the late 1980s, the "foreign" population of Italy—which is understood to include many Italian-born people, including immigrants' offspring and Roma—has become a staple of domestic political and media discourse.[9] The killing of South African refugee Jerry Essan Masslo in 1989 and other violent attacks on immigrants sparked a national debate about racism as a "new" phenomenon in Italy. Still, shopkeepers' and residents' protests against street peddlers and migrant settlements signaled a decidedly anti-immigrant sentiment that influenced the 1990 debate on the Martelli Law, Italy's first comprehensive immigration legislation. Several political parties sought to capitalize on widely publicized hostility toward migrants; notably, the anti-Southern party, the Northern League (Lega Nord), changed its name to simply "the League" and refocused its sights on the immigrant.[10] At this point, immigrants went from being victims of racism to being portrayed by media, politicians, and police as sources of illegal behavior and public disorder.[11] At the same time, Italy's ratification of the 1990 Schengen treaty, which implemented tight control of Europe's external borders, added the frame of "invasion" by masses of undocumented migrants, whom Italian authorities were bound to expel by every means possible.[12] Right-wing and xenophobic parties thus succeeded in imposing a widespread narrative that equates immigration with crime, invasion, and public burden and is now summed up in the pat bipartisan phrase, "the immigration problem."

Prejudice

Given its contemporary political and media discourse, as well as its imperial past, it comes as no surprise that descent-based prejudices have found fertile ground in Italy. Prior to the twenty-first century, opinion polls regularly held Italy up as an example of relative tolerance in Europe. Egalitarian and anti-racist attitudes were commonly professed, although many Italians simulta-neously had little knowledge or curiosity about immigrants and maintained a host of unfavorable stereotypes about them (concerning sexual appetite, lack of discipline, and so on).[13] A 1992 survey in the Piemonte region, for example, found that despite an enduring colonial image of the primitive, childlike, and subordinate African, blacks were not perceived as threatening and instead were seen as pleasant or nice (*simpatici*).[14] Another noteworthy dimension of Italian attitudes in the years leading up to and including the turn of the century was the hierarchy of descent-based groups that emerged from opinion polls. Contrary to their expectations of a "white over black," U.S.-style ranking, Sniderman and his colleagues discovered that the Italians they surveyed in 1994 perceived Eastern Europeans more negatively than Central Africans—for example, when it came to crime, unemployment, housing, and paying taxes.[15] In a 2002 survey, Filipinos (who in Italy are disproportionately domestic workers) ranked highest in likability, followed by Senegalese, Egyptians, Sri Lankans, Chinese, Moroccans, Albanians, and "gypsies."[16] In other words, (Eastern) European groups ranked lowest in a hierarchy headed by Southeast Asian, West African, and North African groups.

Since the 1990s, however, Italian xenophobia has deepened. These changes are partly a reaction to the increased immigration spanning the late twentieth and early twenty-first centuries, including dramatic "border spectacles" like the 1990s Adriatic arrivals from Albania and the mid-2010s Mediterranean crossings from North Africa.[17] According to Neil MacMaster, people who had once been seen as "exotic, distant and external primitive[s]" came to be seen as threatening once they had migrated and become insiders.[18] For

Balibar, the result was "a racism of the era of 'decolonization,' of the reversal of population movements between the old colonies and the old metropolises, and the division of humanity within a single political space."[19]

An equally important driver of descent-based prejudice, however, has been politicians' use of immigration as an electoral issue and the media's amplification of their sensationalist rhetoric; the end result has been apparent in large-scale public opinion polls.[20] In the 2010s, Italians came to regularly voice some of the most—and often *the* most—hostile attitudes toward outsiders in Europe.[21] In 2018, for example, the Pew Research Center found Italians to be the second-least welcoming of diversity (after Greeks) among respondents from Sweden, Germany, Spain, the United Kingdom, the Netherlands, France, Poland, and Hungary.[22] And in 2017, Italians scored at the very top of a field of fifteen European nations on Pew's Nationalist, Anti-Immigrant, Antireligious Minority Sentiment (NIM) scale.[23]

Discrimination

In addition to the prejudices expressed in politics, media, and public opinion, there is ample evidence of descent-based institutional discrimination, spectacular outbreaks of violence, and "everyday racism" in Italy.[24] To start with the state, Italian naturalization law privileges European Union nationals over those of non-European nations, requiring a shorter residence period for European would-be citizens than for Italian-born offspring of non-European descent. And thanks to a *jus sanguinis* citizenship regime, third-generation descendants of Italians abroad can naturalize—and thus vote—more easily than can Italian-born children of Chinese or Nigerian immigrant parents. At lower levels of government, local ordinances and resolutions also resist the advent of a "multiethnic" Italy, for example, by blocking the establishment of Muslim prayer sites.[25] Although these regulations may seem to turn only on citizenship status, they are often intended to combat specific subgroups, like Middle Eastern kebab-shop owners or the Pakistanis and Indians who found themselves banned from playing cricket in Brescia's public parks.

The most blatant form of descent-based institutional discrimination, however, is probably the widespread targeting of Romani people by group-specific policies like forced residential segregation (in what Sigona calls "Guantanamo-like enclosures for latent criminals"), fingerprinting, and special police databases, even for children and individuals who are Italian citizens.[26] And despite the enduring myth of the female gypsy kidnapper of non-gypsy children, it is Romani youth who are particularly vulnerable to separation from their kin: they are seventeen times more likely than others to be removed from their families, and national restrictions on the adoption of children by foreigners are not applied to cases involving young Roma.[27] These and numerous other "state-tolerated, if not sponsored" forms of discrimination against the Roma, moreover, highlight the extreme weakness of Italy's regulatory framework for monitoring and combating "ethnic" or "racial" discrimination.[28]

Individual, interpersonal forms of aggression also coexist in Italy alongside national and local policies of institutional discrimination. Hate crime reports from the Organization for Security and Co-operation in Europe (OSCE), for example, include items like the following: "Two Roma women rummaging through a supermarket's rubbish were locked into the metal cage surrounding the garbage bins and subjected to racist insults by a group, which was filmed and posted on social media," and "The inhabitants of a Roma settlement were pelted with stones and one of the Roma housing containers was set on fire."[29] Similarly, the "racism database" maintained by the Italian nongovernmental organization Lunaria turns up a steady drumbeat of violence toward people of sub-Saharan African origin, like the shooting with an air pistol of a twenty-two-year-old Guinean pedestrian by two people riding by on a motorbike in San Cipriano d'Aversa (Campania) and the fatal May 2018 shooting of the Senegalese citizen Idy Diene by the sixty-four-year-old Florentine Roberto Pirrone.[30] In little over a year, the interactive map of racist attacks that the journalist Luigi Mastrodonato unveiled in June 2018 grew to cover roughly 140 incidents.[31]

And not far behind the instances of extreme aggression that make headlines, moreover, is a daily reality of discrimination, insult, slight, and threat toward the groups that Italians perceive as outsiders.[32] Faïçal Daly's ethnography of Tunisian migrants in the northern Italian town of Modena offers a granular sense of such quotidian indignities and dangers. He recounts that Tunisians would be refused service in local establishments or, if served, handed their coffee in plastic cups for reasons of "hygiene" and then chased out if they complained. He describes Italian employers unilaterally giving Italian names like Carlo, Mario, and Roberto to Tunisian workers with names like Moktar, Fadhel, and Ridha; some even referred to all their Tunisian employees simply as "Ali." Daly also takes notes of explicitly written exclusions—like the job advertisements barring *extracomunitari*, or the sign in a bar stating, "North Africans not allowed here"—that are reminiscent of anti-Southerner postings of the 1950s and 1960s.[33] More recently, autobiographies (and semi-autobiographical work) by black Italians like Pap Khouma and Tommy Kuti also recall myriad experiences of racial epithets, discriminatory treatment at the hands of police, teachers, and neighbors, and not-so-micro interpersonal aggressions.[34] And in his account of *antiziganismo*, Leonardo Piasere reveals the lengths to which some Romani individuals in Italy have gone to avoid everyday stigma and harassment: changing their names to prevent lengthy police document checks, hiding their Romani origins from employers and coworkers to forestall discrimination on the job, and even keeping friends and spouses in the dark. Similar to historical "passing" by African Americans, Piasere sees in these stories "the search for invisibility [as] the main way to avoid discrimination and scorn."[35]

This very brief review of the literature on contemporary descent-based prejudice and discrimination in Italy suggests that they are rooted in beliefs about behavioral difference that are the legacy of classical racial thought. Immigrants and Roma are castigated for acting immorally or illegally, and African and Romani people in particular bear the brunt of aggression targeting them as dirty and subhuman. The patronizing colonial imagery of blacks as childlike has also clearly endured. But to what extent are the supposedly deficient behaviors of Italy's "others" attributed to cultural, biological, or other characteristics? We now turn to the results of our interviews to begin to unpack the varied strands of thought that make up the conceptualization of descent-based difference.

Culture and Belonging

Consistent with the hypothesis of a "new racism" widespread in Western Europe, culture was a fixture of our Italian respondents' commentary on descent-based difference. As we will show, this held true whether the topic was *italianità*, group characteristics and differences, or prospects for integration. The interviews also made clear, however, that the label "culture" was far from sufficient for capturing the many dimensions along which beliefs about difference could vary.

The Markers of Italianità

To avoid imposing our own notions of what constituted a salient descent-based group, the first substantive question we asked our respondents was who, in their opinion, should be considered Italian. Although this query did introduce a category of nationhood, it is one that is already wide-spread in Italian media and political discourse, and so we felt that it could direct interviewees to the topic of descent groups without imposing a new and unfamiliar framing. Equally important, we expected that the question would allow respondents a great deal of latitude in reflecting about difference, and indeed, they drew on varied types of groups in their answers: not just national (or native versus foreign) but also geographic (from the continental level down to the domestic North-South divide), racial (like "white" and "black"), religious (either Muslims or Catholics), and legal (citizen or "illegal"). The range and heterogeneity of the groups that were salient for the students provided a wealth of cases that allowed them to elaborate on what they saw as meaningful markers of *italianità*. In their visions of the Italian people, we ultimately discerned three models of national belonging, each reflecting a particular conceptualization of descent-based difference.

1. *The civic model:* The civic conception of Italianness emphasized individual behavior—often but not always freely chosen—that complied with or participated in national values, norms, laws, or objectives.[36] For a majority of respondents, *italianità* in an individual was indicated by actions such as working, obeying the law (for example, paying taxes and not committing crimes), behaving decorously, and "integrating."[37] For one-third of the sample, anyone who chose to live in Italy belonged to the nation, and a comparable number felt that a decision to live in Italy that was accompanied by a sense of attachment, belonging, and love for the country was more than enough for a person to be considered Italian. Being born in the country or holding national citizenship, even if not by deliberate choice, could nonetheless be included in this understanding of Italianness as a reward for upright behavior.

2. *The nativist model:* Standing in sharp contrast to the civic, voluntary model was what we call a nativist vision, according to which *italianità* was something a person inherited automatically from their forefathers. In this minority perspective voiced by less than one-tenth of the sample, being born in Italy or living there for a long time was not enough for a person

to be truly Italian. As Aurora, a biology major in Naples, stated: "We are the Italians, [we] whose roots are in our country. The others are simply ... visitors, guests." Interviewees who took this minority position had varied notions, however, of what constituted the intergenerational Italian essence: it might be blood, whiteness, descent from historical protagonists, or a special relationship to the land. As Gregorio, a history major in Naples, saw it, "Our homeland, our nation, is the one that sustains us, that we have grown up in, that gave us life. And so basically we should be attached [to it] almost as if it were our parent." Most of the proponents of nativist *italianità* mentioned racial labels or physical appearance in their reflections, but only three— interestingly, all young men studying graphic design at a technical institute in Milan—named whiteness as a necessary condition for being Italian. One of them, Oliviero, argued:

An immigrant, even if they have Italian citizenship, is not an Italian in my view, [and] can never become one. This is not a racist argument, heaven forbid, but we are white, maybe a tiny bit mulatto as you move south, but never black (*di colore*). Like [Ghanaian-origin professional soccer player Mario] Balotelli. As I see it, he plays for Italy, but he isn't Italian; he has Italian citizenship. But no more than that.

And as Riccardo, also a graphic design student in Milan, memorably explained, "Someone who eats sushi while you eat pasta, and [your] identity cards say that both [of you] have Italian citizenship, but you look him in the face and he has Oriental features, you say, 'Okay, you're Italian, but at the same time you aren't.'"

3. *The cultural model:* In between the poles of a voluntary, civic *italianità* and a fixed, nativist version lay a third, ambiguous—or multifaceted— cultural model. In this approach, which was taken by a majority of interviewees, alone or in combination with another, Italianness was equated with certain behaviors and ways of thinking, or simply with a vague catchall reference to "culture." Italians eat certain foods (invariably described as "good" and "right"), display a certain temperament (open, warm, and friendly, yet also closed-minded, individualistic, and selfish), and unquestionably share a single language and (Catholic) religion.

This complex "cultural" combination of both behavioral and attitudinal criteria for being Italian bridged the civic and nativist concepts in three meaningful ways. First, it could be—and often was—paired with one of the other models, notably the civic one. Second, and more importantly, it was highly malleable: culture could be perceived as either inborn (as in the nativist model) or acquired (as in the civic conception). Some respondents portrayed Italian culture as an exclusive community, akin to the Romantic German concept of *Volk*, which one could only be born into. In this view, a person might inherit a particular mentality or temperament from their ancestors at birth, which would predispose them to act in authentically Italian ways. Most commonly, however, interviewees voiced a more inclusive idea of a cultural Italianness whose signal traits—such as foodways, outlooks, or language—could be learned in childhood or even deliberately acquired later in life. Finally, the cultural model was also linked to the civic and nativist concepts in that all three presumed a unitary, authentic *italianità* grounded in both behavior and psychology, even though Italians are well aware of the historical, social, and cultural heterogeneity within their borders.

The three models of Italianness that emerged from our interviews point to two important axes along which concepts of descent-based difference vary. One is the *trait* (or set of traits) that is thought to determine group membership, such as being an upright citizen, having ancestors who ostensibly had lived on the peninsula since time immemorial, or adopting key cultural practices like eating pasta. The other, less obvious axis has to do with the *mechanism* by which a person acquires these membership characteristics. Our interviewees distinguished between inborn, fixed traits like skin color or ancestral geographic origins; characteristics that were inculcated early in life and reinforced through childhood socialization, such as language fluency; and habits adopted later in life, such as patriotic displays or choice of residence. These three kinds of characteristics stem from what we call respectively "essential," "primordial," and "acquired" mechanisms for the attainment of group membership; note that they progress from the involuntary to the voluntary.[38] Although each mechanism was considered by at least some respondents to be a plausible basis for claiming Italianness, it is important to distinguish between them, because there was far from a consensus on which ones led to genuine *italianità*.

Distinguishing Italian from Other

After asking interviewees to tell us who they considered to be Italian, we next asked them to tell us who was *not* Italian—and what the differences were between these two broad groupings. What emerged was a definitive and widely held view of culture as the predominant lens for making sense of descent-based difference.

Interestingly, when listing the groups they perceived as non-Italian, and before we asked them to discuss differences between Italians and others, some respondents spoke about immigration in a way that relied much less heavily on the notion of culture. Instead, socioeconomic characteristics, like living conditions, employment, and legal residence status, were just as prominent in these conversational detours. Two broad narratives held sway. One was rooted in a Catholic, charitable antiracism that portrayed immigrants as needy people who were often poor or marginalized and who had come to Italy to seek a better life and work hard, accepting menial jobs that nobody else wanted to do. The other frame was the product of long-standing media coverage that depicted immigrants—especially those of certain nationalities—as coming to Italy with the intention of engaging in crime, taking it easy, loitering, and drinking beer in public spaces. Many interviewees saw both stories as true, although most of them privileged the account of the hardworking immigrant, and several immediately raised issues of discrimination.

When we asked respondents to detail the differences between non-Italians and Italians, however, the socioeconomic factors that had figured in their generic comments on immigration fell by the wayside. This is surprising in a country where foreign workers are often encountered at construction sites, in tomato fields, or as in-home caregivers for the elderly, while native Italian citizens are found in the offices of companies, the civil service, university departments, and newspapers. It might seem reasonable to expect that the first differences springing to mind would concern the socioeconomic conditions of groups with radically different access to the labor market, housing, education, and other resources. In a related omission, the rights deriving from citizenship were scarcely mentioned, even though this is the primary arena in which foreigners are different by definition.

Instead, inviting reflection on the difference between Italians and non-Italians immediately elicited references to culture. Although one-third of respondents also alluded to socioeconomic differences, almost 90 percent dwelt at length on cultural distinction. About half made generic appeals to "culture," and allusions to "customs" were just as frequent; more than one-third mentioned religion, about one-quarter made references to language, and one-quarter spoke of mentality (values, norms, belief) or character. "I think that the capacity to adapt to the workplace is nowadays the biggest difference between Italians and non-Italians," stated Antonio, a history major in Bologna. And Laura, who was studying tourism in Milan, opined, "The Roma, and the Albanians especially, are the—how do you say—rudest, they're actually a bit on the mean side too, I think. It's actually part of their culture ... also the fact of stealing, they say it's actually part of their culture, stealing. Some people told us that." Such comments illustrated that temperamental dispositions, like being "mean" or having the "capacity to adapt to the workplace," figured in the respondents' imagining of difference and could also be chalked up to culture. In a similar vein, Giovanni, a biology major in Naples, recounted: "On the news, I see that many Muslims, North Africans are closed, perhaps more than towards our culture, towards modern Western culture." Being "open"—which meant "integrating" and interacting with Italians—was another common way of translating ostensibly cultural norms into group psychology.

The primacy of culture was also apparent when we asked interviewees to indicate on a five-point scale the extent to which they perceived the differences between Italians and *extracomunitari* (non-EU nationals) to be cultural (involving customs, religion), social (citizenship, income, education, and the like), or biological (such as somatic or genetic).[39] Although many of the students pointed out that it would depend on the countries of origin of the non-EU nationals, most had no difficulty responding. Two-thirds viewed non-Europeans as very or somewhat culturally different from Italians, while only 5 percent saw them as very or fairly culturally similar (figure 2.1). The salience of culture was further underscored by the length and emphatic tone of respondents' explanations of their numeric ratings and accompanying explanations. For example, Flavio, a cultural heritage major in Naples, observed:

> Our cultural foundations and the cultural foundations of other peoples are completely different. Even on topics that we could bring up here and now, like, for example, the status of women. They are totally different, they are. So culture differentiates a lot. Sometimes it's stupidly believed that it's a thing that's just there, it's not part of us, but in reality, if we actually look into it, culture greatly influences our everyday behavior, our every thought, all our ways of seeing things. So culture is active, and it differentiates us a lot.

Consistent with his university major, Flavio held a firm conviction about the centrality of culture, and he clearly expressed that conviction through

Figure 2.1 Respondents' Views of Non-EU Nationals as Different from or Similar to Italians, by Type of Difference

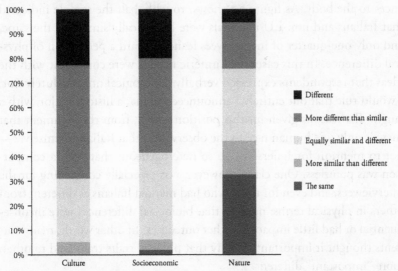

Source: Authors' tabulation.

strong language: the cultures of others were "completely different" and "totally different," and culture "greatly influences ... our every thought, all our ways of seeing things." His words corroborated our previous finding: "culture" was the device that interviewees used to describe and process virtually any form of difference between themselves and those they considered to be not Italian.

Our scale for gauging perceived cultural, socioeconomic, and physical differences between Italians and *extracomunitari* had the added advantage of contrasting quantitative ratings with qualitative accounts. This comparative option proved to be especially useful for taking the measure of respondents' beliefs about socioeconomic or structural differences. The comparison suggested that, even as students were almost as likely to perceive socioeconomic difference as cultural difference between themselves and non-Europeans, they were much more likely to speak about culture, at greater length, and with more concrete examples. In short, socioeconomic status seemed to have a place in their thinking about descent-based difference, yet it had little traction in their talk, crowded out by the preponderance of culture discourse.

If culture overshadowed socioeconomic status in respondents' discussion of difference between Italians and non-Italians, it positively eclipsed references to the body. As figure 2.1 shows, roughly half the sample indicated that Italians and non-EU nationals were biologically similar or the same, and only one-quarter of interviewees leaned toward a perception of physical difference. In this case, the numeric ratings were consistent with the ideas that respondents expressed verbally. "Biological no, absolutely not, I would rule that out entirely," announced Sabina, a history major, with a laugh. The reasons given for this position varied, from the argument that there is only one human race to the observation that Italians themselves—not to mention foreigners—were so heterogeneous that such a comparison was pointless. One claim, however, was especially compelling for the interviewees, and even for those who had marked Italians as different from others in physical terms: namely, that biological differences were inconsequential or had little impact on other outcomes. In other words, many students thought it important to deny that physical traits translated to other, more "important" differences:

No, I think that the big differences concern education and upbringing insofar as there are no genetic rules or bases that force us to do [anything]. *(Francesco, biology major, Milan)*

An African American is totally different from me. After which we are two equal human beings, but we can't reasonably argue that we are the same from a physical point of view. So certainly there are physical and biological differences, but they don't influence a person's culture. *(Martina, chemistry major, Bologna)*

Several students distinguished between surface somatic traits like skin color and internal characteristics, conceding notable difference in the former but not in the latter:

Oh gosh, I mean their visual impact is very different from ours, but perhaps internally they are exactly the same as us. *(Matteo, audiovisual technology student, Milan)*

Each population has characteristic traits, but that is as far as it goes. I've never yet seen anyone whose heart was on the right instead of the left.... It's fair to argue that they have different somatic traits, but obviously we can't say that they're different. *(Edoardo, chemistry major, Milan)*

The bottom line of this "physically different but biologically identical" perspective (as Alice, a tourism student in Milan, put it) remained, however, that bodily characteristics had no repercussions. After all, "they don't influence a person's culture," as Martina put it. The possibility of being a victim of racism owing to one's appearance was peripheral and only occasionally mentioned.

The commentary of young Italians not only revealed a preponderance of "culture talk" in their discussions of descent-based difference but also offered insight into the reasons for this pronounced discursive tendency. To be sure, their exposure to media and political discourse was one proximate cause: decades of messaging about the "right to be different," the "multicultural society," the "clash of civilizations," cultural incompatibilities, controversies surrounding the opening of a mosque or bans on the Islamic veil, and claims about the propensity of people of "certain cultures" to break the law or abuse women had clearly borne fruit. Beyond that, however, the interviewees' words shed light on the cognitive role of culture in their mental models of difference. For one thing, the concept of culture had become so plastic and flexible for them that it provided a ready-made, all-purpose explanation for any behavior or outlook. In other words, it had been made simple and accessible—much as has happened with "race" in the United States. Outcomes that could be explained by individuals' material circumstances—or, even more searchingly, by collective social, political, economic, and legal exclusion—were instead subsumed under the banner of "culture."

Another, related contributor to the primacy of culture was the *determinism* attributed to it. Cultural difference mattered more than anything else in our Italian interviewees' eyes; it explained how people interacted with others, behaved, carved out family roles, approached the world of work, and participated in society. Conversely, physical difference—when acknowledged—was dismissed as irrelevant and meaningless in today's world. And socioeconomic stratification appeared to be out of focus and difficult to grasp, at least when it came to distinguishing Italians from others; perhaps a "class" analysis would have come more readily to mind had the students been asked to contemplate internal divisions among the people they considered Italian. So while the respondents alluded to the import of socioeconomic status, they were at pains to articulate it with the same detail and conviction that they brought to the conceptualization of cultural difference.

Integration against the Fixity of Culture

In addition to the primacy and determinism of culture in students' understandings of descent-based difference, its *permanence* or fluidity was also an important matter of debate. Was culture porous and malleable, or was it fixed, clearly delimited, and attached to its bearers like a second skin? Our interview question "Can non-Italians become Italian?" probed beliefs about the rigidity or flexibility of culture and other markers of descent-based difference, and it served as a gateway to discussions of integration.

According to over two-thirds of the respondents, non-Italians can become Italian; fewer than one-tenth categorically excluded this possibility. The remainder—about one-quarter of the sample, problematized their response, typically invoking distinctions between a citizenship perspective and a values-and-customs perspective, as though to say, "Legally yes, but culturally no." This ambivalent stance was captured in one student's reasoning: "No, in the end if, let's say, a person is of Turkish origin but born in Italy, I don't see why they shouldn't be Italian. After which, it's obvious, they're really Turkish, but legally they're Italian." For these interviewees, and to a certain extent for others, one could be Italian on paper—and even be born and raised in the country, fluent in its language and folkways—without being truly Italian "inside." Even though they described the essence of *italianità* as "cultural," ultimately they saw it as inherited, not learned.

To the majority of respondents who felt that non-Italians could become Italian, we posed a follow-up question: How? When that led to animated conversations about "integration," we asked what that word meant to them. In a nutshell, the word referred to non-Italians' individual efforts to insert themselves into two domains of Italian society: interpersonal relations (integrating themselves into Italian circles of friends, places, and networks; forging relationships with people outside of their group of origin, and generally leaving their non-Italian world behind), and intercultural practices (observing Italian cultural traditions or importing their own culture).[40] Moreover, the students' commentary was not dispassionate observation about *whether* non-EU nationals integrate or not; instead, it quickly turned into a normative judgment that they *should* integrate. As Gaetano, a biology major in Naples, complained: "They don't have our culture, and they don't try to become part of what we are as Italians. Like, for example, the Romanians who keep to themselves, on their own, and have no interest in our culture or in what we are."

Integration, then, was seen as the responsibility of newcomers to Italy and their descendants; very little was expected of Italians. It was clearly up to immigrants to assimilate rather than up to Italians to make changes, either culturally or structurally; our respondents were more than twice as likely to place responsibility on the former than on the latter. The possibility that Italy might facilitate social inclusion or equal access to roles, resources, and rights, or the desirability of such initiatives, almost never came up in connection with the term "integration." Instead, it was the immigrant's individual obligation to display the requisite civic behaviors that would merit equitable treatment: respecting rules, paying taxes, and participating in projects that promoted the common good. Here the lopsidedness of integration norms was exacerbated by the double standard—often freely admitted by interviewees—that foreigners were expected to demonstrate a civic-mindedness that many Italians themselves lacked.

Not only did students rarely reflect on Italian responsibility for integration, but they seemed to have difficulty even imagining that Italians' actions could play a significant role. "As far as the Roma are concerned," Giorgio, a chemistry major in Naples said, "I don't see any particular effort to integrate, or at least the will to integrate, into Italian society. Surely, to a small extent, I mean maybe they home in on the fact that often we are not very forthcoming." In Giorgio's view, the Roma unwillingness to integrate counted more than Italians' habitual reticence, which only mattered "to a small extent." Respondents who felt, like Francesco in Milan, that "a little bit of diversity and variety can only be a good thing for us and that we can only learn [from it]," still expected much less effort from Italians than from others:

Your life is here, your children are growing up here, maybe they were even born here, so it's only right that you should get ... I mean, you live like Italians do. You've almost become Italian, you do the things that Italians do, you don't do what you used to do at home. You have changed your lifestyle to some degree. It doesn't have to be that way, [but] surely it's nice if your origins, your traditions, blend with Italian ones, absolutely. It's nice if an Italian goes into a Chinese restaurant and eats Chinese food. *(Virginia, tourism student, Milan)*

Virginia was addressing an imagined interlocutor who had relocated to Italy, given up what they "used to do at home," and "changed [their] life-style" to become "almost" Italian; in exchange, all Italians had to do to keep their end of the integration bargain was to occasionally patronize a Chinese restaurant.

Our interviewees' ideal integration scenario housed contradictory under-standings of culture as alternately fixed and fluid. On the one hand, their belief that foreigners should adopt the language, customs, values, and rules of Italian society—and that maybe Italians could incorporate a few new habits—made cultural practices and norms seem eminently malleable. On the other hand, they felt that immigrants "should keep up their own cul-ture," and indeed many interviewees thought of foreigners as unable to become entirely free of cultures that they imagined as rigid, backwards, and impervious to the migration experience; that was why, in their view, immi-grants could only become "almost," or "just legally," Italian. And although the students portrayed Italian culture as accessible, modern, and open to change, their expectation was that others would adopt it wholesale, not only learning the language but conforming to a fixed set of existing tra-ditions. It was as if "cultures" were unchangeable, while individuals were entirely flexible, enjoying complete freedom to move between them. Together these competing notions of culture as permanent or changeable resulted in a delicate balancing act for non-Italians. They were expected to embrace Italian culture while preserving their "own" culture of origin, yet only to the proper degree so as to avoid condemnation for remaining "too attached" to that culture.

The permanence and the determinism so often ascribed to culture were also on view when we invited interviewees to comment on how "integrat-able" various kinds of descent-based groups were. More specifically, we asked each respondent for their opinions on three versions of the statement, "Some [cultures/ethnic groups/races] cannot be integrated into Italian society." As figure 2.2 shows, respondents were much more likely to agree that some *cultures*—as opposed to some ethnic groups or some races—were not integratable: almost one-third of the sample, including a majority of the vocational school students, took this position. For this subset, the cultural divide between Italians and non-Italians was an enduring one, whether for individuals or for communities. Moreover, the gulf was hard to bridge, because culture was perceived to have many consequences, as the contrast

Figure 2.2 Agreement among Respondents on the Non-integrability of "Some Cultures," "Ethnic Groups," or "Races" into Italian Society

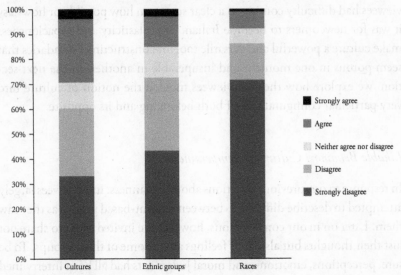

Source: Authors' tabulation.

with race made clear here.[41] Respondents strongly rejected the idea that it might be impossible for a given racial group to be integrated into Italian society; as we heard repeatedly, race was "only skin color," so how could it possibly affect integration? We might as well have asked if redheads·could be integrated; the only factor in play, they insisted, was a superficial physical trait that had no repercussions. When it came to cultural difference, however, students were notably less sanguine about the prospects for certain groups' incorporation; culture simply had greater import. The students' responses to these questions underscored that integration was understood to be an inherently cultural process, so the consensus that "race has nothing to do with culture," as Erika, a fashion design student in Milan, put it, meant that it could not matter in this realm.

By inviting students to reflect on integration or the prospects for non-Italians to become Italian, we were effectively asking them about border crossing: (How) can one move from one side of the *italianità* boundary to the other? Their answer, in no uncertain terms, was that Italy's others could do so through cultural assimilation. But because "culture" took on such a wide array of meanings—standing in for anything from a pleasant disposition to working hard to practicing Catholicism—and because it might appear highly malleable in some instances and rigidly fixed in others, our interviewees had difficulty coming to a clear stance on how possible or how easy it was for newcomers to become Italian. This plasticity and capaciousness make culture a powerful and versatile tool for constructing boundaries that seem porous in one moment and insuperable in another. In the next section, we explore how the interviewees molded the notion of culture into very particular configurations of both belonging and its opposite.

Likable Behavior: Culture or Temperament?

In response to our previous questions about Italianness, interviewees largely attempted to describe differences between descent-based groups as they saw them. Later on in our conversations, however, we invited them to share not just their thoughts but also their feelings about some of those groups. To be sure, perceptions, emotions, and moral judgments had all been intertwined in earlier segments of the interview; after all, individuals not only identify and classify groups but often also like or dislike, approve or disapprove of them. But by asking respondents to tell us explicitly how "likable" (*simpatico*) they found a series of groups, we sought out patterns of appreciation or rejection that could reveal symbolic boundaries integral to the conceptualization of descent-based difference.[42]

Using a quantitative survey measure known as a "feeling thermometer," we offered interviewees a written sheet with a list of nineteen groups and a response scale from 1 ("less likable") to 10 ("more likable") for each group.[43] The list included regional groups (for example, Northern and Southern Italians, to capture the nation's fundamental geosocial divide); peoples that had historically been dispersed around Europe (Jews and Roma); religious majorities and minorities (Catholics and Muslims as well as Jews); and the most salient groups of immigrants, from general categories like *extracomunitari* (non-EU nationals), "immigrants," and "the undocumented" (*clandestini*) to some of the largest single nationalities represented in Italy's foreign-born population, such as Moroccans and Chinese. In selecting these groups, we sought a balance between the objectively most numerous ones, those most often named in public discourse, and those most frequently mentioned in our pilot interviews. To enrich the quantitative data with

Figure 2.3 Respondents' Views of Descent-Based Groups: Mean Likability Scores

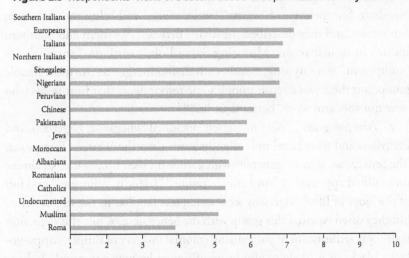

Source: Authors' tabulation.
Note: On the scale from 1 to 10, lower scores represent weaker approval ratings and higher scores represent stronger approval ratings.

more in-depth, qualitative insight than thermometer measures usually yield, we asked respondents not only to assign each group a numerical likability score but also to elaborate verbally on their ratings. A notable drawback, however, was that some students felt uncomfortable making generalizations, especially negative ones; twelve of them opted to either skip the feeling thermometer or assign the same score to all groups.

Strikingly, the rankings to emerge (see figure 2.3) followed two notable patterns. First, there was a clear geographic *hierarchy* of likability: Western Europeans on top; sub-Saharan Africans and Latin Americans slightly below; Asians in the middle; North Africans and Eastern Europeans at the bottom.[44] Second, groups with similar average ratings—but not necessarily shared geographic origins—tended to be described in similar *emotional* or *ethical* terms by the students. More specifically, we discerned the following six clusters:

1. *The "European in-group"*: This group comprised (in descending order of approval) Southern Italians, Europeans, Italians, and Northern Italians. Interviewees generally portrayed (Western) Europeans as open, civilized, and culturally and socially advanced, and they were quick to identify with them.

They often distinguished, however, between "cold," "stiff," and "haughty" Northern Europeans and "warm," "welcoming," and "pleasant" Southern Europeans, and they described the divide between Northern and Southern Italians in similar terms. Mirroring Susan Fiske's work on "warm" versus "competent" stereotyping, Southern Italians emerged as the most likable group, but there was a sense among some respondents that Europeans who were not so warm were "better than us."[45]

2. *"Nice foreigners"*: "Nice foreigners" included Senegalese, Nigerians, and Peruvians and were rated only slightly lower than the Western Europeans. The Senegalese, seen as "generally with a smile on their lips," garnered almost unqualified approval as *"simpatici,"* "polite," "friendly," "honest," and full of the "joys of life." Nigerians were much less familiar to the respondents, but they often equated this group with the Senegalese. While this depiction is strongly reminiscent of patronizing colonial imagery of simple, happy-go-lucky blacks, it is likely to also be conditioned by how commonly Italians interact with Senegalese as vendors who are trying to cajole them into purchases.[46] Peruvians were also seen as friendly and open to social interaction, perhaps facilitated by their sharing a Romance language (Spanish) as their mother tongue. The great store that our respondents put in foreigners' sociability comes across nicely in the praise from Jennifer, a psychology major in Naples: "The Senegalese, the Nigerians, the Chinese ... are all people that I have always looked very kindly on, I find them very nice, they come here to carry out the lowliest tasks, yet I always see joy, love in their expressions, and well, yes, the intention to integrate into Italy."

3. *"Multifaceted foreigners"*: Overall, however, interviewees expressed more ambivalence about the Chinese. Along with Pakistanis, they occupied a median category we call "multifaceted foreigners" because their ostensible merits were balanced with perceived shortcomings. Encountering Pakistanis as rose sellers or shopkeepers gave rise to positive impressions, for example, but these were checked by negative media coverage of Pakistan and recurring Islamophobic accounts of Pakistani fathers rejecting their daughters' choice of a Western lifestyle.

The Chinese community in Italy was subject to an even more variegated set of stereotypes in our interviews. As with the Senegalese, the customer experience of being served by Chinese people (usually in restaurants) led to approving descriptions of them as cheerful, smiling, and friendly. Yet by far the most frequent characterization of the Chinese by our interviewees was as "closed" (that is, to interactions with Italians), often accompanied by allusions to the geographic concentration of Chinese immigrants and their "ethnic economy." Again Fiske's binary is relevant here, because alongside the common perception of the Chinese as lacking warmth was the belief that they were very competent and hardworking ("superhuman," "machines"), an evaluation that simultaneously elicited approval, suspicion, and even a sense of threat. "Practically all the stores," exclaimed Aurora in Naples, "all the things we buy are absolutely 'made in China' [*said in English*], so the Chinese are practically 'colonizing us,' quote unquote, and there are so many of them." Fears of business competition, cultural change, and foreign influence all coalesced in frequent diatribes about Chinese invasion.

4. *Domestic religious groups:* Jews and Catholics garnered lower-than-average ratings (as did Muslims, whom we discuss later as perceived "outsiders"), suffering as a group from the students' impression that organized religions were largely composed of intransigent and bigoted fanatics. Virtually none of our respondents seemed to know a Jewish person, but their generally dim view of Israeli policy in the occupied Palestinian territories seemed to undermine the likability of this group for them. On the other hand, knowing Catholics did not improve the likability of this group for our interviewees but rather definitely hindered it. Viewed by many as priggish, backward, intolerant, closed, judgmental, "not practicing what they preach," and prone to not thinking rationally but rather being too easily brainwashed, this group received positive ratings only from respondents who were themselves practicing Catholics—and not even from all of those.

5. *"Criminalized foreigners":* Moroccans, Albanians, and Romanians were among the nationalities that received the lowest approval ratings. All respondents, without exception, alluded to their reputations as criminal groups, broadcast by the mass media over time as one succeeded the other as the largest immigrant community in Italy.[47] As Adriano in Milan explained, "I've given [a mark of] 6 to Romanians, Albanians, and Moroccans because, instinctively, they seem to be the ones who are more into crime than not." In addition to criminal instincts, these groups were also thought to have other temperamental defects: Romanians, who replaced the Albanians as the focus of negative news stories from the mid-2000s onward, given their later arrival in Italy, were described by some as unfriendly and cold, yet hotheaded.[48] Despite their disparate geographic origins, respondents often saw Romanians and Albanians as cultural similars, as well as comparable

to the Roma. Sabina, a history major in Milan, labored to connect all four as follows:

> So Romanians and Albanians are part of Europe. Although I don't see them, but that's my personal feeling, I don't see them as very different to the Moroccans. Well, maybe that could also be due to the fact that they're usually Muslims. But I also know Albanians who are Catholics. Yes, there are, there's a part of Albania that is Catholic. But I also associate them a little bit with the Roma, because [my] experience [of them] hasn't been so good. Sometimes, at the [train] station, I feel as though I have been singled out, literally.

After a religious commonality proved elusive, Sabina settled on unpleasant and threatening personal experiences—reported by several female interviewees—as the common denominator between these least-liked groups.

6. *"Outsiders":* Finally, the "outsiders" included the most stigmatized groups, none of which were nation-based. If we exclude the categories that are not descent-based but rather legal (for example, undocumented migrants), we are left with two groups that have a long history in Europe, and in Italy in particular, yet are resolutely depicted as grave threats to the social order: Muslims and, in a bottom league of their own, the Roma. Students saw Muslims as the extreme of religious intolerance, in line with Catholics but worse for being, in their stereotyped view, violent and backwards, religious warriors, and oppressors of women.

If Muslims represented the worst of humanity, however, the Roma stood for those who were less than human and could be denigrated without any compunction whatsoever. Interviewees equated Roma "culture" with stealing and making their children beg; with nomadism, dishonesty, brazenness, rudeness, and unwillingness to work; and with being closed to integration, opportunistic, and quick to draw the knife. These stereotypes were ironclad; respondents dismissed any individual exceptions to this "rule" as people who were no longer, or not really, "gypsies." The hostility, contempt, and revulsion that our interviewees expressed toward the Roma had no parallel with any other descent-based group. Moreover, denunciations of the Roma—which even included expressions of a wish for their elimination—were unique in that somehow these pronouncements alone seemed to be immune to any potential charge of racism. "They are a race that I just can't stand. Because they're rude, or in any case they're people who don't even have much respect for the people around them," said Romina, a tourism student in Milan, who felt free to vent. "Believe me, I'm not racist," Francesco in Milan assured us, "but the Roma are true parasites: not because I think so, but on account of what they do." He then added, "I wish they didn't exist, only because they are, I think, the only social class in the world that does no good to anyone."

This profound rejection of Muslims and Roma—widespread elsewhere in Europe—highlights the salience of descent-based groups that do not easily fit into traditional racial categories like "black" or "white." They lie outside the scope of the classic Linnaean race taxonomy but are no less powerful for it, exercising an unmistakable pull on the Italian social imaginary.

From the rich, detailed, and often emphatic commentary of the Italian students we interviewed about various descent-based groups in their country, we distilled four interrelated criteria that drove their evaluations: sociability, integration, respect for others, and upright contribution to society. Although each of these criteria was invariably attributed to "culture," we can discern in them not just beliefs about culturally valued behaviors or norms but also far-reaching notions about temperaments or dispositional tendencies that the respondents imagined to be fixed and monolithic group traits. The prized criterion of social interaction and integration with Italians was largely attributed to intrinsic warmth, friendliness, openness, and even happiness; conversely, coldness, detachment, or arrogance—rather than any contextual or structural factors—were often seen as impeding such interactions. Similarly, both "behaving well" and "not creating problems," on the one hand, and acting rudely, "doing whatever they like," and being violent, intolerant, or bullying, on the other, seemed to be attributed to cultural "mentalities" (such as norms, values, and outlooks) as well as deep-seated group dispositions toward respect or contempt for others. In the same vein, being an upright member of the community—for example, by working, maintaining "legal" status, and staying away from crime—was seen as a natural proclivity for some groups, but as a near-impossibility for others like Moroccans and, above all, the Roma, who were portrayed as inherently dangerous and parasitic. In short, under the rubric of "culture," interviewees demonstrated great interest in the inner psychological and emotional states of others, whether in the form of habitual thought (mentality) or feeling (temperament). All of these traits, moreover, were evaluated along a spectrum of proximity to or distance from the Italian, or Eurocentric, standard.

Discussion: The Myriad Dimensions of Difference

Across multiple questionnaire items, a series of important findings emerged regarding the role of culture in our young Italian interviewees' concepts of descent-based difference. First and foremost was the undisputed primacy of the language of culture to make sense of everything from who was Italian to who could become Italian. Whether discussing processes of integration or the likability of specific groups, a common set of criteria revolving around sociability, openness, and good behavior were largely ascribed to culturally determined actions and mentalities. The wide-ranging application of cultural explanations, however, raised the question of what—and how much—"culture" actually meant to the respondents. As it turned out, culture could stand in for behaviors, traditions, norms, values, outlooks, and even temperaments—an opaque mix of ostensibly learned and inborn traits.

The complexity of culture as a discursive and conceptual tool was evident in other ways as well. In addition to the implicit question of how individuals acquire their group's cultural characteristics (at birth or through years of socialization?), interviewees also varied in their depictions of culture as fixed or fluid. And evaluations of groups based on cultural criteria gave rise to varied hierarchies and new groupings. "Culture" was ambiguous and plastic, then, not just in terms of its ostensible manifestations—as behavior, mentality, and so on—but also in the qualities it could take on: essential or primordial, fixed or fluid, hierarchical or horizontal. What never wavered, however, was the determinism or consequence ascribed to it. The centrality of culture—paired with the conceptual flexibility it has been accorded—gives it tremendous range and explanatory power, making it an appealing and useful interpretive tool for everyday Italians as well as for political and media elites.

The Limits of Culture: Biology and Society below the Surface

Still, cracks appeared in the edifice of cultural discourse on descent-based difference that we encountered in Italy. Although cultural explanations largely crowded out alternative accounts centered on factors like socioeconomic status and physical appearance, they were not all-powerful. For one thing, cultural interpretations were often flimsy, based on little or only superficial knowledge of any culture other than Italian culture. In the absence of personal familiarity, the colonial and media stereotypes often echoed in popular wisdom became the basis for respondents' pronouncements about culture. "Going on the little that I know about the Roma," the University of Milan sociology major Cecilia told us, "I really don't like their culture in general. It's usually said about them that they steal a lot, then they don't have a fixed location, no, I don't, I just don't like them." For another thing, students applied selective criteria in gauging cultural similarity and difference: pairings from different corners of the globe, like Nigerians and Peruvians, or Romanians and Moroccans, could be seen as culturally alike based on prioritized characteristics like their ostensible friendliness or deviance. The most important reason to question the hold of culture on our interviewees' concepts of difference, however, is simply the indication that these beliefs were often molded, if not superseded, by unacknowledged structural conditions and classic racial taxonomy. If the conceptualization of descent-based difference can be likened to an iceberg, culture is what is visible, rising above the waterline, while social structure and physical race are hidden from view. Contrary to any simplistic reading of Barker's "new racism" thesis, biology and social stratification are not eliminated so much as submerged by references to cultural difference.

Throughout this chapter, we have seen that students did not deny or ignore altogether the socioeconomic disadvantages that non-Italians faced in Italy, or the structural processes shaping these disadvantages, such as the granting of citizenship or access to employment. The interviewees did tend, however, to minimize or discount structural factors, and above all, they were much less invested in and animated about structural accounts than they were about cultural ones. Discrimination in the labor market or the educational system, for example, rarely entered into their reasoning. Yet their comments and experiences invariably pointed to everyday social boundaries that colored their perceptions of others. Their limited and asymmetrical interactions with people of other descent-based groups contributed to the perpetuation of stereotypes. The funneling of immigrants to the lowest stratum of the economy colored our respondents' thinking about "desperate" arrivals, their involvement in work and in crime, their integration, their likability, and the "burden" they imposed on Italians.

We also saw that "race" as well as biology were either routinely dismissed or largely ignored when respondents discussed *italianità*, differences between Italians and non-Italians, integration, and likability. Physical appearance was of little consequence for societal outcomes, interviewees reasoned. The hierarchy of likability that we (and other researchers) discovered seemed to bear this out, as it located whites both at the top (Italians and other Western Europeans) and at the bottom (Eastern Europeans). Race also seemed to hold little personal meaning for our all-white sample: when we asked about their own identities in terms of "ethnic group, race, or nationality," most respondents settled on "Italian," and the few who engaged the topic of race did so with reluctance and embarrassment.

Yet, as with socioeconomic stratification, there is ample evidence that the interviewees' thinking was influenced by beliefs that stemmed from the classic Western ideology of race. For one thing, the stereotypical temperaments that students ascribed to others—the happy Africans, the saturnine Asians—were of a piece with the humoral dispositions (like "phlegmatic" or "melancholy") that Linnaeus and other early scientists attributed to human races. For another, their ranking of West Africans as more likable than Eastern Europeans was in no way inconsistent with a racial perspective; as the work of Sniderman and his colleagues suggests, a ranking of intelligence, competence, or overall superiority would probably have put Eastern Europeans ahead.[49] The mark of classic race thought was also visible in at least three other tendencies displayed by our Italian subjects: the privileging of blackness over cultural characteristics; the depiction of nonwhites as the epitome of otherness; and relatedly, the invisibility of whiteness.

In several instances, blackness trumped culture—for example, with respect to religion—as the most salient descriptor of Africans. This held uniformly true for Senegalese and Nigerians, who were never seen as Muslims even though Islam is the majority religion in both countries.[50] Interviewees associated North Africans, Pakistanis, and Albanians with Islam to varying extents, and they extended their criticisms of Muslims to them accordingly. Race seemed to override their attention to West Africans' deep roots in Islam, however, and so a colonial imagery of blacks as simple and *simpatici* precluded the lumping together of Senegalese and Nigerians with other, supposedly fanatical and dangerous Muslims. The primary importance of physiognomy over culture was also asserted by two respondents who took up the case of francophone Africans when discussing "ethnic" difference later in the interview. Both felt that somatic characteristics like skin color were a more accurate indicator of such groups' ethnicity than their language fluency. Tommaso, a psychology major at the University of Naples, explained that "those with Afro-American [sic] features can be English speakers as well as, I don't know, French.... So language, yes, [denotes ethnicity], but in a minimal part. But the physical characteristics, right." The primacy of race over culture when it came to classifying blacks was doubly evident here: not only did Tommaso minimize the importance of language compared to physical traits, but he conflated West Africans with African Americans.

The students' depictions of Moroccans also illustrated the potential for culture to recede in importance when racial framing came into view. As we have seen, Moroccans were often linked to Eastern Europeans as possessors of ostensibly "criminal" cultures or dispositions. An exception arose in Naples, however. In that port city, whose population is long accustomed to the presence of North African communities and where illegal activities such as drug trafficking are tightly controlled by the Camorra (the local criminal organization), Moroccans were decriminalized and thus became simply Africans. There respondents regularly associated Moroccans with other African nationalities and with traits believed to be characteristic of Africans in general:

> Moroccans, Senegalese, all these people of color are ... all the faces you see, you hardly ever see a sad Moroccan. Even though they've got nothing, right? [Even if] they haven't got money for food, they always go like: "Hello! How are you?!" So I think they're nice. I really have a thing for them. I always say that if I could be born again, I would be born black. Then I like their color, the fact that they seem.... They're just born with a great physique.
> (Alessandra, biology major, Naples)

Alessandra's comment clearly indicates what it means for Moroccans to go from being a criminal nationality or a threatening Muslim culture to being racially black. No longer scary predators or oppressors of women, they become alluring physical specimens who are always happy, regardless of their poverty.

Long-standing Western beliefs about race also seemed to lie behind our respondents' selection of particular descent-based groups to represent "otherness." Analysis of the groups named most frequently when respondents discussed difference and integration revealed a striking landscape of visibility—and invisibility. For despite being by far the largest foreign-born group in Italy, with distinct languages, religious customs, and political histories, Eastern Europeans were rarely held up as examples of a different culture. Simply put, they seemed to be associated with a whiteness that spared them from being symbols of the other. Instead, when asked to identify non-Italians in their society, our interviewees thought first of smaller communities like the Chinese, Africans, and, of course, the Roma (even though roughly half of the Roma are Italian citizens).[51] When asked who was not considered Italian in his country, for example, Gianmarco, a psychology major in Naples, replied, "Surely Roma, black people (*gente di colore*), whoever in short could seem not Italian at first glance, clearly." Taking into account the population size of various descent-based groupings, we found that African and Asian peoples were named more often than their demographic presence in Italy might warrant, while immigrants from Eastern Europe and South America received markedly less mention than the size of their respective communities would lead us to expect. In short, the nonwhite races that Linnaeus described—namely the "black" and "yellow" races—routinely stood in for nonbelonging, rather than a much larger domestic community of Albanians, Romanians, and Slavic peoples.

Finally, the hypervisibility of nonwhites as cultural others was also apparent in the recurring formula that "even" a Chinese or African person could be integrated into Italian society. In a common turn of phrase, Lisa, a psychology major in Bologna, asserted, "A person can be Italian ... even if they come from Africa." No one ever said, "... even if they come from the United States," or "... even if they come from Russia." Several respondents also referred to a hypothetical black or Asian child adopted and raised by (presumably white) parents in Italy as an illustration of how people with phenotypic differences from the majority could acquire the same cultural traits as their parents and become Italian. Although such statements sought to distinguish physical and cultural differences, they also elided them by suggesting that the former might be expected to signal the latter:

> I think that a culture can be pliant, it can blend with another culture, I mean to say.... Well, also here in the South, we have examples of this, quite obvious ones, I mean.... From the past and not from the past, for example, black Americans who left us children of color, who in the end became integrated. *(Clara, tourism student, Milan)*

Clara's remark was ostensibly about the blending of cultures, but she illustrated it by referring to color. In pointing to "black" Americans—and not white American soldiers, who also left children behind in Italy after World War II—she assured us that integration must be possible if even *i mulattini* (as mixed-race children were known after the war) could eventually be accepted.[52] In this way, the racialized body becomes "the signifier of radical difference," as Colette Guillaumin puts it, and Asian and African people mark the extremes—or limits—of an assimilation that respondents insisted was cultural.[53] Although the phrase "even a black person can become Italian" was meant to support the frequent assertion that "physical characteristics don't matter for integration," it undercut that premise every time.

The subtle interplay between biological, social, and cultural notions of descent-based difference that we encountered in our interviews with young Italians calls for a rethinking of the "new racism" premise. To be sure, their preferred language for discussing difference was that of culture, which is consistent with the proposition that Western Europeans approach the topic with a culture-oriented mindset. But as we have shown, both social structure and, especially, physical traits nonetheless provided salient frameworks for perceiving, organizing, and reasoning about difference. In addition, another type of characteristic unexpectedly surfaced in our respondents' "mental maps": namely, group temperament or disposition. This idea that descent is linked to particular personality or psychological traits was invoked to explain a wide range of behaviors, regardless of whether interviewees adopted a civic, cultural, or nativist concept of group belonging. Taken altogether, these findings show that simply labeling Italian concepts of difference as "cultural" would be grossly inadequate for fully grasping them.

A blanket "cultural" designation would also fail to capture the many meaningful dimensions along which our respondents' beliefs about difference varied. In this chapter, we have noted that interviewees offered competing accounts of the fixity or fluidity of cultural traits and signaled diverse paths or mechanisms for obtaining them; the signature characteristics of a given group might be essential (inborn), primordial (learned early in childhood), or acquired (deliberately adopted) later in life. Where the students stood in unison, however, was on the affirmation that culture was consequential or deterministic: it mattered a great deal, they insisted, for a wide range of outcomes. Even the fact that biology, in contrast, was repeatedly dismissed as inconsequential alerts us to the importance of determinism as another facet of the conceptualization of difference that merits attention.

Finally, the respondents' ranking of groups' likability based on their perceived sociability and civic-mindedness—rather than, say, their skin color, as we might expect in the United States—points to the myriad ways in which hierarchies can be constituted, as well as undone. All of these elements of the conceptualization of difference will be taken up again in the book's conclusion.

Gaining a more nuanced picture of what might at first appear to be a monolithic "culture" concept holds out the promise of better understanding its appeal and widespread embrace in contemporary Italy. As we saw, its ambiguity and fluidity—culture could be invoked to explain any and all perceived differences between descent-based groups—made it a useful rhetorical tool, if not always the sole conceptual framework in play. But contrasting culture with socioeconomic, civic, biological, and temperamental notions of difference is equally telling. Culture talk—including frequent references to temperament—avoids the taboo of speaking about race or the body, but it does not disrupt enduring ways of perceiving and categorizing human beings along classic racial lines. Cultural—and even civic—discourse also serves to explain social inequalities as the result of the characteristics of non-Italians rather than of structural mechanisms of power in which Italians ("we") are implicated. In short, the wide-ranging use of culture to understand difference preserves Italians' self-image as *brava gente*: never racist, and innocent of any role in producing the gulf in life outcomes between insiders and outsiders. Culture, then, is enlisted to justify the exclusion of others, just as race has been; it is currently the visible face of a larger juggernaut of concepts that distinguish "us" from "them."

The words of Europarliamentarian Mario Borghezio, with which we began this chapter, play on the dividing line between what "you can say" and what "you can only think." In the open-ended conversations we had with young Italians about descent-based difference in their country, culture was clearly on the side of what could—and indeed, should—be said; in contrast, social structure could be mentioned but more often was not, and physical difference should not be spoken at all. Yet just as much as culture, social structure and physical difference were elements of what people thought.

In the next chapter, we move to an entirely different arena: we asked interviewees in both Italy and the United States to talk explicitly about "race." That reshuffling of the discursive terrain led to a new configuration of how and when culture, biology, and society should be spoken and thought.

CHAPTER 3

"Race" Talk

Maybe I link [race] a lot to Hitler and the Second World War, as far as what I've studied. So linking it so much to a really ugly fact, which struck me so much the first time I studied it, because however much you can hate someone, can hate the fact that they're different from you, I can't understand how a man could think about hurting so many people. So tied to this factor, to the suffering that took place, it brings me to reject the word "race," it really makes me sick.

—FLAVIA, graphic design student, Milan

In particular school worries me, as the primary educational agency in a civilized society, which—as emerges from the words of these kids—is not even able to teach them to distinguish form from substance, the word from its contents. To not be racist, all you have to do is never say the word "race." If you don't say "race," there won't ever be gas chambers again, and we're all set and happy with our consciences. This is the sole message that school has succeeded in inculcating in them. So when a new Hitler arrives, instead of "race" he'll call it "baloney" (*mortadella*), millions more will be killed in defense of baloney, and again no one will realize anything is going on!

—ELENA SKALL, transcriber and daughter of Holocaust victims,
in email comment on the interviews, June 25, 2013

AT THE start of each of our interviews with young Italians, we tiptoed around race and ethnicity, avoiding the use of these words ourselves. But once we had listened to the students' open-ended commentaries about "Italianness" and, we hoped, given them the chance to get used to talking with us, we asked them to reflect on precisely those terms. For both words, we requested a definition, illustrative examples, and an explanation of how varied groups (ethnic or racial) differed among themselves. We even asked for their reactions to a statement taken from another survey: "There are biological races within the species *Homo sapiens*."[1] Prodding the interviewees to engage with the terms "ethnicity" and then "race" allowed us to gauge their reactions, both emotional and intellectual, and to learn something about how they conceptualized these ideas, observed certain norms about their expression, and conveyed notions of difference even when eschewing such language.

Overwhelmingly, our Italian interviewees recoiled from the word "race." Again and again, we heard them reject it as *una brutta parola*—"an ugly word." The reaction of Flavia, the student quoted at the start of this chapter, was typical. When asked to define *razza*, her thoughts immediately turned to Hitler and wartime genocide. Not only did "race" conjure up the most horrific crimes against humanity for the bulk of our respondents, but this association placed the blame on another era and another country. "Race" was also understood by many as a matter of the individual prejudice of one powerful man with an inexplicable hatred of those who were "different." All that was terrifying, unimaginable, and unconscionable about the Holocaust was distilled into the word "race," making a young person like Flavia feel "sick." In contrast, "ethnicity" carried little of that charge for our interviewees, and indeed, "ethnicity" was often seen as an unproblematic substitute for "race."

For Americans who are used to hearing, talking, and reading about race in everyday life, it may be hard to understand how viscerally distasteful the word is for many Italians (not to mention other Europeans). The closest example we have come up with in American English is the word "mulatto." Like *razza* in Italy, "mulatto" conveys an idea about racial difference that we associate with another time (and even another place for many of us): the antebellum slave society of the U.S. South. Not only does "mulatto" sound anachronistic to American ears, but it is heavily associated with the overt, government-sanctioned, and brutal white supremacism of that period.[2] For all these reasons, it is hard to imagine Americans seriously referring to anyone as "mulatto" in this day and age.

There is another, more profound parallel between *razza* in Italy and "mulatto" in the United States: as cringeworthy as these words may be to most people, they do not necessarily reject their underlying meanings. Even though we do not refer to Barack Obama as "the first mulatto president" of the United States, Americans have no reservations about noting his mixed-race ancestry or labeling him "biracial." Their current speech norms do not prohibit that. In short, Americans have discarded the word "mulatto" but not its fundamental concept of multiraciality; other terms have simply come into play to replace it. Can the same be said of *razza* in Italy?

Elena Skall, who transcribed most of our audiotaped interviews in Italy, thinks so. In the reflections she shared with us after having listened closely to many interviews, she conveyed her fear that young Italians have been taught to shun the word *razza* without having learned to recognize the many forms of exclusion it can underpin, both present and future. As she put it in the chapter epigraph, the message young people receive is: "To not be racist, all you have to do is never say the word 'race.'" Our interviews suggest, however, that an array of discursive strategies for dealing with race are used by both Americans and Italians, that these go beyond simple silence, and they do not always map onto actual beliefs about descent-based difference.

Posing to Italian students the same questions on race that Morning had asked of Americans allowed us to compare their concepts of descent-based difference, which we categorized as antibiological, biological, constructivist, or culturalist.[3] In this way, we address this book's central question about the roles of culture, biology, and other perceived bases of group difference in the American and European imaginaries. What we have called the "new racism" hypothesis suggests a more biological take on race in the United States and a more cultural perspective in Western Europe.[4] And in the preceding chapter, we reported that "culture" was indeed the dominant element in our Italian respondents' discussions of Italianness and group difference; it was the go-to explanatory framework when biology was deemed unacceptable and structural socioeconomic difference went unnoticed.

Yet in this chapter and the next, we discover the limits of the Italian students' culturalist discourse—and thus of the new racism hypothesis. Though prominent in definitions of "ethnicity," the notion of culture effectively hit a wall when it came to definitions of "race" in Italy—but curiously, not in the United States. Moreover, the centrality of biology to both American and Italian respondents' reasoning about race also cast doubt on the transatlantic distinction that has often been suggested. Finally, as we will show, our U.S. and Italian respondents were more alike than not in the minor place held by the notion of race as socially constructed in their understandings of difference.

A Shared Biological Approach to Race

In stark contradiction to any claim that Americans and Europeans hold very different understandings of the word "race," our interviews in Italy and the United States revealed highly similar definitions. First and foremost, biology was the primary lens for making sense of racial difference in both countries. Our two samples were also comparable in the degree of their agreement on the existence of "biological races" in the human species. And both sets of students recognized the potential sensitivity and moral concerns associated with the topic of race. Finally, we found that definitions of race varied in similar ways within each sample, notably along the lines of field of study and political leaning.

Not only were both Italian and U.S. interviewees more likely to adopt a biological definition of race than any other kind of definition, but the two samples did so at similar rates. Fifty-six percent of the U.S. respondents equated race with biology, as did 48 percent in Italy.[5] In fact, if we limit consideration to only the Italian university students, excluding the Milanese vocational students in order to make a more appropriate comparison to the U.S. college sample, we find that the Italian undergraduates were just as likely as their American counterparts to define race as biology: 56 percent of them did so as well.[6] Biological concepts of race focused on physical difference, whether expressed in surface phenotypic traits like skin color, manifested in physiognomy or anatomical structure, or residing in underlying genetic variation. An example came from the biology major Angela in Milan: "Race as ... as a biologist [laughs], a subgroup of a species ... a ... a group of individuals who have similar morphological and genetic characteristics and so who can be grouped together. For example, skin color, particular somatic traits.... That's a race ... which exists in man, in dogs, it exists in all animals."

U.S. and Italian respondents were also similar in the extent of their agreement with the statement on the existence of biological races that we took from a survey by Leonard Lieberman.[7] Thirty-eight percent of the Americans agreed with the statement, compared to 35 percent of the

Milanese vocational students and 32 percent of the Italian university undergraduates. The Milanese vocational students were also similar to the Americans in the rates at which they selected the intermediate, neutral, or unsure position: 26 percent did so, compared to 31 percent in the United States and only 15 percent among Italian college students. Across the board, moreover, respondents in both countries employed similar arguments when supporting the claim that biological races exist in the human species—pointing, for example, to the role of genes in producing different shades of skin color.

The disjuncture in both countries between the share of students defining race as biological, on the one hand, and the share of those agreeing that biological races exist, on the other, speaks to a shared sensibility. Although roughly half of both samples equated race with biology when offering their open-ended definitions of the term, only about one-third of each sample agreed with the statement on biological races—a notable drop-off. The bald-faced assertion about the existence of biological races seemed to make U.S. as well as Italian interviewees uneasy, provoking negative feelings, raising ethical concerns, and probably heightening anxiety about social desirability to an even greater degree than the question about defining "race" did. Seeing the statement on paper made Eileen, an Ivy University anthropology major who disagreed with it, "angry," "unhappy," and "suspicious," as if its author were about to go on to propose harm to other people.[8] Other American students, echoing their Italian peers, called the statement "loaded," "dangerous," "racist," "very shifty," and capable of being "abused" and "taken out of context" to fuel "social Darwinism."

Finally, we found similarities in the sociodemographic characteristics associated with biological understandings of race in Italy as well as in the United States. In particular, having a right-leaning political orientation and majoring in biology at college were linked to biological definitions in both countries. Conversely, gender mattered little, and the impact of class background was ambiguous. In Italy, Northerners were markedly more likely than Southerners (and even those born in the North to Southern parents) to adopt biological definitions of race, but regional patterns could not be investigated in the U.S. sample, which was smaller and heavily skewed toward Northeasterners. Moreover, the majority-white samples precluded an exploration of the role of racial identities in the conceptualization of descent-based difference.

Despite the impossibility of making sweeping statements or any national estimates based on these small interview samples, their results clearly call into question the notion that Americans have an especially biological understanding of race that is absent in Western Europe. It is hard to maintain that the biological race concept has been abandoned in Western Europe when, depending on the measure, one-third to nearly half of our young Italian respondents subscribed to it.

The Italian Rejection of Race

Despite the evidence that the classic Linnaean notion of biological races retains an unmistakable hold in Italy as it does in the United States, we also discerned a vocal rejection of race that was much more pronounced among Italians than Americans. Although the American students were no less aware of the dark history of racism—and were arguably more attuned to its contemporary realities—they generally did not perform the rejection of race in the same ways or to the same extent that their Italian counterparts did. Among our Italian respondents, this stance blended discursive strategies like the refusal to use the word "race" with moral evaluations of its content, making it difficult to discern the extent to which their rejection of race was linguistic, ethical, or conceptual. The ways in which Italian interviewees continued to espouse biological notions of descent-based difference—for example, when labeled as "ethnicity"—and even the conceptual framework of classic racial taxonomy suggest that their rejection of race was more apparent than real. Above all, our findings make clear that those distancing themselves from the word "race" are not necessarily discarding long-standing Western beliefs about descent-based physical difference.

Dissenting from the Race Concept

Although our Italian interviewees were no strangers to the biological interpretation of race, as we have seen, there were two ways in which they were notably more resistant to it than our American respondents were. First, if we exclude the Milanese vocational students and compare only the Italian college students to their U.S. counterparts, a marked divergence appears in their attitude toward the Lieberman statement on the existence of biological races. Whereas fewer than one-third of the Americans interviewed disagreed with the notion of biological human races, more than half of the Italian undergraduates did. Interestingly, Italians were more likely to invoke the broadly authoritative idea that "science shows" or "scientists have said" that there is no such thing as biological race, whereas Americans were more likely to reference specific scientific findings, especially the claim that more than 99 percent of our DNA is common to all human beings.

Second, the Italian respondents were more than twice as likely as Americans to espouse "antibiological" definitions of race, often encapsulated in the refrain, "there's only one human race." That is, they more often asserted that race is *not* grounded in physical difference or that it does not exist—where existence was equated with being biologically real. Such negative refutations about what race is not—rather than positive declarations of what it is—constituted the second-most frequent approach to defining race in the Italian sample, but the least common approach in the U.S. group. And if we focus only on the interviewees who employed some kind of biological reasoning when defining the term "race," a much greater share of the Italians did so to refute a biological definition compared to the Americans. Of the eighty-nine Italian interviewees who referenced biology, thirty-seven (or 42 percent) argued that race was not grounded in biological difference, whereas only seven of the thirty-six comparable American interviewees (less than 20 percent) did so. In other words, when arguments about the human body came into play, they were more likely to sway Americans than Italians toward a biological reading of race.

Linguistic and Moral Distancing from Race

Although ethical reservations about the race concept arose in our interviews in both countries, Italians were noticeably more vehement in their moral condemnation of it. Tallying up all the race definitions that made reference to hierarchy, inequality, power, racism, or simply a negative opinion, we found that only one-quarter of the U.S. interviewees made such criticisms, compared to nearly 60 percent of the Italian interviewees. We also noticed a striking difference in affect; the Americans' response came across as anemic compared to the immediate and intense discomfort and rejection expressed by the Italian students. Most of the Americans did not seem to bat an eye when it came to the mention of "race," demonstrating a sangfroid that was astounding compared to the Italians' heated denunciations. Put differently, race seemed to have lost its power to shock in the United States, whereas in Italy it incited the performance of a morality play with a familiar script. In this repertory lay several regular linguistic set-pieces, including the avoidance of the word "race" and varied semantic strategies for distancing the speaker from any mention of it. As in the interpersonal interactions that Stefan Timmermans and Iddo Tavory dissected using semiotic analysis, the specter of racism required subtle (and not-so-subtle) management.[9]

THE REFUSAL TO ENGAGE "RACE"

Throughout our interviews in Italy, respondents rarely used the word *razza* spontaneously before we had broached the subject ourselves; only 11 of the 106 respondents did so. Moreover, in the context of the opening conversations about *italianità* that we described in chapter 2, the term usually came up as a synonym for nationality or people and was not strictly linked to Linnaean color-coded taxonomy. "In my class," a tourism student told us, "there's the Chinese guy, the girl from Angola, the Iraqi, the Egyptian, the Peruvian, the Filipina. There are all the races. The Italian, the Tuscan (*laughs*).... We're all ... the races."

When we explicitly asked interviewees to provide examples of racial groups, the Italian students were more reluctant to do so than the Americans were, and in fact, almost one in five refused to name any race, arguing that the question was dangerous or nonsensical. In addition, a little more than one-quarter of the Italian respondents provided a list meant to reflect others' beliefs while underscoring that it did not reflect their own views because they would not use the concept of race. Amid these and other ways of expressing doubt or consternation, fewer than half of the Italian interviewees provided examples of racial groups in a straightforward and apparently untroubled manner. And a handful either refused to define "race" or made vague references to difference, opting instead to simply condemn it with phrases like, "I don't like it as a word," or "I find it a very derogatory term," and linking it to racism, hierarchy, or Hitler.

SEMANTIC DISTANCING FROM "RACE"

When we pressed the Italian students to discuss "race"—for example, by asking them for a definition of it, or for a reaction to the Lieberman statement on the existence of biological races—we were effectively breaking a linguistic taboo for many. To repair this normative breach, respondents often adopted what Bonnet calls "the discursive strategies of non-racism—how people manage implicit or potential accusations of racism."[10] In France, Bonnet found distinct ways of coping with the "stigma" of violating "colourmute" speech norms.[11] Chief among them was contrition, "the expression of sorrow and repentance, which is a way for respondents to signal that they respect, understand, and usually abide by, the dominant norms of nonracism.... In numerous instances, respondents become demonstrably apologetic in their explanations of talking directly about race, anxious that they are violating speech norms."[12] In our conversations with young Italians, we also encountered a mix of emotion and rationalization when they were prodded to speak of race. They exhibited anxiety, uncertainty, embarrassment, indignation, and incoherence and used multiple rhetorical tactics to distance themselves from the concept of race, including denouncing race, marking a boundary between themselves and the use of race, and relegating race to other eras or societies.

The vehement, spontaneous exclamation that we repeatedly heard from Italians when asked to define "race"—*Che brutta parola!*" (What an ugly word!)—conveys their deeply negative sentiment toward it. Their visceral animosity also came out in other ways: for instance, Claudio, an anthropology major in Bologna, said that just hearing the word made him feel "sick." In a similar vein, Anna, a history major in Bologna, said, "It's a term I absolutely repudiate, that I can't stand, that I don't use." Part of what bothered the respondents was that in Italian *razza* is also the word for "breed," as in animals, and so it seemed inappropriate for human beings. More often, however, the Italian interviewees denounced race as linked to racism, historical inequalities, hierarchy, unease, and obsolescence; more than half (63 out of 106) did so. This association was so strong that at times the students interpreted our request to name racial groups that came to mind as a question about "racist" groups and offered examples such as the Ku Klux Klan and skinheads. These instances underscore how little conceptual distance there was between "race" and "racism" in the minds of many of our Italian respondents.

The moral or scientific unacceptability of race—or the fear of being labeled racist—often led our Italian subjects to position themselves discursively as outside or beyond its realm. "I've never used [that word] for humankind and never will," declared Donato, a chemistry major in Bologna; "I tend not to use it as a category," remarked Luna, a history major in Naples; and Oliviero, who was studying graphic design in Milan, asserted, "I really don't have the race concept." For these reasons, some suggested, they could not offer a definition of race. "I don't know, for me it's difficult to define," said Beatrice, a chemistry major in Naples. "It's that I don't have it as a concept, so I'm not able to." For Daniela, a tourism student in Milan, defining race was impossible because "it's not in my vocabulary to say to a person that they're of a [certain] race."

Such self-positioning took on added force when respondents contrasted their own approaches to race with that of others. These respondents drew a moral boundary between the self and those who trafficked in the illegitimate concept.[13] Others saw and thought about race, these interviewees suggested, but they did not. As the tourism student Elisabetta put it, "Surely [race] exists in the imagination of many people. Not in mine, so I can't even define it." After a long commentary on the social acceptability of labels like "white" and "black" (including "I don't believe that a black should feel offended by being called black because it's silly—in the sense that we're called whites but no one gets offended"), biology major Francesco in Milan responded as follows when Morning asked whether he considered these terms to be racial labels:

> Well, let's say that in society they are [racial labels], but not in my thinking, in that sense there. That is, I know that outside, even here probably, there are many people around who have these racial labels and then probably just to say, "Oh, the blacks...." Who knows what they think and all that. But ... like, I'm aware of the fact that outside of these walls it's like that. But at least inside me it's not at all.

Another interviewee who emphasized the specificity of her own thought by contrasting it with others' was Maria, a biology major in Naples:

> There are quite a few people who are very ... fixated on the fact of race, and so aren't able to see beyond it. But my own thought is, for example, [that] race is a derogatory term, and so I don't like to use and make this difference. But for example, society nowadays leads us to make this distinction between various people, also the difference in skin color, for example. They haven't influenced me much.

After hearing countless respondents describe race as a "derogatory" term, it is striking to us that Maria believes this to be her own personal standpoint, and that she is convinced that others' views have little influence on her. Her position speaks, however, to the moral urgency of distinguishing one's own engagement with "race" from the illicit uses of the concept by others—namely, those who are "fixated" and can't "see beyond" it, those who "make this distinction between various people."

Finally, our Italian interviewees frequently managed the discomfort of race talk by displacing it in time and space, often simultaneously. In disagreeing with the idea that "certain races" could not be integrated into Italy, Elena used a memorable image:

> Because race is just the calling card, no? The person who presents themself in front of you. Maybe if we lived in Nazi Germany, I'd almost agree, but fortunately we no longer have a Nazi or Fascist culture, so I think that races ... it isn't that there's a need to integrate the races. Culture yes, but race no, they're already pretty integrated, I think, like we see them every day, so there's no need to integrate them.

This depiction of race as an ideology that held sway only in the period leading up to World War II, and then largely in Germany, is one that we heard time and again in interviewees' comments.

A more subtle yet recurrent projection took place when students regularly used the term "African Americans" (*afroamericani*) for other blacks, whether referring to those in Italy, Africa, or elsewhere, thus making race a singularly U.S. phenomenon. Recall, for example, the consternation of Tommaso, the University of Naples psychology major mentioned in the previous chapter, over the ethnic designation of francophone Africans, given their "Afro-American" facial features. Later in the interview, he transported black Americans to Italy as well, placing them in occupations associated with immigrants to his country: "So if we're used to seeing the white guy, I don't know, professor, engineer, etc.... we tend instead to see the Afro-American guy like, I don't know, the worker, the construction worker." Tommaso was not alone in this translation: when asked to list races, undergraduates Alberto, Stefano, and Martina all named *afroamericani* alongside groups like whites and Asians; Vanessa, a vocational school student in Milan, even described "an African American who lives near the equator, it's obvious they'll have darker skin than mine." Unless she was thinking about black people in Florida, it seems likely that Vanessa viewed "African American" as globally synonymous with "black." These all-purpose uses of Americans to stand in for blacks everywhere not only speak to the world diffusion of U.S. cultural models but also reflect a geographic—and historically colored—displacement, one that locates race and racism in the United States, seen as the home of slavery and Jim Crow.

The positioning of race as historically and geographically distant involved a kind of national boundary-marking around contemporary Italy rather than a merely personal self-positioning. Consider the bright line that Fabrizio, a psychology major in Milan, drew between past and present:

> In my view [race] doesn't exist so much anymore. I have this feeling because anyway like . . . the concept of race—at least I say, talking in an Italian, European context, right—because anyhow the concept of race, let's say it leads to much bigger outcomes than what can happen today. Today the most that happens—which is serious enough in itself—is a beating, maybe a Molotov cocktail thrown into a Romani camp, that is, in that sense, while the concept of race leads, in my view, to well, other . . . to well, other consequences, but really at the level . . . not so much at the level of behaviors, but really at the level of ideals. . . . So the race concept, in my view, in this moment in Italy, for better or worse. . . . Yes, you could say . . . even saying racist, in itself, is not so true anymore, because anyhow one doesn't have an issue with race so much as with behaviors in this sense. Excluding extremists of course.

Despite some disjointedness, Fabrizio placed race firmly in the past, describing it as an ideology with large-scale consequences. No doubt he had Nazi concentration camps in mind as "much bigger outcomes than what can happen today." Fabrizio minimized today's beatings and arson of Romani homes as not really racist and "the most that happens," even as he acknowledged that these acts were "serious." Again, the place of race was diminished and displaced to the past—or to the "extremist" fringe.

Students like Fabrizio turned repeatedly to a well-stocked toolbox of rhetorical strategies for managing eruptions of explicit race speech. With these tools, they aimed to assure their interlocutors—and likely themselves—that race was absent not only from the contemporary Italian social landscape but from their own inner mental worlds as well.

*When Biological—and Even "Racial"—Concepts of Difference
Become Acceptable*

For all the recoil from the word "race" and heartfelt arguments challenging
its biological reality that we registered among the Italian respondents, it
became quickly apparent that these reactions did not preclude a belief in
meaningful biological differences between groups historically known as
"races." Instead, as long as these ideas were discussed under the rubric of
"ethnicity," they were not subject to any of the scrutiny or semantic maneu-
vering that race talk had required. Similarly, classic racial labels like "black"
and "white" seemed unproblematic, unless the word *razza* was mentioned.
In short, a complex set of norms governed our Italian interviewees' expression of beliefs about race, ethnicity, and the human body.

Although "culture" was far and away the most important touchstone
for Italian students when we asked them, "How would you define the term
'ethnicity'?," biology and race were the second-most important association.[14] More than three-quarters of these students linked ethnicity to culture,
custom, religion, language, or mentality. But a sizable minority—roughly
one-third—defined it as either the equivalent of race or a matter of physical
difference. Damiano, a history major in Bologna, ventured, "Ethnicity ...
I don't know, synonym of race." Eugenio, a psychology major in Milan, did
not refer to race but incorporated antiquated racial labels in his definition
of "ethnicity":

> Well, I'd define it as genetic, physiological, and very often personality char-
> acteristics, maybe, of a given people. I don't know, I think of the stocks
> (*ceppi*)—we're born from the Negroid, Mongol, and another stock, I think
> it's European, I don't remember now.

Fifteen of the respondents combined both biology and culture in their
definitions, like Tatiana, a biology major in Milan, who described ethnicity
as "the set of morphological, cultural, social traits that characterize a people."
The tendency to incorporate biological reasoning was not random, moreover, but was particularly characteristic of Northern-born university students
majoring in psychology or biology, like Tatiana, and of the offspring of relatively well-educated and highly skilled parents. In other words, biological
reasoning appealed to the more privileged segment of our Italian sample.[15]

For many of our Italian respondents, then, the concept of ethnicity incorporated notions of difference that have traditionally been the hallmarks of Western ideas of race. These signature beliefs included the importance of physiognomy (and at times, temperament) as a marker of group membership; the depiction of group traits as essential or fixed; and references to large-scale, continental groupings. With respect to bodily characteristics, for example, Diana, a student of audiovisual technology in Milan, described differences between ethnic groups by providing a detailed comparison of Italian, Greek, German, and Chinese physiognomy (among others), adding, "There's also the culture, but the first thing you notice is appearance."

Ethnicity was also associated with processes of intergenerational transmission that could be either primordial—that is, involving socialization from a young age—or, like the classic race concept, essential—a matter of inborn or hardwired traits inherited from biological parents.[16] Both mechanisms might be at work, for example, in this definition from Antonio, a history major in Bologna:

> Ethnicity is your roots and your belonging, what you are, what your ances-
> tors were and what, with the passing of generations, you became and what,
> if you feel like you belong, you want to be passed down to your children,
> your heirs, I don't know, your ... the generations that will be born of you,
> in short.

Similarly, Giacinto, a history major in Naples, saw ethnicity as "something in which one grows up, independently of their free will," and Samuele, a chemistry major in Bologna, saw it as "a question of tradition: what my parents teach me. Ethnicity is something that is passed down, not something personal." On the one hand, the language of intergenerational transmission in these quotes evokes a primordial mechanism, where parents pass along ethnicity to their children through their teaching and modeling of cultural practices. On the other, however, this language takes on such an infallible, inevitable, and unchanging air that it approaches an essentialist permanence. In this vein, one has "roots" that ordain "what you are"—which is unequivocally "what your ancestors were." The process is deterministic, infallible, independent of one's "free will," and "not something personal"—much as race has been understood in the West.[17] While the American interviewees often regarded culture as a matter of superficial trappings that could be shed from one generation to the next, the ethnicity that

· our Italian respondents generally equated with cultural difference took on a greater air of permanence, owing perhaps to its entwinement with race.

The classic Linnaean race notion was even more clearly present in the kinds of groupings that Italian respondents deemed "ethnic." For one thing, just as race was constructed to mark nonwhites as inferior or problematic, ethnicity in our interviewees' eyes was fundamentally about others, not about "us." Many definitions of ethnicity underscored this point, presenting it as involving people who came from another country—or as Milanese tourism student Romina put it, people who "come from other cultures, traditions, different from ours." Ethnicity was also seen as about people "who have problems," in the words of University of Naples chemistry major Giordano, and about those who "live in a place that is not civilized, [who] live in a different world from the cities that are more modern," according to Daniela. Iacopo, a sociology major in Milan, gave the example of "the aborigines who still share, I don't know, the totems, see the god of rain, stuff like that; then, if I'm not wrong, there are also ethnic objects, like wood carvings, that stand out from other objects." Isabella, a student of tourism in Milan, offered another indigenous example:

The children of Native Americans, for one, even if now they've been influenced by America, the arrival of the English, the colonies and all, but anyway they were a fantastic ethnic group, and at least some of them must have preserved the traditions, so there are all these cases of kind of particular ethnicities.

As these comments suggest, ethnicity was so far projected beyond the borders not just of Italy but of the West more broadly that even American Indians, as a "particular" (though "fantastic") ethnic group, were positioned outside "America," which became the province of the ethnically unmarked English. This way of mapping ethnicity was so powerful that even those interviewees who wished to challenge it found themselves resorting to the recurring formula that "even we" could be considered an ethnic group.

Traditional Western racial taxonomy was also apparent in the students' cataloging of "ethnic" groups. They routinely associated ethnic groups with the broad continental collectives that have been the mainstay of racial thought, like "Orientals," Africans, and indigenous Americans, rather than the specific, smaller-scale national or subnational communities that are more likely to exhibit the distinctive cultural practices—for example in language, dress, or culinary practice—that they claimed were at the root of ethnicity. The most frequent examples of "ethnic groups" we heard were, in descending order: "Africans" (in 23 of the 106 interviews); "Roma," "gypsies," or "nomads" (in 21); "Chinese" (20); and (South Asian) "Indians" (in 16). "Africa" remained for the most part a monolith, undifferentiated by nationality or indigenous language, as is so often the case in the West. "Chinese," though a national label, similarly homogenized a population of over one billion people that comprises multiple minority groups. In keeping with a racially inflected understanding of ethnics as nonwhite "others," European groups whose cultural practices were probably most familiar to Italians— whether Eastern Europeans (the largest foreign-born community in Italy, as we saw in chapter 2), Western European neighbors like the Swiss, French, or Austrians, or Italy's own regional minorities like Sardinians or Piedmontese— rarely figured in the respondents' mental maps of ethnicity.

In fact, the Italian students often appeared comfortable with traditional racial labels or groupings, as long as the word "race" was not mentioned. For example, their resistance to identifying "racial" groups was nowhere to be found when asked to name "ethnic" groups, even though they frequently listed the same groups for both questions. In both cases, African, Asian, and European ancestry—the taxonomic touchstones of the eighteenth century— came to the fore. And although only a handful of respondents brought up "race" spontaneously before we asked them about it, more than twice as many introduced racial labels like "white"—or especially, "black"—without any prompting, bringing the share of interviewees referring to race or color early on in the conversation up to nearly one-quarter.

In summary, we found that what made race so objectionable for so many of our Italian interviewees was not the content of the concept. Emphasis on physical difference, the "othering" of non-Europeans, and even the classic Linnaean taxonomy could all be invoked without hesitation as long as they were not explicitly linked to race. Moreover, even those students who most staunchly insisted that race did not exist in biological terms were at a loss to explain why; their responses rarely ventured beyond the formula, "there's only one human race." Reasoning about whether or how race was incorrect or inaccurate as a concept was in short supply. As a result, our Italian interviewees often depicted race as morally flawed, or an invention of people who were "sick in the head," as Virginia put it, rather than as factually wrong. When Morning asked Flavia, for example, why she had said that it was never "appropriate" to use the word "race," she immediately replied, "Because it's ugly," then added, "Also because Hitler used it to define who wasn't pure, all the Jews, like that. It's never been seen as a nice word." She did not say, for example, that "race" incorrectly alluded to discrete biological clusters in the human species or that it mistakenly presupposed hard-wired behavioral tendencies among groups. Similarly, when Rosa, a student of cultural heritage in Naples asserted that "it's better not to use the term 'race,'" she also confessed, "I don't know if it's right or wrong, though." The conceptual content or logic of the word was not the problem; instead, students' equation of race with unjust hierarchy provoked an immediate rejection of the term that headed off a deeper examination of whether they actually subscribed to any of its elements.

Our Italian sample's widespread rejection of race, then, was both deeply felt and yet superficial. As respondents themselves were often the first to acknowledge, they were reacting to the connotations of the word rather than its substance. Time and again they let us know that the same concept of descent-based difference that they embraced when labeled "ethnicity" would be unacceptable if called "race." According to Benedetto, an anthropology major at the University of Bologna, "ethnicity" was the "evolution of the race concept in politically correct terms." "The word 'race' had to be eliminated," he explained, "but there was the need to indicate with another term what was eliminated, the good parts of the race concept." In contrast, the "negative parts" to be discarded were those "tied to all the discriminations that took place over the course of history, in the most different, diverse ways, over differences that in the end were cultural differences, differences of custom." The central tenet of classic Western race—the division of the human species into a handful of color-coded groups ascribed fixed physical and temperamental qualities—seems to have been left undisturbed. As Giuseppe Faso puts it, ethnicity has become a "lexicon of dissimulation" in Italy, owing to the unacceptability of "race."[18]

The Fortunes of Constructivism in Italy and the United States

Challenges to the biological reality of race, as posed by many of our Italian interviewees, can take two forms. One is the antibiological approach we have seen: a negative rebuttal that race is *not* biological in nature. The other is a social constructivist stance: a positive assertion of what race *is*—namely, a collective human invention. Neither approach is better than the other; they are simply two sides of a single coin that repudiates the biological conceptualization of race. As Morning discovered among U.S. social and natural scientists, however, few people marshal both perspectives when they argue against a biological understanding of race. Whether due to their training, their social status, or something else, people tend to emphasize one line of argument over the other.[19]

Antibiologism and Social Constructivism in the United States and Italy

In our interviews, Italians and Americans differed in their use of antibiological as opposed to constructivist arguments. When Italian students sought to challenge the biological notion of race—and in our samples, they were almost twice as likely as Americans to do so—they relied almost exclusively on an antibiological line of reasoning. An example of such logic would be the observation of Eleonora, a history major at Bologna, that "it's not like there are some [men] with six legs and others with two." Conversely, only 4 of our 106 Italian subjects developed a social constructivist framework when asked to define race, making it the least-cited type of definition among them. In contrast, the U.S. students were almost five times more likely than their Italian counterparts to adopt a constructivist approach—but less than half as likely to mount an antibiological argument, making that viewpoint the least-cited in their definitions of race. Steve, an anthropology major at State University, illustrated this U.S. leaning when he defined race as "socially constructed" and went on to explain, "The concept of race is the idea that there are differences between groups of people based on biology essentially, but that in reality those—the ideas that are— the attributes or stereotypes that are associated to people based on biology, which isn't even really that accurate to begin with, is [*sic*] culturally formed or historically formed."

Both the American constructivist mantra, "Race is a social construct," and its Italian antibiological counterpart, "There is only one human race," often took on a limited or superficial quality in our interviews. We have already seen that Italian challenges to a biological reading of race rarely went beyond declarations of the unity of the human species, assertions that scientists had refuted race, or simply admonitions that it was not "appropriate" to speak of race. Similarly, U.S. students' constructivism was quite passive and thus incomplete: race was invented, they maintained, but it was not clear when, where, by whom, or under what circumstances. Italians invariably attributed the "race" idea, wrongly, to Adolph Hitler, but Americans generally did not even hazard a guess about which society or societies actually gave rise to it. The construction of race thus became an ahistorical fact for our U.S. respondents, unmoored from any specific sociopolitical context.

Constructivism and Its Similars

Although they were more common in the United States, social constructivist definitions of race were infrequent in both countries, appearing in 19 percent of the U.S. interviews and 4 percent of the Italian ones. Notably, none of our Italian interviewees ever used the formula "race is a social construct" in their definitions (although the phrase "social construct" popped up a few times elsewhere in those interviews). This may come as a surprise to students and professors in U.S. higher education, where the phrase has become something of a commonplace, but in Italy most undergraduates seemed unlikely to have ever heard it.[20] Even in the United States, social constructivism appeared less often in respondents' definitions of race than one might expect, given that anthropology students made up one-third of the sample; Morning found that coursework in that discipline was associated with undergraduates' adopting a constructivist view of race.

Although social constructivist definitions of race were rare, we found in both countries "almost-constructivist" interpretations that we call the "similars" of social constructivism. These are descriptions of race that embody some element of social constructivism while lacking others. To classify a definition as social constructivist, we looked for two sets of elements, both of which stem from the label itself:

1. A reference to *construction*, invention, creation, classification, and so on, or recognition that the concept is not a simple reflection of an objective reality (in other words, that it is "arbitrary" or "not real")
2. Identification of the collective (*social*) origins of the concept

For example, in Steve's definition, he presented race as an "idea" that is not an "accurate" representation of biology—that is, as a construct—and one that is "culturally formed" or collectively created. In the United States as well as in Italy, we heard several descriptions of race that captured some aspect of these characteristics—including the word "construct"—while missing others.

In the absence of the language of "construction" in Italy, three kindred types of discourse flourished instead. First, there was a recurrent "individual constructivism" that regularly depicted a single person—Hitler—as the creator of racial thought. A second individualist approach took racial thought or racism to be the inevitable product of universal human emotions or psychological traits, such as fear, insecurity, or ignorance. In this view, race was a natural way of thinking about the world—and racism a natural way of acting in it—for individuals under certain circumstances. Stefania, a tourism student in Milan, provided an example. "The term 'race' is probably used because someone is afraid of what is different," she declared. "And whoever defines a race, it's really because they're afraid, sees something different, and thinks that what they are is right." This perspective is ahistorical; since human beings over the ages have felt anxiety, disdain, and so on, why does race thinking arise at a particular point in time? And both approaches depart from constructivism because, rather than point to the communally created and sociopolitically driven nature of racial ideology, they emphasize individual psychological motives (such as scapegoating or the desire to maintain hierarchy) that give rise to such classification, epitomized yet again in the reviled figure of Adolph Hitler.

Conversely, the third alternative to social constructivism that we found in Italian definitions of race could be said to incorporate a societal focus while dispensing with the construction. In lieu of references to the creation of the race concept or classifications, we often heard young Italians talk about the *uses* of race as a term or an idea; the emphasis here was on race as a tool rather than an invention. While this instrumentalist viewpoint certainly shares with social constructivism the notion that ideas can serve particular purposes, it does not necessarily maintain that race is a subjective human creation. In this perspective, race could well be an objective feature of the human body that is "abused" to the advantage of a powerful group in the same way that height might privilege tall people in the workplace. This ambiguity about the constructed nature of race is apparent in the comments of Davide in Milan: "There, on its own the word 'race' isn't dangerous in itself, I believe. It's been used in a very dangerous way, and has degenerated [into] all this logic of racial hierarchization in everything we know." Davide's view of race as not dangerous in itself but as having been used abusively or as having "degenerated" from a previous acceptable state suggests that there might actually be certain racial dividing lines out there in the world that need not be contested. We do not know what that prior, acceptable racial schema was based on; we just know that since then, race has "been used in a very dangerous way." Condemning certain "uses" of race, then, leaves unanswered the question of whether there are other uses or outcomes of race—either as word or worldview—that are objective and unproblematic.

In the United States, we came across yet another similar of social constructivism, one that might be labeled "cultural constructivism." This was exemplified in the occasional use of the phrase "cultural construct" to mean that racial difference was based on people's cultural characteristics or practices. Despite the semantic similarity, this way of thinking is at odds with a fundamental premise of social constructivism: that racial categories say more about the classifying society than they do about the individuals classified. In other words, this U.S. culturalism, dressed up in the language of constructivism, was yet another way of saying that racial membership emanates from an individual's characteristics, whether in terms of their dress, their foodways, or something else. In contrast, social constructivism maintains that racial membership is projected onto individuals; to paraphrase Tukufu Zuberi, race is a social relationship and not an individual property.[21]

That a social constructivist understanding of race has made little headway in Italy as well as in the United States is yet another similarity in the conceptualization of descent-based difference that we encountered, though in both nations we saw various substitutes or near-misses for such an interpretation. The differences in their approaches to challenging or condemning the biological race notion, however, were telling. The Italian students may have been more likely to advance antibiological arguments because their American peers were more exposed to popular discourse affirming biological racial differences (for example, in medical outcomes).[22] Yet at the same time, the idea that "race is a social construct" seems to have gained more traction in the United States than in Italy. In its absence, our Italian respondents found other ways to convey the idea that race was not rooted in biology but in the human imagination. The American students' approximation of social constructivism, however, was much less skeptical of race. As we will see, they found it appealing to portray racial difference as an uncontroversial matter of culture.

Recasting Race as Culture in the United States

Despite the new racism hypothesis that a cultural language of race predominates in Western Europe, in our study it was the Americans who were most eager to transform race into culture. Fully one-half of the U.S. interviewees equated race with cultural difference (alone or in addition to other forms of difference), compared to only 15 percent of the Italians (whether at universities or vocational schools). Maria, a psychology major at City University, emphasized foodways, dress, and language when she contended that race had to do with "everything from like how you eat, what you eat, to what you wear to like, I mean, the language, everything." And because so many of the American respondents also linked race to physical difference, they commonly defined race by combining references to culture and biology.

"Race" in the United States as "Ethnicity" in Italy

Bringing cultural practices, beliefs, or values so heavily into the picture when defining race, alongside references to physical traits, made American "race" a lot like Italian "ethnicity." In fact, we found that the cultural dimensions of race perceived by American students were indistinguishable from the forms of ethnicity described by their Italian peers. Food, dress, religion, ancestral customs, language, and ways of thinking all figured prominently in both. In addition, cultural practices in the United States were as closely associated with family as they were in Italy. As Pilot University biology major Wendy put it when defining race: "I think there's a little bit of your culture, your background, kind of those values that your parents teach you."

The twin concept of U.S. race/Italian ethnicity, which blended physical with cultural traits, was distinct from what Italians meant by "race," and very likely from what Americans meant by "ethnicity" as well. For our Italian interviewees, "race" overwhelmingly denoted a purely biological concept of descent-based difference (even if they took issue with it). And their tendency to equate race with ethnicity seemed to allow the physical differences they associated with race to permeate their understandings of ethnicity.

In contrast, the U.S. respondents referred to ethnicity much less often than Italians did when defining race, suggesting that the two terms were more conceptually distinct for them. Had Morning asked the American students to define the word "ethnicity," they might very well have reserved it for cultural traits alone, consistent with how the term has often been used in the United States over the last century.[23]

The American "culturalization" of race that we observed is probably due in part to the institutions to which the college interviewees were exposed. Most of them resided on a large university campus with considerable descent-based diversity, and as a result they encountered peers from different backgrounds on a daily basis in dormitories, classrooms, dining halls, clubs, and athletic facilities. In contrast, Italian undergraduates generally did not live on campuses, but rather commuted to them, and they were members of student bodies that were much more homogenous in their ancestry. The Milanese vocational students probably occupied a social space somewhere in the middle: like Americans, they took classes—and had a range of relationships—with "all the races" (as Virginia put it), but like their university-educated compatriots, they did not live in dormitories and so did not necessarily have the experience of sharing every aspect of daily life with peers from diverse backgrounds. As a result, the U.S. college students were probably exposed to a greater range of everyday experiences with people of varied descent-based backgrounds, and those experiences would have fueled their observations not just of phenotypic differences but also of unfamiliar behavioral practices. At the same time, the exposure of American students to the widespread U.S. institutional practice of classifying individuals by "race"—much more than by "ethnicity"—gave them a ready-made classification system to which they could peg their campus observations of physical and cultural differences. No such institutional equivalent obtained for our Italian interviewees.

Racial Culturalization as a Semantic Move

Americans' frequent rendering of race as culture was also a linguistic strategy, however, akin to Italians' discursive rejection of the word "race." When Morning asked her U.S. respondents to give examples of races, they largely named the broad Linnaean groups (white, black, Asian) that number in the millions if not billions worldwide and are enshrined in the federal government's official classifications; they rarely mentioned groups that are actually delineated by cultural practices like language, religion, or custom. Furthermore, references to culture were usually add-ons to other definitions of race (often combined with biology, as we saw) in both Italy and the United States, as if it were a supplemental or secondary feature rather than a primary or self-standing one. (This was also true of the references to geographic origins we heard in race definitions in both countries.) In other words, there were limits to the American students' depiction of race as depending on culture; as in the Italian case, they spoke about culture more as a semantic maneuver than as a deeply rooted conceptual framework.[24] And also like the Italian interviewees' discourse, the U.S. sample's culturalist approach served the purpose of defusing the anxieties or sensitivity associated with race by distancing the speaker—and her society—from it. Given the different historical and contemporary realities of the United States, however, our American respondents had to take a different tack than their Italian counterparts took.

Countering the long U.S. history of imposing racial labels on people deemed nonwhite in order to exclude them from full citizenship and its benefits, the American interviewees' culturalization of race made race seem voluntary, fluid, and inconsequential. If race was about freely chosen, optional styles of dress, food, or music, it was unlikely to entail discriminatory social penalties—or at least, it could always be refashioned to avoid them. The question of individual choice, and particularly of the interplay of internal (or self-) identification and external (observer) identification, was a recurring theme among the U.S. respondents (and virtually absent from the Italian interviews); more than one-third of them commented on it. When asked how she defined "race," State University anthropology major Rosanna responded, "I guess it's the group of people and the place that you—the group of people and the place and the practices of that place that you most identify with. You know. And the—just sort of the social practices and the interpersonal organizations and the attitudes and the religion and—that you most identify with." After equating race with "cultural background," Linda, a biology major at Ivy University, went on:

> I wouldn't know how to classify anybody. I mean, everybody would have to classify themselves, I suppose. You know. I couldn't—I couldn't do it. I can only do me.... Some people don't really feel that they have a race, and that's just fine too. Like, I don't consider myself having a religion and

that's—you know, so I think there should be like an open-ended kind of classification and not, like, restrictions.

Linda's comparison of race to religion was telling. First, it made racial categorization optional: just as a person might refuse a religious affiliation, they could—or should be able to—pass up a racial label as well. Second, the principle of religious freedom, foundational in the United States, also applied here: no one could dictate to someone else what their race was, just as no one could mandate another's religious belief. Instead, the individual in question was the ultimate authority; they alone could determine their racial membership. According to Rosanna, "It's very personal for each—like, what each person wants to decide how far and, you know, in how much detail they want to identify with any particular group to be that race."

Needless to say, the belief that individuals are free to simply choose the racial affiliation that suits them most is at best highly aspirational in the United States today. To be sure, the decennial census and many other forms now allow Americans to check off whatever box(es) they like. But recent cases of individuals being publicly excoriated, socially ostracized, or economically penalized for identifying with a race other than the one that others ascribe to them make it clear that lived racial identity is still far from voluntary.[25] What is important here, nonetheless, is the American students' embrace of a cultural vision of race that transforms it into a matter of individual agency and egalitarian freedom from tyranny—sacred tenets of the national patriotic imaginary. In this rosy version, everyone gets to decide their race for themselves, perform it in whatever way they prefer, and enjoy the right to do so without any outside interference.

For the optional cultural-race scenario to work, however, our American respondents had to recast the United States as a nation where race did not matter, much as Italian respondents had labored to displace race to other countries or time periods. More than one-third of the American students interviewed thought that either race had taken on a special meaning in their country—or that it had lost meaning there. As Marion, an anthropology major at Pilot University, put it:

I mean it's—I think it gets particularly complicated in an American context. A lot of times I tend to associate race with, like, a geographical or
nation-state ... and in America that doesn't really apply. And I would tend
to—I mean, I guess there—you know, there are color lines or birthplaces

or historical origin. But, I mean, I think more and more it's something that has to do with completely, you know, self-definition, what group you kind of identify with.

In Marion's words we encounter again the optimism that race depends on individual preference, particularly "in an American context." David, a student of meteorology at State University, also put forward the sunny vision that color "doesn't really matter" in the United States:

> I would have to say that race is probably defined, at least in our culture, as I guess mostly like as the color of your skin. I mean, that's how it is. I mean, obviously Americans, I guess, really, it doesn't really matter what the color of your skin is because, you know, it's American. It's a melting pot and it doesn't really make a difference. But unfortunately it exists still. So, but I—in my opinion, I guess that's what it is. It's the color of your skin. But it's really— that's all it should be. Like it shouldn't be anything more than that. That's it. And I think some people take it more than that. You know, they make it culturally I think. But as Americans, what makes our country so great is that it doesn't matter—it doesn't matter what color of skin you are. You're an American. So in my opinion I don't think race should be an issue ever. For anything, anymore, but unfortunately there are some people who think that—that think it should be. So I don't think—on the outside it's the color of your skin, but other than that, that should be it.

David's words clearly convey a tension between an idealized America where race does not matter and an actual one where "unfortunately there are some people" who think differently. In the "melting pot" image, however, he has a grandiose national narrative to fall back on, which—like Italians' faith in themselves as *brava gente*—aims to confirm that descent-based difference is no obstacle to full acceptance and inclusion in society.

Conclusion: The Conceptualization of Race and Society in Italy and the United States

Without a doubt, our Italian and U.S. interviewees' definitions of "race" upended any "new racism" claim that biological race is the sole province of Americans and cultural difference the exclusive domain of Europeans. Most of the Italian students linked race to biology, and it was instead the

American students who routinely associated it with cultural difference. Moreover, we found important similarities in the two samples' conceptualizations of race rather than sharp divergences. Both groups associated race with physical difference more than any other characteristics, and they often drew on its classic color-coded taxonomy. In addition, both gravitated to a model of difference that combined physical and cultural characteristics: what the Americans called "race" and the Italians preferred to call "ethnicity" (while frequently acknowledging it to be the equivalent of race).

Rather than a culture-versus-biology contrast, then, other facets of the two groups' conceptualizations of descent-based difference were sites of meaningful divergence. For one thing, our Italian respondents expressed much more hostility to hierarchical frameworks of diversity than Americans did. For another, the U.S. students attributed a greater fluidity and lesser consequence to culture than their Italian counterparts did. This greater flexibility was also apparent in the American interviewees' suggestion that racial identity was a matter of choice. Such a concept of race stands in stark contrast to the essentialist and primordial models we saw emphasized in the last chapter; in these models, one gained membership in a descent-based group either through birth or through early training. The U.S. respondents often gravitated to a third mechanism: the acquisition of group membership through deliberate action, such as engaging in particular cultural practices.

These divergences do not diminish, however, the most fundamental convergence of all between our Italian and U.S. interviewees: their shared inability—or unwillingness—to define race as a contemporary societal force. This was evident in the fact that both samples offered a social constructivist account of race only rarely. Circulating in its place in the two groups were varied "similars"—that is, definitions that borrowed some but not all elements of social constructivism. Tellingly, all of the concepts of race that the students were most likely to embrace—whether biological, cultural, or even antibiological—sidelined consideration of how it might structure the societies they lived in. On the one hand, Italians' antibiologism— simply asserting that physical race did not exist—left open the question of whether race existed socially as an enduring belief that shaped present-day outcomes. If anything, this stance presumed that it was better not to ask rather than invoke an evil ideology that had ostensibly been laid to rest. On the other hand, Americans' culturalism asserted that social race—one that was involuntary and exclusionary—no longer existed, at least not in their country. Race was simply a matter of personal choices that concerned no one else. Finally, it must be kept in mind that the majority of respondents in both countries were content to equate race with bodily characteristics. In all of these cases, there was virtually no opening for contemplating the social nature of race, let alone for addressing the inequalities that it continues to leave in its wake.

The preference that both Italian and American students showed for nonsociological understandings of race jibes with the work of scholars on both sides of the Atlantic. The hallmarks of Bonilla-Silva's "linguistics of color-blind racism," for example, appear in our respondents' shared projections of race to other countries and in their tendency to minimize its importance.[26] Curcio and Mellino describe the "discursive foreclosure" of race, while Skarpelis writes of its "enclosure" and "bracketing"; Giuliani sees in Italy a "tendentious dissimulation, in colloquial as well as scientific language, of much of the terminology [of late Fascism] without a real process of investigation or deconstruction."[27] Petrovich Njegosh likens Italy to the rest of Europe in its "difficulty to categorize race and thus to use it as an analytical category to deconstruct discourse on racism." She continues:

> Faced with the paradoxical or "double" status of race—according to which race exists or doesn't exist, or in Marxian terms, is a "true appearance" . . .— in both the specialist debate and in popular discourse, old binary grids based on the opposition between true/false, real/inexistent, ignorance-lies/truth, past/present seem to predominate.[28]

The same authors insist, however, that this depiction of race as nonexistent or unimportant masks what is actually a deep underlying engagement with it. Picker contends that "race essentially functions by obfuscating and dissimulating itself, in the sense that its chief *raison d'être* has become the shaping of forms of domination that would not be identified as 'racial' or 'racist.'"[29]

Among our Italian and U.S. subjects, discounting the enduring social realities of race was an important way of grappling with the ethical questions that it raises. Describing this approach as "racelessness," Picker illuminates its connection to notions of "goodness" and "sinfulness":

> Racelessness, in short, can be viewed as the politics of inherited reflexes of silence and oblivion that, moving from their irreflexive stance, suppresses insurgent race-aware politics. As such, racelessness is constantly in the

making, a continuous confirmation of its own stance, identity, belonging, roots, whiteness: a doxa. The internalization of goodness coincides with the externalization of sinfulness, blaming the racially deemed for their own social conditions as they themselves represent a crack in the system of purity: ultimately, squaring the circle of bright-looking white social order.[30]

Picker's words highlight the moral boundary work at stake that emerged so powerfully in our interviews. Racelessness is not just a sociopolitical worldview; it is also an identity, a self-image, and one that is infused with faith in one's own goodness. Shoring up their "raceless" self-representation required special efforts when respondents were faced with the discomfort of explicitly engaging with the term "race": that is, when we asked them to define it, to list racial groups, or to react to the affirmation that human biological races exist. Our respondents on both sides of the Atlantic most commonly met this challenge by switching race talk onto the rails of biology, culture, or a performative but limited antibiologism.

Moreover, their structural contexts made it especially feasible and appealing for both Americans and Italians to simply weld culture to biology when reflecting on descent-based difference. The "biologization" of ethnicity in Italy worked because there was little in the way of an immigrant second generation in Italy to challenge the close association of physical and cultural otherness. Conversely, the "culturalization" of race in the United States was plausible despite that nation's long experience with the descendants of immigrants because residential and social segregation has preserved the appearance and reality of distinct subcultures associated with phenotype. Despite the substantial differences between their societies, both our European and U.S. interviewees demonstrated just how hard it is to break with the canonical eighteenth-century concept of race that married physical traits to behaviors.

Our respondents also illustrate how difficult it is to move beyond the classic race notion without a clear and comprehensive education on its fundamentally social nature. The young people we spoke with on both sides of the Atlantic had clearly absorbed the message that race—or at least racism—was "wrong." But they were much less sure about why and how. As our transcriber Elena Skall lamented of the Italian interviewees at the start of this chapter, schools were "not even able to teach them to distinguish form from substance, the word from its contents. To not be racist, all you have to do is never say the word 'race.'" In both countries, however, our finding that young people possessed only limited discursive and conceptual tool kits for reasoning about race suggested that they had been exposed to only sporadic, inconsistent, or superficial pedagogy regarding descent-based difference in their societies, if any. What Morning described in the United States—namely, varied and at times contradictory messages about the nature of race coming from different quarters, whether schools, families, doctors, scientists, or the census, just to name a few—has parallels in Western Europe. Young Italians have to negotiate diverse signals from professors, the Catholic Church, the media, and politicians, for example, about what group labels and terms like *razza* or *etnia* mean and how they should (or should not) be used.

If their education, formal or informal, largely excludes a rigorous and sustained examination of race as a long-standing societal force in the West, young Italians and Americans are left to their own devices to cobble together explanations for much of what they can observe in the social world around them. They must reckon with present-day disparities in social status and material well-being, everyday patterns of social interaction, and the subtle, often unspoken discursive codes embedded within these patterns by weaving together media accounts and popular wisdom on disadvantaged groups' biological predispositions or cultural predilections. Educators on the whole seem largely to have renounced the project of bringing into view overarching social structures and their attendant power relations.

CHAPTER 4

Difference in Play

Sport and Descent

> In my view, it's a purely physical and scientific question, in the sense that Africans'
> physical structure permits [them] to develop a certain type of musculature, or anyway
> a certain stamina that the other races or other ethnicities, if you like, aren't able to
> develop. So if it's possible in track for the musculature of Africans or anyway ... yes,
> of Africans let's say ... to allow [them] to reach very high levels, it's not possible in
> individuals belonging to other races.
>
> —CHRISTIAN, anthropology major, Bologna

BELIEFS ABOUT descent-based difference do not reside solely in our abstract definitions of terms like "ethnicity," judgments of others, or imagined national boundaries; they also inform our interpretations of events and outcomes in the world around us. As Richard Apostle and his colleagues note in *The Anatomy of Racial Attitudes*, how we *explain* social differences is closely bound up with our perceptions and evaluations of them.[1] In this chapter, we focus on the ideas about descent-based difference that respondents in Italy and the United States formulated when asked to account for diverse group outcomes in one area of "real life": the world of sports.

Athletics offer a rich site for reflection on difference for several reasons. First, in both countries, sports occupy an important niche in popular culture, whether through the viewing of (or attendance at) professional matches or participation in amateur or simply recreational games. The playing field therefore has at least some familiarity for most people, regardless of whether they regularly watch or engage in athletic activity. Second, stadiums have repeatedly been home to debates about national membership, from the cries of *Non esistono negri italiani* (Italian n*gg*rs don't exist) hurled at African-descent soccer players in Italy to the furor over African American athletes "taking a knee" during the U.S. national anthem in support of the Black Lives Matter movement.[2] So everyday people are likely to have been exposed to some degree to ideas about the relationship between ancestry and difference in the context of athletics. Third, sports have simultaneously been a fertile site for popular speculation about race differentials and their relationship to multiple factors, including bodily traits, cultural values, and structural opportunities.[3] Finally, the myriad levels at which competition is joined—from international meets like the FIFA World Cups to neighborhood pickup games—offer varied types of descent-based groups to explore. In short, sports provide a spacious arena for investigating concepts of difference that are grounded in diverse rationales—cultural, national, biological, geographic—and that draw on varied groupings, from continental ones like Asians to national populations like Brazilians and subnational communities like African Americans. In addition, the association of athletics with play and leisure may offer the methodological advantage of reducing some of the sensitivity that is often attributed to the topic of difference.

Christian, the anthropology major at the University of Bologna whose commentary we feature at the start of this chapter, offered an illuminating and representative example of the ways in which we heard many young Italians—and Americans—talk about sport and descent. First and foremost, in a display of what Morning has called "black biological exceptionalism," he was quite confident that Africans are categorically distinct from all others; no non-African athlete could ever achieve what blacks can.[4] Also typical was Christian's attribution of both visible traits (musculature) and invisible characteristics (stamina) to Africans; indeed, muscles inevitably figured in the respondents' descriptions of black bodies. Whether this distinction was racial or ethnic was unimportant to Christian; he used the terms as synonyms, where ethnicity could replace race "if you like." His assertion that this was "a purely physical and scientific question," moreover, aimed to stave off any ethical qualms about what followed, invoking a disinterested, impartial approach that was free of bias in taking the measure of the natural world. Finally, Christian felt comfortable not just with arguing that Africans are biologically unique in the athletic domain, but also with introducing the word "race" here—even though he had termed it "vulgar" when asked to define it earlier in the interview. In fact, at that moment he had allowed, "Maybe it's a term [that is] a bit derogatory, let's say; it can also be a bit derogatory if not used in the right context." Christian's remarks thus leave us with the fascinating question of why the sporting realm would be "the right context" for the language of "race."

Our Italian interview conversations about sport and descent were anchored in the questions that Morning posed to college students in the United States about National Football League (NFL) players. After indicating that she would ask about "the overrepresentation, or underrepresentation, of certain racial groups in certain sports, compared to their share of the total population of the country," Morning continued:

> To give you an example from football: in the NFL, blacks make up 67 percent of the players and white athletes are in the minority. But in the total population of the United States as a whole, whites make up the majority and blacks count for only 12 percent of the population.[5] In your opinion, what could be some plausible explanations for why the racial composition of the National Football League is so different from the racial makeup of the country as a whole?

After hearing respondents' range of potential explanations, Morning asked them to identify which one they thought "most likely" and to explain why. This line of questioning yielded what was without a doubt some of the most vivid commentary on race that Morning garnered from her interviewees. And those results in turn persuaded us to include a comparable question when collecting data in Italy.

For our Italian sample, however, we sought an athletic domain that would be more familiar than U.S. football, and one that incorporated greater descent-based diversity than Italian professional soccer, the nation's premier sport. Accordingly, we developed a question about the Olympics, which offer a highly varied setting to reflect on, whether in terms of the myriad descent-based groups represented or the wide range of sports included. Specifically, we asked:

> In world or Olympic competition, certain sports are dominated by particular population groups. For example, athletes of African origin ("blacks") have dominated speed events in track for many years. Yet they are rarely found in other sports like swimming. In your opinion, what are possible explanations?

This approach differed from the one taken in the United States in a couple of ways. First, we chose to split in two what was originally a single question about whites and blacks in the NFL. If Italian respondents gave a physical explanation for the Olympics question about African-descent athletes, we followed up with another, separate question about European-descent competitors: "How would you explain, then, the predominance of athletes of European origin ('whites') in sports like swimming?" In that way we hoped to avoid the asymmetry Morning had encountered in the United States, where interviewees focused overwhelmingly on blacks' ostensible characteristics and paid relatively little attention to whites' supposed traits. Second, in Italy we also systematically asked the students who suggested biological causes for sports differentials to explain where such physical differences came from, or how they came about. This decision was also prompted by Morning's findings: her U.S. interviewees' offhand accounting for sports differentials had tapped a rich vein of thought about human evolutionary history and its implications for the present. Finally, in Italy we did not refer to "race" or "racial groups," unlike in the United States, because we did not want to impose that particular terminology, although we did mention "blacks" and "whites," as Morning had done in her American interviews.

Despite the differences in question wording, the results of our Italian interviews were virtually identical to those obtained in the United States when it came to sports. When reflecting on African-descent athletes' over-representation in certain athletic fields, respondents in both countries focused overwhelmingly on the ostensible properties of black bodies. Conversely, they had real difficulty fathoming why or how biology might play a role in European-descent overrepresentation in other sports. Italians and Americans also proved to be quite similar in how colorfully and creatively they speculated on human evolutionary histories that would have led to present-day asymmetries in continental sports representation. Many of the American and Italian beliefs flew in the face of what biologists have known for decades about the extensive genetic and phenotypic variation within the groupings popularly known as races, as well as the overwhelming genetic overlap between them.[6] Their imagining of human physical adaptation to the environment also defied some basic tenets of evolutionary theory—for example, with respect to the time scale on which it operates and the hereditary mechanisms involved. What the students' remarks *were* faithful to, however, was a centuries-old Western ideology of race, one that attributes intelligence to whites and reserves brute strength for blacks.

We begin this chapter by detailing the dominant discourse of African-descent physical superiority that emerged in both American and Italian interviewees' ruminations on sports. Then we turn to what is likely a less familiar domain: the portrayal of European- and Asian-descent athletes, in which cultural and structural reasoning took precedence over the biological. We draw attention throughout, moreover, to the renditions of human evolutionary history that respondents shared as a way to make sense of the contemporary representation of varied descent-based groups in diverse sports. The enthusiastic sports talk we encountered frequently contradicted, however, the respondents' previous comments on race and its links to biology. Accordingly, our last empirical section aims to explain why certain notions of human difference are articulated in response to certain questions, focusing in particular on the play of rhetoric versus conceptualization. We conclude the chapter with our observations on the deep similarities between our Italian and U.S. interviewees in both regards. Without a doubt, their thinking about athletes upends any presumption that a wide gulf exists between European and American notions of descent-based difference.

Explanations for African-Descent Representation in Sport: The Black Body and the Colonial Archive

More than in any other area of discourse that we can compare between our Italian and American samples, the ideas we heard about sports on either side of the Atlantic were virtually indistinguishable from each other. To put it bluntly, there was practically no daylight between American and Italian interviewees' accounts for black athletes' overrepresentation in some fields and white athletes' overrepresentation in others. In both countries, students converged heavily on the idea that a high share of African-descent athletes in a sport could be chalked up to their unique physical properties. In fact, our Italian respondents were even more likely than those in the United States to raise that argument: over 80 percent did so, compared to 74 percent of the Americans.[7] And in both samples, structural or socioeconomic circumstances were the second-most frequent explanations offered, followed by cultural accounts. Finally, Americans were no less creative and animated than Italians when it came to imagining how human evolutionary history shaped today's athletics—and no more familiar with the fundamentals of evolutionary theory.

Biological Accounts Reign Supreme

The U.S. and Italian interviewees' shared convictions about the special athletic properties of black—and usually male—bodies were evident in several ways. Without a moment's hesitation, they were able to launch into detailed descriptions of African-descent physiognomy that would favor sports success. They spoke with considerable certainty. And they also had vivid back stories at the ready; in these accounts, they believed, the physical evolution of African ancestors helped explain today's athletic outcomes.

In both countries, muscle was central to the interviewees' heavily biological reasoning about African-descent athletes; it was the premier locus of physical difference.

Yeah, no, I knew that the African race has a muscular density and many more tendons, as a result they have a much more explosive force. On the other hand, they have much more resistant and heavy bones, so they don't swim well. So there's this difference due to purely physical characteristics, of a genetic kind. *(Samuele, chemistry major, University of Bologna)*

For starters, like I was saying before, it's clear that there are differences between ethnicities at the physical level, so clearly I can think of a person of African origin who has longer legs, maybe greater musculature, greater physical resistance, so they can somehow run faster. *(Tiziana, psychology major, University of Bologna)*

I'm going to sort of concede to some of the biological data, because there are certain studies, that I'm not exactly sure on their validity or not, but they show something like the density of muscle and there are certain things that would affect performance in sports like density of muscle. I don't know if you know anything about slow twitch versus fast twitch or anything like that. For example, there are people that would be better marathon runners than power lifters just because of the type of muscle they have, and I think certain genetic groups or races probably have different proportions of those kinds of muscles in the populations. *(James, history major, City University)*

That genetically they're absolutely superior, but they're also superior in body building. Anyway they have different melanin, they have different DNA, they're more powerful, more developed [*ipertrofici*], faster. Like, physically they're superior to—as Hitler used to say—the Aryan race. In fact, in Berlin in '36 he lost the Olympics, Hitler did. (*Ludovico, audiovisual technology student, Milan*)

Other characteristics like height, stamina, or DNA came up, but much less consistently than musculature.[8] Although there were occasional minor variations that were voiced in one country and not the other—for example, references to pelvises in Italy, stories of extra leg muscles or different cardiovascular systems in the United States—the students' descriptions of black bodies were virtually interchangeable regardless of nationality.

These quotations illustrate another recurring tendency that was common to both Italian and American interviewees' explanations for the track-and-field prominence of African-descent athletes: the certainty and even expansiveness with which they warmed to the topic. Phrases like Samuele's "I knew that" and Tiziana's "it's clear that"—like Ludovico's "they're absolutely superior"—left little room for doubt. James, moreover, presented "the biological data" as so compelling that even though he was not sure of their validity, the facts about "genetic groups or races" warranted his concession. Overall, respondents in both the United States and especially Italy appeared to be much more comfortable on the terrain of sport than when they had discussed race, color, or physical difference earlier in the interview, and they often plowed ahead with little self-consciousness while discussing sport.

The interviewees' discussion of sports also stood out for its use of humor, which may have reflected a certain comfort level. It might also have been a strategy for ensuring such ease, but it is striking that humor was used less often in other circumstances; in other words, joking seemed a feasible or appropriate social tool when it came to sports but not in other conversations about descent-based difference. A recurring example was the "joke . . . they always told me," said Romina, a student of tourism in Milan, about Africans becoming fast runners to escape from lions. "So it's something a little funny," she explained, "and it makes me smile, but on the other hand it's also true, because the ones I've seen in the Olympics, they're lightning, absolutely no one catches them."[9]

Such ostensibly humorous accounts contained a subtle mix of both embrace and rejection.[10] On the one hand, portraying these accounts as jokes is a distancing move, as if to say, "I don't really believe this." But on the other hand, respondents often simultaneously recoup and reassert the content of the account, as Romina did: the "funny" tale that makes her smile is "also true." The same ambivalence colored the version told by Riccardo, a graphic design student in Milan: after airing the possibility that Usain Bolt, a Jamaican whom Riccardo mistook for Ghanaian, had to run from lions, he laughed and conceded, "Well, it doesn't make sense." And after his interviewer, Maneri, replied, "I don't know," Riccardo answered, "Me neither, it's stupid [*una stupidaggine*]." In short, Riccardo reversed himself, backtracking from his opening statement. Whether "funny" or "stupid," however, several respondents could not resist sharing this "joke," suggesting that it was quite compelling to them even if they had to rhetorically mop up afterwards. The genre of the joke provided them with the necessary deniability.[11]

The power of such "jokes" becomes even more apparent when we realize how widely known such imagery of Africans was for our respondents on both sides of the Atlantic, and how sincerely they believed in its explanatory power. It was precisely this colonial-era imaginary of Africans as the primitive inhabitants of a dangerous and harsh natural environment, with few trappings of human civilization, that undergirded the students' thinking about black overrepresentation in certain sports. For when we asked them why or how African-descent athletes had acquired their ostensible physical superiority, the answer was invariably that Africans past and present had had to adapt biologically to the natural and structural hardships of their environments.

It was not always clear whether the adaptation that Italian and American students had in mind had occurred over a multitude of generations (as evolutionary theory would contend) or was simply a process of individuals building their physical capacity today. When asked what had caused the continental biological differences that he had mentioned in connection with sports, Alessio, a psychology major in Milan, confidently named "evolution due to the environment in which we live." But his present-tense account left unclear whether he had in mind the historical and generational mechanism of selective adaptation or a contemporary story of individual capacity-building instead. "Maybe in Africa, for example," he continued, "seeing as African athletes are ... always first in track competitions, there's the need to move quickly from one place to another and so.... Or given that you never see them in swimming, there's no need to swim." Similarly, although Massimo, a business student in Milan, invoked evolution (with some help from his interviewer, Daniela), his present-tense description of Africa suggested instead the individualist, speed-training perspective:

MASSIMO: Kenyans, for example, have immense spaces to run in; the more indigenous populations matter here, because in Africa they have immense spaces to run in and the indigenous populations run to hunt—something that we don't do—or maybe they have a village really far away from a well, so instead of walking there, which would take two days, they run. So the bodily change, like Darwin said about ... I don't remember the term now ...

DANIELA: Evolution.

MASSIMO: So the body evolves as a function of necessity.

In other words, Massimo's comment seems to focus on the individual body that evolves—that is modified by the practice of running—in a person's lifetime rather than on change in a population over generations. This conceptual fuzziness in terms of what evolutionary theory predicts, and the flattening of the time scale on which it operates, may be exacerbated when Westerners think about Africans because the continent is so often portrayed as timeless and ahistorical.[12] Our interviewees made little distinction between the circumstances they ascribed to modern-day African people and those of their ancestors; lions, "immense spaces," and distant wells could be a feature of life today or millennia ago. As the anthropologist Eric Wolf put it, they were perceived as "people without history."[13]

The one historical experience that all interviewees but especially the Americans could connect to African peoples was transatlantic slavery, and it made its way into their accounts of sports representation today. While speculation about how enslavement had affected the physical constitution of African-origin people in the Americas materialized in a couple of Italian interviews, it did not have nearly the purchase there that it had in the United States. As Morning noted, this narrative took two forms. One had to do with the perils of the Middle Passage, which Serena, a chemistry major in Bologna, described succinctly:

Since initially black slaves were brought to America, only the strongest came to survive, and so, exactly because of natural selection, the blacks who live in America now are those who come from the most adapted, strongest, most resistant ones who had initially been transported to America.

The other hypothesis about the evolution of African bodies in the Americas imagined the purposive breeding of slaves. Again, although this idea was much more frequently voiced in the U.S. sample, it was an Italian student, the anthropology major Claudio, who summed it up neatly: "Maybe a strong black guy was forcibly mated with a strong woman, and so a strong child would be born." Not only are these Italian accounts indistinguishable from their American counterparts, but they share the semantic feature of using the impersonal voice to describe the atrocities of slavery. Slaves are "brought to America" and "forcibly mated," but the perpetrators of this violence go unnamed. Nor do mass rapes by white slaveowners ever figure into speculation about the impact of slavery on the African American gene pool. Instead, black people and bodies alone remain at the center of the tragic story. In that way, the transatlantic slave trade comes to be the only historical event that marks the otherwise timeless, ahistorical horizon of African people's existence as imagined by both young Americans and young Italians.

The popular biological accounting for the current preeminence of African-descent competitors in particular sports is deeply flawed. First and foremost, the category "black"—like "whites" or "Asians"—contains hundreds of millions of people who are spread across wildly varied environments and who embody a wide range of physiological and genetic features.[14] There is simply no uniform black physical essence or trait to associate with athletic prowess. Second, as the biologist Adam Rutherford details, a closer look at sports—and genetics—also pokes holes in this folk theory.[15] Although African-descent runners from North America and the Caribbean have come to dominate international sprinting competition, the West African populations from which they descend are barely represented in such events. In fact, athletes from sub-Saharan Africa have been about as successful as white ones in short-distance running, according to Rutherford. He also points out that if blacks had a special capacity for the explosive speed needed in track, we would expect them to be overrepresented in other sports like squash, cycling, and tennis—or for that matter, in U.S. Major League Baseball.

The conjecture that slavery selected U.S. and West Indian blacks for athletic ability is similarly problematic. For one thing, it ignores the fact that population gene pools evolve over much longer time frames than a couple of centuries. "Indeed," Rutherford reports, "one 2014 study of the

DNA of 29,141 living African Americans showed categorically no signs of selection across the whole genome for *any* trait, in the time since their ancestors were taken from their African homelands."[16] The conventional wisdom also overlooks the true nature of slaveowners' "breeding" efforts. Plantation owners and overseers hardly sought to cultivate running speed in their enslaved workforces. Instead, what they accomplished was the large-scale injection of their own DNA into African-descent populations throughout the Americas. The biological accounts for contemporary sports representation to which young people are exposed, then, cobble together superficial observations that fail—or refuse—to examine what we know about human history and physical variety.

Structural Accounts and Stereotypes

After the predominant biological view, interviewees gave socioeconomic or material explanations for African-origin athletes' representation at the top echelons of track and field. Here U.S. approaches diverged somewhat from Italian ones. As the quotation from Massimo above hints, our Italian respondents largely attributed structural differences between Africans and other competitors to material conditions that favored blacks' development of the needed physical skills. For that reason, Italian reflections commonly cited hard labor, which built muscle or endurance; distant wells and schools, which required physical exertion to reach; or the absence of facilities that allowed for necessary training:

> I've always thought that African kids, also to go to school, have to cover many kilometers. At least I've always been told something like that; also from various documentaries I saw that. So I think they have a much more developed physical stamina than ours, so they also have the possibility of running much more through open fields, not on tracks. *(Eleonora, history major, Bologna)*

> Maybe, I don't know, being used to the savannah, they run and there's no water, so they don't do it, they just don't have a way to practice swimming, but rather the proximity of ferocious animals maybe, I'm talking . . . I have in mind the savannah with the lions, these things, like I've mixed these things up a bit, but maybe also the nearness of environmental danger. *(Emiliano, psychology major, Bologna)*

So physical capacity could be due to conditions ... to heavier labor, to a harder life. Like how I heard talk that for example, the pelvis of black women is more developed because they give birth to more children on average. *(Daniele, history major, Milan)*

In short, for young Italians imagining the trajectories of African-descent athletes—whom they invariably thought of as foreigners, despite a history of blacks on Italy's own premier teams—socioeconomic inequalities might have played a role only insofar as they materialized in bodily characteristics. What was largely missing was the recognition of institutional structures—like state-funded programs and elite training academies—that channel African-descent athletes into track and field. "In Kenya and Ethiopia," which are both noted for long-distance champions, "running is an industry," Rutherford notes.[17]

In contrast, the U.S. interviewees, who were asked to compare white and black football players in their own country, thought about structural differences in the opportunities that the two groups had to embark on sports (and other) careers. First, the (mostly white) American respondents often thought about the appeal of a sports career for their black compatriots, reckoning that it offered an enticing ladder of social mobility for people they saw as mired in poverty and social dysfunction. As a student at State University related:

I read a lot of articles in *Sports Illustrated* about [black] athletes, and they always grew up in, like, poor settings, so they found sports is their only outlet to, like, get away from the drugs and the violence and whatever was associated with their lives. That was the only thing they could do, so they got really good at it. And then they would be recruited by colleges and then they would ... you know, they got really good and then they eventually become the pros. Whereas, whites typically don't grow up in those kind of settings, where they don't need sports as an outlet to rescue them from, you know, dangers and stuff like that, from the streets.

This description also illustrates a related observation that was common among our U.S. interviewees: that there are institutional mechanisms in place for recruiting African American athletes into the professional leagues. In fact, one out of five believed that blacks benefited from recruiters' bias in their favor. Americans were more likely than Italians to attribute a particular psychology or temperament to blacks, seeing them as more "intimidating" or "aggressive" than white players—and thus more attractive to recruiters. In contrast, institutional structures that have discouraged black participation in certain sports—such as the exclusion of African Americans from swimming pools—were much less apparent to the interviewees.

Differences between U.S. and Italian reasoning about social structure are no doubt due in part to differences in how we posed our questions: the question about the National Football League that Morning put to her U.S. respondents had a domestic focus, as opposed to the international focus of the question about the Olympics that we gave to those in Italy. Compatriot athletes pointed to the role of one's own society—and thus of social factors generally—in shaping sports outcomes, a mechanism that might have been harder to envision when global competition was in play. Interviewees may have been more familiar with the trajectories of their conational sports figures—thanks to domestic media coverage by outlets like *Sports Illustrated* and *La Gazzetta dello Sport*—than those of star athletes from abroad. And given the American penchant for "bootstrap" stories of social mobility, it is not surprising that rags-to-riches accounts would be especially familiar to and resonant for U.S. respondents. Added to this is the conviction among many Americans that "reverse discrimination" favoring blacks is a major force in contemporary life. Finally, another particularly American overlay here is the depiction of blacks as "aggressive" and frightening, echoing the ongoing criminalization of African Americans; no one ever suggested that the belligerence of white hockey players was scary.[18]

What the U.S. and Italian structural accounts of African-descent sports overrepresentation have in common, however, is a deep reliance on well-worn stereotypes about black living conditions, which they invariably portrayed negatively. Whether speaking of "the drugs and the violence" of African American life or the sparse wells of rural Africa, students depended on the white supremacist archive of colonialism and slavery, and its afterlife. They seemed to know little of contemporary life for the second-largest continental population in the world (after Asia), where more than 40 percent are city-dwellers.[19] Nor did they appear to be aware, for example, that drug use is as prevalent, if not more so, among white Americans as among their black compatriots.[20] In the absence of much factual knowledge about the socioeconomic conditions that African-descent people face around the globe, let alone a firm grip on the workings of human evolution, both

Italian and American students pieced together accounts for contemporary black overrepresentation in certain sports from the stories, stereotypes, and assumptions to which they had been amply exposed.

Blending biological with structural factors at times in a search for a superficially plausible back story, our interviewees were more likely to create a tenuous web of free association than a masterpiece of reasoned, well-informed logic (as confidently recounted as it might be). Consider this rumination by Flavio in Naples: "It would come to me a bit like how the Chinese, who have almond-shaped eyes, were set to gathering rice or whatever on the reservations, always in the sun, so their ... their traits were ... so maybe a certain activity [Africans] did daily, right for developing the musculature suited for track and all that."[21] Flavio's comment highlights that these accounts were ultimately little more than just-so stories cobbled together from disparate elements that were salient to their authors. It is no surprise that when thinking about the factors behind Asian physical characteristics, Flavio would immediately mention "almond-shaped eyes": this facial trait was a ubiquitous feature of the Italian students' commentary on Asians, even though it had no obvious link to sports outcomes. Nor is it surprising that he reached for another kind of observation common to the interviewees in making a comment about food, particularly a food like rice, which is not as central to the Italian diet as pasta. Although his explanation might raise evolutionary biologists' eyebrows (rice cultivation led to the epicanthic eye fold?), the point here is that Flavio tried to weave together a plausible story about human evolution using signature objects that he—like many of his peers—associated with Asian people. He took what he had at hand, conceptually speaking.

Cultural Accounts Unimagined

As with definitions of the word "race," culture surfaced in different ways in American and Italian respondents' explanations for African-descent overrepresentation in track and football. Here again, moreover, it was the Americans who surprisingly embraced cultural accounts much more than the Italians, who had favored them so heavily when it came to discussing Italianness—and who, as Europeans, would be predicted to be the culturalists in the study. Yet, in both countries, "culture" turned out to be a somewhat hollow explanation for black sports representation.

The Italian interviewees seemed to have difficulty imagining how culture might shape African dominance in a sport. When they did invoke it, it was in very vague terms, with nothing like the granularity and zest they brought to dissecting biological arguments about black sport. Tommaso, a psychology major in Naples, spoke, for example, of "a certain tradition" of track competition in Jamaica, noting that "the inhabitants of that area will tend to be directed toward a certain sport"—but he was unusual in naming a specific area or even a particular sporting "tradition." More typical was Veronica's broad guess that "maybe black people don't have swimming in their culture," or Rosanna's general reference to "different customs" among Africans:

> But they have many talents, then exactly having anyway different customs, different tendencies, maybe they've concentrated on this in their country, and so it turns out well for them. Also with dance, they're much better compared to Italians. It's maybe also a question of passion. Most of the group is attached to something, and so practicing and practicing it, they're born with these passions through and through.

Rosanna's reflection is telling because, although she mentioned "custom," her comment was more of a psychological portrait of "passions" or temperament that veered toward an essentialist picture of Africans being "born with" certain "talents" and "tendencies." It was as if the Italian students had little in their collective imagination that associated blackness with any form of human culture—perhaps not surprising in the wake of Italy's imperialism in East Africa.

Conversely, their American counterparts did have a notion of "black culture," which is also not surprising given the long history of an African-descent presence in the United States. Yet the way in which they applied this imagined "black culture" to explain sports outcomes was unmistakably similar to the Italian temperamental version, unmoored from any specific practices. It turned out that to the largely white American interviewees, black culture did not signify an attachment to or valorization of a particular sport, or even sports in general. Instead, it stood in for a kind of mind-body dualism, in which black appreciation of physical activity (athletics, dancing) was contrasted with whites' ostensible appreciation of intellectual pursuits. As Susan, an anthropology major at City University, said of "African culture and African-American culture" (eliding them), "they might just be more in tune in with their bodies and know how to use them better." Joshua, a biology major at Pilot University, speculated that

> there's more of a stress on, you know, blacks, I guess more as a culture, then, to perform well athletically as a means of bettering themselves, versus whites being, you know—there's a big emphasis on education and studying. Staying in the library as you're growing up and reading books. Not as much on being outside and running around.

Joshua summed up this contrast as a matter of blacks' valuing "body knowledge" versus whites' prizing "book knowledge."

In both Italy and the United States, then, the association between black athleticism and biology remained ironclad, even when culture or socioeconomic status were brought into the equation. A plentiful array of long-standing stereotypes were available to cement this connection. For our Italian interviewees, socioeconomic inequality was relevant only insofar as it reinforced or inhibited blacks' physical abilities, and culture was a way of talking about inborn temperament. For their U.S. peers, structural arguments relied on stereotypes of black athletes needing to "better themselves" (to paraphrase Joshua), and their cultural arguments sketched out a mystical connection between African Americans and their bodies that also posited an impressive affinity for scholarly pursuits among European Americans. Now, it might seem only natural to explain a particular group's overrepresentation in a given sport by bringing up biological traits and even standard tropes about racialized bodies. The American and Italian students' comments on Asian and especially European athletes showed, however, that sports talk takes a very different turn in the absence of such a well-stocked repertory of stereotypes.

Explanations for European- and Asian-Descent Representation in Sport: Good and Bad Cultures

When we asked Italian and U.S. interviewees to explain why European-descent athletes dominated certain sports, like swimming and ice hockey, it was as if we had flipped a switch that drove the respondents in the opposite direction from where they had been heading when thinking about African-descent athletes. Suddenly, physiognomy had nothing to do with sports representation anymore, and the cultural and structural accounts that had been secondary and superficial with respect to blacks took on primary importance for whites. Although we did not ask the students as consistently to comment on Asian-descent athletes, their ideas on this topic proved highly valuable for understanding how whites were constituted as the implicit and superior reference group in the interviewees' concepts of difference.[22]

White and Yellow Sporting Bodies? Europeans, Asians, and Africans along a Scale of Biologization

Italian as well as U.S. students remained so tightly focused on black bodies that even *white* underrepresentation or overrepresentation in a sport was regularly accounted for through the lens of African physiognomy. Indeed, in both places we heard more than one respondent wager that blacks would dominate every sport if they had equal opportunity to train in them. In this way, white athletic outcomes almost never came to be explained by reference to their bodily characteristics. In between these two extremes of African biologization and its European opposite, Asians occupied a middle ground: respondents did not hesitate to refer to this group's ostensible anatomical characteristics, but they were less likely to see these as consequential compared to their interpretations of black athletes. This held true in the United States as well, although we draw here from our more abundant examples from Italy. The ultimate effect in both places was still more of the black biological exceptionalism that Morning first described among the American respondents.[23]

THE MARKED ASIAN BODY

In Italy, Asians stood out to our interviewees for a concise set of somatic traits that seemed particularly salient. "When we think, like, about China," said Diana, a student of audiovisual technology in Milan, "you always imagine these little people [*piccolini*], similar, with yellowish skin, not quite white but not dark either, [and] eyes: big, bright, almond-shaped." Respondents occasionally linked their presumed body type to sports outcomes—like excellence in diving, "because they're lighter, they're miniscule," as Pietro, a student of audiovisual technology in Milan, put it. More commonly, however, the athletic potential of Asian bodies was described when they were contrasted with black bodies. "The Chinese is smaller in stature ... while the African is generally more built [*piazzato*], with musculature maybe more adapted to physical activity," according to Massimiliano, a business student in Milan; Sara, a history major in Milan, contrasted willowy Ethiopians with "the Asian girls who are very minute, and are very talented for gymnastic sports of agility." Oliviero, a student of graphic design in Milan, put it this way:

> Anyway you see that black people, like from central Africa, are taller, more imposing. I think they have physical characteristics that anyway lead them to obtain certain results in certain disciplines. Like, it's difficult to see ... the Chinese, no? The Chinese are champions in gymnastic floor exercises, in rings, because anyway they have characteristics that lead them to be like that. Maybe central Africans have maybe firmer, harder, more resistant, more dynamic ligaments in their legs for running.[24]

Striking here is the disparity in the degree of detail accorded the African versus the Asian body. Oliviero ruminated on black people's height, size, and four aspects of their legs' physiognomy, but does not specify any corresponding trait for Chinese gymnasts; they simply "have characteristics" that favor their success. The gap between his descriptions of the two groups speaks to the abundance of a Western cultural repertory of stereotypes regarding African physicality and its athletic consequences, alongside the relative absence of a similar archive for Asians, whether in Italy or the United States.

It comes as little surprise, then, that our interviewees often discarded biology outright as a factor in explaining Asian athletic outcomes. What was undeniable for African-descent competitors seemed irrelevant for their Asian-origin counterparts. Simona, an anthropology student in Milan who reported having heard that "the skeleton of black people is heavier, and so they couldn't swim as fast as, I don't know, a white person, let's say," discarded such biological explanations when reflecting on the successes of Chinese athletes at the Beijing Olympics. "So I don't think that it's because Chinese as people with almond-shaped eyes have a physique that is predisposed for certain sports," she declared; instead, she was persuaded that "Chinese children were trained twelve hours a day, 365 days a year." Similarly, Matteo, a student of audiovisual technology in Milan, started off responding to our question about black Olympians in track and field by guessing, "Maybe it's due to their physical configuration, maybe." But when we asked if he could think of any other potential explanations, he turned to the Chinese for a nonbiological mechanism. "[In] platform diving it seems to me that there are Chinese who are very strong, so I think that a person training can reach high objectives." Here Asian athletes were intrinsic proof of the fruits of hard work rather than of innate corporeal abilities.

THE INVISIBLE EUROPEAN BODY

If the link between sports success and the body was tenuous in our interviewees' discussions of Asian athletes, it was virtually nonexistent when they were asked to account for the dominance of white athletes in fields like swimming. Simply put, it was nearly impossible for our respondents to even recognize, recall, or describe any European physical traits that might stand out, let alone have an impact on their sports performance. In other words, it seemed inconceivable to most students that bodily characteristics could affect Europeans' athletic prowess, even though these characteristics seemed all-powerful when it came to understanding the success of African competitors. Typical explanations for European-descent predominance in Olympic swimming included:

> Simply just because it is practiced more so maybe children start when they're small and so become very good ... because no physical characteristics for which they should be better come to mind. *(Ilaria, psychology major, Milan)*

> I don't know, maybe more dedication to what they want to do. *(Flavia, graphic design student, Milan)*

> I don't believe that Europeans, like the French, like the Dutch, are, how to say, predisposed for swimming. It's a question in this case of structures that allow high-tech training and that allow the development and identification of those athletes who have more of that potential compared to others. In fact, it's no coincidence that if you look at the winners in these categories they're very varied. *(Christian, anthropology major, Bologna)*

These examples reflect the reasons that interviewees generally gave for the disproportionate presence of white swimmers: greater "dedication"; a cultural habit of swimming; better facilities for training; and institutional mechanisms for the selection and cultivation of athletes. They also show

how quick respondents were to dismiss physical explanations out of hand when it came to European athletes. For Ilaria, the reason for their success was "just" habit; "no physical characteristics" suggested themselves. And Christian, who expanded on the uniqueness of African sports ability at the start of this chapter, immediately rejected the notion of a natural European talent for swimming, particularly since he was mindful of the internal variety in that category. As a result, "in this case," it was athletic institutions that were decisive.

As we saw with direct comparisons between Asian and African athletes, juxtapositions of European and African competitors were also telling. After a long disquisition on African bodies and the genes they passed down to black Americans, Massimo, a business student in Milan, allowed that he only connected physical traits to African descendants. In contrast, he went on, "a European who focuses on soccer, it's not because he's genetically predisposed, it's because he focuses more on that." The disparity between the amount of attention lavished on the ostensible details of black physiology and the inability to apply the same lens to the white body was particularly apparent when Carlo, a biology major in Bologna, groped, like many of his peers, for an account of European swimmers:

> Well, I would … I'm thinking a moment … I don't know, maybe because from the point of view … honestly, I couldn't say; it would be easier for me to understand why Africans are more suited, faster in track, because beyond the geographic point of view, also from the anatomical point of view, they have greater stamina…. Then you get into the weeds, from the biochemical point of view, I mean. Anyway, there are a lot of characteristics in their favor. Also, skin color is one of their advantages, so resistance to heat, so a lower body temperature and a greater efficiency from the point of view of effort and therefore work. For Europeans I couldn't say why swimming is favored, honestly.

As was the case when respondents compared Africans to Asians, it is striking how accessible a catalog of black physical traits was for this young student of biology. But the disparity in richness of detail is even more remarkable in this case, as Carlo and his peers were talking about the group to which they themselves belonged: white Europeans. Why would they be so knowledgeable about the bodies of the inhabitants of a continent that few if any of them had ever seen, and so incapable of identifying any particular bodily properties of the people around them? Here their own distinctiveness was washed out by the socially constructed markedness of the other.[25]

Given the hypervisibility of black biological traits coupled with the invisibility of the white body, it comes as no surprise that even explanations for *European* domination in sport were grounded in notions about *Africans'* physical characteristics at times. With the athletic qualities of whites being so difficult to envision, interviewees often turned to the more familiar terrain of black physiognomy to figure out why people of African descent might be *under*-represented in a sport. Their accounts of European overrepresentation in Olympic swimming thus turned out to be mostly about—Africans:

African women have a somewhat lower pelvis, and so this disadvantages them a lot [in swimming]. *(Alessandro, biology major, Milan)*

Maybe [Africans] are too long, and so they do laps too fast and it doesn't count. *(Alice, tourism student, Milan)*

I was talking with some other guys who work at our newspaper, [and] they were saying that practically the problem comes from the fact that the skin of black people is much heavier than the skin of whites, and so they have less floating capacity compared to that of whites and have to make more of an effort. *(Martino, business student, Milan)*

They have a different way of breathing. *(Gregorio, history major, Naples)*

As far-fetched as these explanations might seem, they underscore how much easier it was for the respondents to reflect on black rather than white bodies. Tellingly, they did not reverse these conjectures to apply them directly to Europeans; we did not hear, "Europeans have lightweight skin and so can float more easily," or "My friends and I were talking about it, and they told me that white women have relatively high pelvises, which makes swimming easier." Even when asked expressly to account for European-descent athletes' overrepresentation in a field, they could not really do it—at least, not in the biological terms they had applied so liberally to others. So despite their distaste for the word "race," these young Italians relied on an old colonial archive in which people of African descent are strongly associated with their capacity for physical exertion and labor.

The disparity between the respondents' biologization of blacks versus whites was also strongly evident in their affect. Both American and Italian students generally projected great certainty and even ease when describing African bodies, but they were largely tongue-tied when it came to talking about European bodies. For example, the biology major Aurora had not hesitated to explain the place of African-origin athletes in track as follows:

> But there I think it's really, there are really genes—talking about biology—that develop, not specific muscles, let's say, but a particular capacity in the legs. In fact, they always have muscular legs, all of them. That's why they stand out in track.

Aurora was thoroughly convinced of her answer, emphasizing that there "really" are genes that govern African sports outcomes; that "they always have" the requisite musculature, "all of them"; and that this is why, she said unequivocally, "they stand out in track." But when it came to accounting for European overrepresentation in swimming, she was at a loss to project the same assurance:

> I don't know how to answer this question for you. Maybe, maybe it could be linked to a lifestyle, I don't know ... what they can do there, obviously.... I don't know how to answer this question for you. I don't know. I'll think about it.

What is striking here is not only the fact that Aurora could not conceive of an answer to this question—for example, by continuing the genetic line of reasoning she had embraced vis-à-vis blacks—but that her confidence of just a moment earlier had deserted her. She repeated "I don't know" four times, and in contrast to her tight, complete sentences on Africans, here her speech trailed off more than once, with an unfinished sentence dangling in the middle.

Aurora's uncertainty edged toward the kind of incoherence that Bonilla-Silva attributes to the "linguistics of color-blind racism" (see chapter 1).[26] A more pronounced example of such semantic confusion—again in response to our question about white athletes—came from Gaetano, a biology major in Naples:

> Because ... of European origin.... But let's say also those Americans, like Michael Phelps, for that matter. But why? Because maybe—now I don't know anything about swimming—but what do I know, we who live by the sea are more trained compared to ... we're more ... we have more ... yes, we're more predisposed.

Again, the contrast with commentary on African athletic prowess is instructive; in this realm, Gaetano readily offered a much more fluid account:

Well, they evolved in a different way because they had to, because if we Italians in order to live had to . . . we found the way to raise cows and hens. In contrast, Africans didn't discover the method, when we were evolving on that they still had slaves, etc. etc., they hadn't found the way to raise livestock, so to live they had to hunt an antelope. We would never have been able to chase an antelope, [but] they, with their running, maybe they could absolutely do it. That's why they had to . . . are faster in this case.

While it has some breaks, this account about black athletes is much less disjointed and follows a more consistent narrative thread. Although incoherence may seem to be simply a manifestation of uncertainty, it marks especially treacherous shoals, where deeply embedded assumptions, norms, and interests must be navigated without ever allowing them to surface. In examples from Aurora and Gaetano, as well as from Carlo and others, it was whiteness—represented here by European athletes' bodies—that could not be confronted head-on and so gave way to babble. Letting "whiteness seep through discursive cracks," as Bonilla-Silva puts it, would challenge the "color-blind image" to which both individuals and institutions aspire. Incoherence thus signals the presence of the "unspeakable" and of the unthinkable.[27]

Positioning Europeans in between African and Asian Cultural Extremes

Culture played only a peripheral role in our interviewees' accounts of African-descent sports representation, as we saw, despite its prominence in the Italians' thinking about descent-based difference in general and in the Americans' definitions of race. When it came to explaining the outcomes of European- and Asian-origin athletes, however, both cultural and structural accounts reasserted themselves and the body took a backseat. For some students, like Anna, a history major in Bologna, there was a simple explanation for the dominance of European-origin athletes in swimming: in Europe, "pools are widespread." In a related vein, many alluded to disparities in athletic training between Africans and Europeans, frequently in vague terms that obscured whether these disparities were the result of different structural *opportunities for*, different cultural *preferences for*, different temperamental *predispositions toward*, or even different physical *capacities for* such training. Gianmarco, a psychology major in Naples, wondered whether "we have more capacity for training, or we're better at training, or we have a tradition in that particular sport that is more advanced than theirs, or maybe we whites are better at swimming." But because whites' sports performance was hardly ever attributed to their innate characteristics, its imagined basis tended to shift back and forth between a structural, material account, where socioeconomic difference in opportunity was at work, and a cultural, traditional one, where local preferences were in play.

When focused on European- and Asian-descent athletes, cultural explanations took on the detail and confidence that the respondents brought to their descriptions of African physical traits (but not to their accounts of white physical characteristics). Much of the richness of these accounts lay in their interweaving of stereotyped assumptions, normative judgments, and parallels drawn across diverse domains. Consider the following two commentaries from Isabella and Virginia, both students of tourism in Milan:

> Eh, each one of us has a knack for something. For example, they also say that *persone di colore*, blacks, are more talented in dance, because they feel the rhythm inside. But why? Because, I think, for years their way of celebrating, their rituality was based on movements, on dance, on dances. So it's something that you really carry in your DNA for centuries. Something that maybe Italians don't have, even if maybe you study dance your whole life, a particular kind of dance, you'll never dance like a person who never studied it who is maybe black that really has it inside, feels this rhythm thing inside. Same thing for music. Asians are monsters, I'm talking about classical music. They have methods of very targeted and severe study, also, in fact they know how to play musical instruments, the classical instruments, pretty well. Italians have a different study method, maybe not as severe, but they have a different musical culture, the history of Japan's classical music isn't a history like Italian classical music. So you already have inside something of yours that pushes you to do something better—unfortunately it's like that—better than other groups. Same for sports, but I don't know, those are things that are a bit biological, when you're talking about sports, and a bit traditional. *(Isabella)*

> Maybe it's a stupid thing, but the swimmer, the Italian swim team, the swimmers were [once] young swimmers, they were child swimmers, they were

little fish that Mommy and Daddy took to the pool to train to swim. That then the kids fell in love with swimming is maybe also thanks to the parent. Maybe in Africa there isn't the parent who takes you swimming. I don't think that happens. I think they learn to swim in the sea on their own. There isn't the dad who teaches them with inflatable water wings. Instead, maybe here it's because the culture of raising one's children, of having them take up certain sports, is more of a European thing, is more of an American thing, is more of a Western thing. I don't know, in general. *(Virginia)*

These lengthy quotations are packed with comparisons between Italians or Europeans and other continental groups (Africans and Asians) that favor the former, both explicitly and implicitly. When Isabella brought up Asians, she immediately cast them as "monsters" for their "targeted and severe" musical training and offered only a lukewarm assessment of the results (they played "pretty well"); when she turned to Italy's musical culture, she saw it as a case of one group doing "something better" than others.[28] In Virginia's rumination on swimming, there is a sharp contrast between the warm family scenario where "Mommy and Daddy" are personally involved in a child's upbringing and the imagined African landscape, with no parental involvement at all. "The culture of raising one's children," she concluded, "is more of a Western thing."

In these and other interviewee discussions of sports, the figures of both Africans and Asians served jointly to place Europeans in a flattering light. To borrow Claire Kim's insight, together they "triangulated" the European position in the middle of a continuum where Africans and Asians represented opposite extremes.[29] This was the case when interviewees opined about child-rearing and education on the path to sports. In Virginia and Isabella's comments, we see the loving, involved European parent flanked by the negligent, absent African parent, on the one hand, and a severe, overly demanding Asian regime—not even family—on the other. Alice in Milan was one of several students to link Chinese sports outcomes to rigid, impersonal institutions:

Also the Chinese are little fish in swimming, they're strong, or in ping pong, or what's it called, like rhythmic gymnastics, artistic, because anyway in China they have a mentality, the culture, the schools, the rules are very regimented [*quadrate*, literally, "square"]. The Chinese don't have an easy life, in China.

This configuration of Europeans in between Africans and Asians serves to define the intermediate position as "just right." Asians train too much, Africans do not train enough, relying on raw ability, and Europeans train just the right amount.

The juxtaposition of Asians to Europeans is particularly important because it shows how easily culture-based explanations for the same outcome can be colored in positive or negative ways depending on the party in mind. With Africans firmly relegated to the realm of the physical—for example, in Isabella's notion that blacks have natural rhythm in their DNA, as opposed to study being at the root of Asian and Italian musical success— Asians are left contending with Europeans for cultural supremacy. As we have seen, our Italian interviewees had many tactics for taking these Asian competitors down a peg. First and foremost was the minimizing or dismissal of their achievements: the history of Japanese classical music is not that of Italian music; Asian classical musicians are just "pretty" good; Chinese Olympic victories are the result of unconscionable training practices, or even doping, as one student recalled. In fact, the same actions that could be seen in a positive light when attributed to Europeans were put in a negative light when ascribed to Asians. Many respondents suggested that the predominance of European-origin athletes in swimming was due to their "dedication" in training, but such devotion among Asians was routinely portrayed as excessive or detrimental. Giorgia, a biology major in Milan, thought that the accomplishments of Chinese gymnasts were due to their being "subjected to heavy training because maybe in their country they focus a lot on sports specialization rather than forming more complete people who can be students and athletes at the same time." This was a very different rendering than Virginia's affectionate invocation of the Italian parents getting their small children started early on in swimming and thus launching their future careers on the national team.

Exploring the different ways in which interviewees positioned Asian, European, and African athletes relative to each other also made clear that white superiority could be conveyed through varied constellations. The European-Asian-African ordering along a scale of biologization, with whites virtually never described in terms of their physical traits and blacks almost always being depicted in that light, follows a hierarchical model in which whites are at the apex of intellectual ability. In contrast, the cultural continuum—with Africans being devoid of culture, Asians having excessive, state-directed regimes, and only Europeans in the middle having the right balance of social customs—is a horizontal configuration in which centrality is the hallmark of white superiority. Regardless of the structural framework, however, whites retain the privileged position as the optimal standard to which others are compared, even if only implicitly.

The Evolution of European Mental Superiority

When thinking about why European-descent athletes might predominate in certain fields, respondents pointed to a "culture" that was not limited to particular customs or values; they also generally ascribed to whites a life of the mind that they did not perceive among other groups. This was suggested by American students' attribution of a penchant for study to white "book culture," and it also came out in Italians' association of "technique" with Europeans. For example, Damiano, a history major in Bologna, chalked up the track-and-field successes of blacks from the Americas to the happy marriage of African physical prowess and European know-how:

> One explanation should be physical in nature, because I don't know if it's true or if it's an urban myth, I don't know, but I believe that black people have a structure different from ours, so maybe in speed, in stamina they're better.... Then, okay, black athletes, the ones that win, are all American and now Jamaica [sic], because they have European trainers. They went with technique on top of greater potential.

This depiction neatly mirrored long-standing ideas of European intellectual ability versus African bodily strength—and of the former's domestication of the latter.[30]

Just as the U.S. and Italian students had promptly offered accounts of human evolutionary history that explained black physical prowess, they also had fanciful images of European history that they linked to modern-day sports outcomes. Tellingly, however, these tales did not involve the development of any particular bodily traits; the respondents' inability to identify any features of white bodies that might favor athletic achievement precluded any evolutionary account of their genesis. Indeed, the interviewees' mentions of European evolution generally discarded the notion that white bodies had adapted to their environments. If anything, the image of the European body that emerged from these depictions of human evolutionary history was of a singularly frail or vulnerable type. When recalling "the usual stuff they give you when someone tries to explain [environmental adaptation]," Azzurra, an anthropology major in Bologna, quickly reeled off a list of climatic dangers against which Europeans were defenseless: "Where the sun beats down directly, a white person dies. In Tibet they need bigger lungs because, if not, you don't breathe. The Eskimos have a greater fat layer." And Erika, a fashion design student in Milan, was persuaded that Africans "have to be physically stronger than us" because "they're more in contact with nature, going back generations," and have developed more robust immune systems than Italians.

Instead of white *physical* evolution, both Italian and U.S. respondents routinely posited a uniquely *intellectual* adaptation in Europe to the exigencies of the environment. Consider the two starkly different tracks for change over time in Europe and Africa that the biology major Francesco imagined:

> But above all, we Europeans, let's say, learned to distinguish ourselves by our mind and by our social class. In an African place where maybe it doesn't matter so much how intelligent you are and how open you are, but how strong you are counts, where maybe the law of nature still prevails, so as a result the strongest wins. Consequently, it's normal that they predominate, these very tall and strong people, because they're . . . the law of Darwin is the law of survival in which the strongest wins.
>
> And then, exactly, maybe we have had the fortune to have people who governed and who wanted more to develop us culturally and all that. They understood that knowledge is man's real strength and what truly sets him apart.

Here Francesco articulated a way of thinking about human evolution that seems to sum up well what we heard from other students when reflecting on sports and the body. "The law of nature" (or the law of "survival," or of "Darwin") applies to black people but not to whites. "In Europe, where there was economic development," maintained the chemistry major Donato, "strength wasn't necessary to survive." European intelligence and technological know-how had spared them any evolutionary pressures to adapt biologically.

According to our Italian and U.S. interviewees, over time Europeans had developed, not physical strength, but good governance, cultural distinction, knowledge, and prosperity. As a result, they frequently attempted to account for whites' sports outcomes by alluding to European technology or skilled occupations, in contrast to the sparse infrastructure and hard manual labor they had invoked for Africans, or the coerced and dogged persistence they associated with Asian athletes. Consider the contrast evoked by Sara from Pittsburgh: "I have images of Africa, of, like, walking around ... buckets of water, pails of water. And like, Europeans, I just see them as like judges, I don't know why, I'm just getting a big judge." When Alessandro (the biology major who had suggested that black women's lower pelvises inhibited their swimming) imagined the ancestors of Europeans and Africans, he envisioned that, "while we went around in carriages, they kept running in order to escape from the lion." Similarly, Pilot University biology major Wendy recounted, "When I think of Caucasians, where they originated, the first thing I think of is medieval times, where they're all kind of domesticated, they're wearing clothes, and they're just not being, not really running around, and riding horses or something." And to account for Europeans' overrepresentation in Olympic swimming, the psychology major Gianluca speculated, "Maybe because always being people surrounded by water, being navigators and so on, they developed the ability to swim." Since the African continent is also surrounded by water, what seems to be distinctive to Gianluca is European skill in navigation. In short, our interviewees imagined that European technologies and institutions allowed them to master their environments, thus overcoming the natural features that other people could only cope with via their own physical transformation.

As colorful and even fanciful as they were, our respondents' imaginings about the human past and its implications today adhered to a recognizable framework. At its core was the centuries-old conviction that Europeans are unique in their intellectual history, accomplishments, and capacity, and thus in their ability to sidestep the challenges posed by nature. Other people— in Africa, Asia, and the Americas—were seen as being at the mercy of the elements and able to respond only through bodily change, not through technological, economic, or political innovation. Although the rigor and logic of evolutionary theory were elusive in these accounts, it is not their coherence that is important. Instead, what is meaningful is the pervasiveness of imperial-era beliefs about Europe as a shining beacon of progress and civilization in a world that is otherwise harsh and threatening: "a more hostile environment than the one we live in," as Tiziana in Bologna put it. Africa in particular remains the "heart of darkness" of colonial lore, and the black sporting body its symbolic home.

What Sports Talk Makes Possible: Rhetoric versus Conceptualization

By offering a way for young people to talk about difference that did not hinge on abstract concepts like "race" or "ethnicity," conversation about sport gave us an additional tool or measure of conceptualization. The change in topic and in question format ushered in both new ideas about group differences and a new attitude toward discussion of "blacks" and "whites." Simply put, the discomfort that so many interviewees had shown when asked for their views on "race" was much less in evidence when talk turned to athletes. As a result, notions of difference that had not emerged previously colored respondents' accounts, often contradicting statements they had made before. Contrasting their sports talk with prior definitions and taxonomies of race and ethnicity, as well as with their opinions of the Lieberman statement "There are biological races in the species *Homo sapiens*," this section examines how both the content and form of race-related talk varied depending on which question was being posed.

Question Context and the Spectrum of Racial Biologization

We begin our comparison by juxtaposing how the Italian interviewees accounted for African versus European differentials in international sports representation, on the one hand, with the kinds of differences they had previously associated with the term "race," on the other, both in their definitions of the word and in their reactions to the Lieberman statement on "biological races." Putting these commentaries side by side, it is clear that there was a continuum in terms of the embrace of biological models of difference that depended on which question was asked. Only one-third of the respondents agreed that biological races exist in our species, yet nearly half included biological difference in their definitions of race, and more than four out of five believed that physical makeup was a factor in African- and European-descent athletes' Olympic successes.

As a result of the divergent perspectives on physical difference that our questions elicited, what a student said at one point in the interview might well contradict what they said later. Perhaps most strikingly, twenty-two (or nearly 60 percent) of the thirty-seven respondents who had insisted, when asked to define the concept, that race did not exist in biological terms ended up attributing black or white sports outcomes to physical difference, as did three of the four interviewees who had embraced a constructivist definition. Similarly, more than half of those who had disagreed with the Lieberman statement on the existence of human "biological races" nonetheless offered physical explanations for African or European sports representation. In fact, the *majority* of students who drew on biological accounts when answering the sports question had said that they disagreed with the statement on biological races in our species.

Regardless of which rationale respondents gave for their antibiological or constructivist definition of race—that is, whether they claimed that "race doesn't exist," that "there is only one human race," or that race applies only to (nonhuman) animals, or whether they simply viscerally rejected the word "race"—in multiple instances, we found, they went on to speculate or assert that black bodies were fundamentally, innately different from white ones. Such juxtapositions of race definitions and sports explanations included:

[*Defining "race":*] For me it's hard to talk about race.... Like, race in what sense? Human race? ... I feel sick when I hear this term.... Because anyway talking about human race doesn't make any sense, I think ... in the sense that there is no biological race. We can talk, right, about ethnicities or nationalities, communities ... but races ... that is, I wouldn't even know how to define them. [*On sports:*] Probably, for example, like we were saying before, due to the fact that in America for many years blacks were, let's say, taken there, accustomed and therefore forced to live in certain ways. That is, to be able to work in the coffee fields or whatever it was, you had to be in perfect physical condition. So basically ... like, at least I think, there was a kind of selection ... a eugenics, if we can call it that. So with the passage of time, let's say that the black, especially in America at any rate, became strong. *(Claudio, anthropology major, Bologna)*

[*Defining "race":*] I think race only means the human race, because I don't think there exist the white race, the black race, the yellow race, so to speak. The human race exists. There's just one. Then you can talk about different ethnicities, different skin colors, but in any case I think that the [only] race

is human, we're all human beings. [*On sports:*] I think it all goes back to ...
anyhow you see that black people [*persone di colore*], like from central Africa,
are taller, more muscular. I think they have physical characteristics that anyhow
lead them to achieve certain results in certain fields. *(Oliviero, graphic design
student, Milan)*

[*Defining "race":*] No, the term "race," let's just say it's inapplicable, because
also from a really biological, genetic point of view, I think it's very hard to
apply, probably because it's not so simple; I think it's always been impossible
to distinguish different races. [*On sports:*] So there's a struggle over this thing
about Africans who have more—how do you say—possibility I could say, propensity to win track races, which derives simply from a biological characteristic
that is obviously linked to an aspect we could call racial, but obviously this
word is only connected to the biological aspect. Because let's say that some biological characteristics—maybe even despite various mixtures [*contaminazioni*]
between groups that present different biological characteristics—maybe last
and so in some cases can turn out to be favorable, in certain specific activities.
But obviously recognizing a difference—maybe I don't know the role of this
question in the research—but obviously a concrete difference, between various
groups, obviously doesn't jeopardize the principle of equality. *(Giacinto,
history major, Naples)*

These side-by-side comparisons reveal several puzzling inconsistencies.
Claudio claimed that it was so hard for him to talk about race that the
word made him sick, yet he did not hesitate to expound on the belief that
African Americans had developed superior strength owing to the "eugenic"
results of slavery. For Oliviero, "there is no black race," yet there were "black
people" with marked physical properties. And although Giacinto started off
arguing that race was "inapplicable" from a biological point of view because
it was impossible to distinguish races, when the talk turned to sports, he
allowed that Africans won at track owing to "a biological characteristic that
is obviously linked to an aspect we could call racial."

Not only did the content of interviewees' concepts of descent-based
difference vary depending on which question they were asked, but the
affect and semantics they brought to it also differed noticeably. For one
thing, the trepidation and even indignation that respondents (especially in
Italy) displayed when asked to define "race" or, even more, when invited
to comment on the notion of "biological races in the human species" all

but evaporated when talk turned to sports. In that realm, beliefs about biological differences between racialized groups like whites and blacks could be discussed with great confidence and gusto, even humor. Moreover, the students effectively shifted from the discursive strategies of avoiding, minimizing, or distancing race (and racism) when defining the word or considering its impact on their societies to embracing, asserting, or justifying its relevance in the sports domain—at least for black competitors. When it came to applying biological reasoning to white athletes, in contrast, the uncertainty, discomfort, and incoherence that came to the fore also indicated the workings of a classic Western racial logic in which whiteness remained the unacknowledged point of reference. This oscillation between comfortable and uncomfortable topics, between what could be boldly declared and what could only be reluctantly admitted, traced out a moral landscape for discourse on difference that did not always map directly onto the underlying terrain of belief.

Accounting for Contradictory Answers

Explaining the apparent contradictions between responses to different questions thus requires grappling with norms and habits that steer interviewees' comments in particular directions, at times away from the fundamental concepts that appear to structure their thinking about descent-based difference. Focusing here on our interviews in Italy, where we employed a wider range of questions on descent-based difference (touching, for example, on "Italianness" and "ethnicity"), we identify two main factors that seemed to drive a wedge between respondents' discourse on descent-based difference and their actual conceptualization of it: "race-blind" speech norms, on the one hand, and powerful stereotypes, on the other.

NORMS FOR EXPLICIT "RACE" TALK

The disjuncture between nonbiological race definitions and biological sports accounts that we illustrated earlier, using Claudio, Giacinto, and Oliviero as examples, is no doubt due in part to disparate discursive norms in the two question contexts. In the first exchange, interviewees defining "race" (or commenting on "biological races" in our species) were largely trying to signal their ethical distance from a historically destructive ideology. Italian students did so by saying that they rejected "race," that it made them sick, or that there simply was no such thing other than "the human race." Their American peers distanced themselves in similar fashion by routinely recasting race as a matter of individual preference for particular cultural practices or, to a lesser extent, as a social construct. But when talk turned to sport, there was no similar taboo on the idea that black people naturally had more muscles and were better athletes than whites. So despite the apparent contradiction of logic between these two stances, in most cases respondents did not seem to feel that they were in tension with each other.

In fact, Giacinto's closing comment on sport illuminates how normative coherence, rather than logical consistency, could reconcile an antibiological definition of race with the conviction that African athletes benefit from "racial" physical characteristics. Such "concrete differences," he maintained, did not call into question "the principle of equality." The common thread of his ideas, in other words, lay in their shared commitment to egalitarianism; the precise relationship of race to biology was of less importance. Conceptual confusion, uncertainty, and incoherence could thus remain undisturbed and unexamined, in both his comments and those of many of his peers on either side of the Atlantic. What took precedence was the norm of distancing oneself semantically from the word "race" and its implied hierarchy—but not necessarily from labels like "black" and "white" or from the traditional biological conceptualization of racial difference.

The absence of the word "race" altogether in our Italian interview question on the Olympics may have further accentuated the difference in the normative context.[31] Perhaps the interviewees did not feel that they were talking about race when speaking about African and European athletes, even though we and they used classic racial labels like "black" and "white." Note that both Claudio and Oliviero, after insisting that "there is no biological race" and "I don't think there exist the white race, the black race, the yellow race," used almost exactly the same formula: "then you can talk about ethnicities." In other words, race does not exist—but ethnicity does. And since, as we saw in the previous chapter, a substantial minority of the Italian interviewees—more than one-third—equated ethnicity with biological difference and/or race, it is conceivable that Claudio, Oliviero, and other students believed that the "black people" to whom they attributed superior athletic ability were not a race but an ethnic group. This was clearly the case for Tiziana, the psychology major in Bologna whom we quoted earlier: "There are differences between ethnicities at the physical level," she said. In other words, she interpreted our question about blacks and whites in Olympic sport as one about "ethnicities"—and this semantic translation may have been sufficient to shift the discussion onto less ethically fraught ground.

Other aspects of our interview questions, common to both the Italian and U.S. samples, are also likely to have contributed to the conceptual contradictions between them that we encountered. One factor might have been the question format. As the questions moved from the most blunt but also the most constrained ("Do 'biological races' exist, yes or no?") to the least direct and least constrained ("What are some potential reasons that black or white athletes predominate in one sport or another?"), respondents grew noticeably less inhibited about voicing long-standing stereotypes linking race to bodies. Our questions also spanned a spectrum of formality, from the most ostensibly scientific realm (with a statement about *Homo sapiens*) to the everyday domain of sports, which for many respondents was the province of leisure and idle conversation with friends and family. Our question requesting their definitions of race was somewhere between these two domains, in that it combined a direct reference to "race" with an unconstrained, open-ended response format; students could answer whatever they liked, rather than being limited to only yes/no or preset menu options. This question was also in the middle of the formality spectrum, in that it could be viewed as a somewhat intimidating academic exercise (in coming up with the "right," dictionary-type definition), but also perceived (as it often was) as a request for a personal opinion: "How would *you* define it?" we asked.

Finally, our questions about sports may have seemed to be a morally safe space for our U.S. and Italian interviewees alike. For one thing, they may have thought of sports competition as pure meritocracy—the ultimate level playing field—in which descent-based differences in representation could only be the objective (and thus indisputable) result of racial traits. For another, the students may have thought that their black biological exceptionalism was in some way flattering to people of African descent and was thus an antiracist challenge to historical white-over-black hierarchy rather than a rehearsal of old stereotypes about black intellectual limits.

THE IRRESISTIBLE PULL OF STEREOTYPES

Despite the antiracist norms that many if not most of our interviewees, American and Italian alike, sought to observe, they were also saddled with a large repertory of Western racial stereotypes that ultimately prevented them from articulating a consistent understanding of descent-based difference. As often as they rejected the term "race" or the notion of "biological race," their images of black people remained in thrall to long-standing beliefs about the physical properties of African bodies. The strong association between blacks, strength, and sport that Frantz Fanon reported from his research in the 1950s seemed impossible to overcome.[32]

The power of these stereotypes comes as no surprise given the myriad ways in which young people are exposed to them. Textbooks, documentaries, cartoons, museums, and sports media were just some of the influences that our respondents cited.[33] Just as importantly, if not more so, the interviews revealed that this well-known repertory of narratives was constantly being told and retold in their social and family circles. There were the friends' stories about black women and their pelvises, the recounting of news reports on African runners' leg muscles, the family jokes about voracious lions, and the assertions of black physical superiority by authority figures like coaches. The students' accounts made clear, then, that the classic racial framework they had imbibed was no mere legacy; it was actively reconstituted on a daily basis. Indeed, as we saw, the interviewees themselves easily worked up accounts of black and brown bodies that drew on these sources of information, their own observations, and a loose understanding of evolutionary theory.

The familiarity of such stereotypes is not enough, however, to explain their apparent appeal. Some old derogatory images—say, of Africans as primitive cannibals—still circulate yet seem less urgent today. So we have to ask: Why are the supposedly extraordinary properties of black bodies such a constant and widespread object of everyday speculation? Here the typical profile of the interviewee most likely to expand on this theme—a young white man—offers a clue. Not only had the male respondents in general most likely been more socialized into sports discourse, but the white ones in particular may have been fascinated—"unnerved and excited," to paraphrase Stan Thangaraj—by the hypermasculinity and hypersexuality attributed to black men.[34]

RHETORIC VERSUS CONCEPTUALIZATION:
THE LIMITS OF SPEECH NORMS

Weighing the importance of speech norms, on the one hand, and stereotypes, on the other, points to the conclusion that while the former shaped respondents' discourse, it was the latter that deeply informed their conceptualization of difference. What seemed at first like conceptual discrepancies—for example, asserting that "there is only one human race" yet arguing that "blacks can run faster, jump higher"—can thus be explained as disjunctures between how individuals spoke and how they thought. How do we know, however, that it was not the other way around? That is, did students truly believe that there is only one human race, for example, and paid only lip service to the notion of black physical superiority? Here both the students' affect and the normative language they used when discussing the term "race" provide important clues. Both the Italian interviewees' heated, even stricken, denunciations of race as "an ugly word," without dissecting its flaws, and their American peers' wariness toward the statement on biological races signaled a morally inflected rhetoric rather than a deeply grounded conceptual positioning. Their sports commentary showed that norms that produced discourse hostile to any mention of race or claims of racial biological difference did not actually impede the conceptual embrace of such claims or of racial classification more broadly.

If anything, it is striking how much classic racial thought—and even discourse—is left unchallenged and untouched by moral prohibitions on the language of "race." When the normative specter of "implicit or potential accusations of racism" is lifted, almost anything goes.[35] Or as Italians put it, these ideas are *sdoganate*: they clear customs and make their way into the world at large.[36] There is no taboo, for example, on asserting that Africans, Europeans, or Asians have fundamentally different biological makeup—different muscles, pelvises, stamina, or genes—or that whites represent the apex of humankind's evolutionary intellectual development, as compared to black physical ability and mindless Asian discipline. Nor is there any prohibition on applying eighteenth-century color terms like "white," "yellow," or especially "black" to people. As Giorgia in Milan explained, these terms are "neutral, because [they have become] part of everyday speech now," in contrast to "race," which, she said, "unconsciously makes me think of racism.... So ... yeah, it's not a neutral thing."

Scholars in the United States have noted how "coded" language allows discussion of race but provides it with deniability, thus circumventing speech norms. The result, according to Robin DiAngelo, is that "racial misinformation that circulates in the culture and frames [whites'] perspectives will be left unexamined."[37] Similarly, Anna Scacchi challenges the claim that Italians "lack a racial vocabulary":

> Or rather, is such a lack a fiction deriving from the myth of innocence? In reality, as shown by the names for *caffè macchiato*[38] that are widespread throughout Italy, like *marocchino* [Moroccan] or *moretto* [little Moor], and by the expressions used by various Northern League representatives to refer to African immigrants, like "baluba," "bingo-bongo," "Bedouin," "Hottentot," or "Zulu," we do have a way of speaking about race. In daily use there survives a vocabulary that is the legacy of the Italian 'of the empire' analyzed by Laura Ricci,[39] with which, through travelogues and propaganda, an exotic, hypersexualized, and primitive colonial world was constituted in the collective imaginary, [a] true paradise of the senses counterposed to the racial, moral and cultural superiority of Italians.[40]

Scacchi's observations on coffee and on the xenophobic League Party's speech suggest that in everyday realms of life, especially those associated with leisure and pleasure (like coffee and athletics), or where denigration is socially acceptable, a highly racialized language with an unmistakably colonial pedigree can be introduced without trepidation.

Conclusion: The Sports Arena, the Preserve of Race

The remarkable convergence of American and Italian students' commentaries on black and white athletes, across an ocean and a decade, and despite differences in the questions posed, is of crucial importance to this book's central research question. It heaps further doubt on the claims that Western Europeans think of descent-based difference in radically different ways than their cultural cousins across the Atlantic, and that they have decisively discarded the classic racial thought of their eighteenth-century forebears.

How is it that American ideas about the National Football League in the early 2000s are virtually identical to Italian thoughts about Olympic competition ten years later? The overwhelming similarity speaks to their shared roots in a global ideology that changed little in the early years of the twenty-first century—and has probably changed little since the 1700s. The rock-solid conviction that Africans are best suited for physical exploits and Europeans for intellectual accomplishments, convenient during the era of slavery and imperialism, endures in our young interviewees' interpretations of sport. Its matter-of-factness was conveyed, moreover, in the ease and expansiveness with which both American and Italian respondents approached the topic.

The similarity in the ideas about sports representation that we heard from students on either side of the Atlantic also reveals how few conceptual or rhetorical tools they had for challenging old stereotypes. Consistent with their "race" definitions in chapter 3, the antibiological views that these students had heard were not deeply rooted enough to overcome the black biological exceptionalism that they had imbibed since childhood, starting with cartoons and family jokes about Africans escaping from lions. Arguments like "there is only one human race," for example, may have been too superficial to actually help the Italian respondents reason about concrete examples like Olympic sport, a terrain already mined with media accounts of black biological superiority. Similarly, in the United States the mantra "race is a social construct" was of little help when undergraduates were asked to explain black overrepresentation and white underrepresentation in the NFL. In neither country did young people commonly have ready approaches for thinking or talking about the kinds of differentials between continental descent-based groups that everyday sports talk evokes. They could offer no counternarrative challenging the stereotyped biological and cultural uniformity of the category "African," nor could they show a firm grasp of evolution; only occasionally did they reveal a recognition of changing patterns of sports representation over time. Instead, what everyone had within reach was a stock account of blacks' special muscles.

In summary, these questions about sports revealed a void in both Italy and the United States in the training that young people are given to assess enduring and widespread claims about the nature of racial difference. The gap is enormous between the normative rhetorical training they have received and the education on human variation, whether biological, cultural, or social, that they have not. Even experience with anthropology or biology coursework was no guarantee against stereotypical notions of human bodies and their evolution over time, as Christian's comments at the start of this chapter attest. Instead, what had clearly been very effectively drilled into the students in both countries was an ethical rejection of overt, state-led, color-based discrimination as well as personal color prejudice—and even more, a fear of appearing to be a "racist" who condoned these. As Bonilla-Silva wrote of the United States, "Younger, educated, middle class people are more likely than older, less educated, working class people to make full use of the resources of color blind racism." This is no surprise given that "they are the cohort that has been ingrained from day one with the ideology of color blindness."[41] What may be surprising, however, is that so little work has been done to equip these young people—Italian or American—to question, let alone oppose, hoary categories and stereotypes that recycle simplistic, derogatory, old, and inaccurate ideas about people whose origins lie outside the West.

CONCLUSION

Rethinking Race

A New Model of Descent-Based Difference

> Biological difference and cultural difference are in no way separable; they are perceived in the same time and the same register. If a group is constituted in a coherent and stable way, it will appear under the bicephalic sign of the biological and the cultural.... The distinction between the two levels is an intellectual, intentional, corrective act that follows perception, [which remains] still marked by the original unity.
>
> —COLETTE GUILLAUMIN, *L'idéologie raciste* 2002 [1972], 95–96

MUCH OF the impetus for this book came from Martin Barker's groundbreaking work on British Conservatives' "new theory of race."[1] Barker argued that "new racism" incorporated a "pseudo-biological" culturalism that maintained that human beings have "natural homes" in bounded communities marked by unique traditions and ways of life, and that they instinctively defend these against outside encroachment. In this new outlook, the source of group distinctions shifted from biology to culture, and hierarchy seemed to give way to neutral, sometimes even admiring, allusions to simple "difference." As described in the introduction to this volume, the eventual spread of scholarly ideas about "new" or "differential" racism fueled a largely taken-for-granted association of this novel, culture-based racism with Western Europe, as well as a sharp contrast to the apparent persistence of "old" biological racism in the United States.[2]

These depictions of racial thought on either side of the Atlantic led us to formulate the two main questions that drove this book. First, are ideas of difference in Italy—as a significant case study of ideas circulating in Western Europe—the ideas predicted by the "new racism" hypothesis? Are they indeed more culture-based and less biology-based than ideas of difference in the United States? And second, how else might beliefs about the nature of difference vary across the ocean? Though inspired by Barker's study of racism, we saw in his and related work an argument about what we call "concepts of descent-based difference," meaning people's understandings or theories about the distinctions they believe demarcate communities of descent.[3] Little empirical research has directly focused on such notions among everyday people, however, so our in-depth interviews with young people in Italy and the United States offered a rare opportunity to explore them.[4] This study also pushed beyond the limits of local notions of "race" in order to examine the broader terrain of belief about descent-based difference.

In the pages to follow, we review the key findings of our cross-national comparison and draw on them to outline a new theoretical framework for the study of concepts of descent-based difference. We then apply the proposed approach to our own data in order to refine the analyses of Italian conceptualization in comparison to American conceptualization. Finally, we consider how this new model and the empirical findings on which it is based help us rethink the debates with which we opened this book: namely, scholarly and political conflicts over the place of race in our understandings and governance of society.

Comparing Concepts of Descent-Based Difference in Italy and the United States

Our interviews led us to the clear conclusion that despite Italians' emphasis on cultural difference and prompt rejection of race as an "ugly word," their ideas about descent-based groups are not as different from Americans' as has often been imagined. As we will detail in this chapter, the prediction of Americans' overwhelming reliance on a biological concept of race, and of Italians' rejection of it altogether, simply does not hold. If anything, it is the rhetoric used to produce socially desirable statements, grounded in norms about admissible or unacceptable discourse, that changes starkly across the Atlantic. Conceptually, both biology and culture have real purchase on notions of difference in Italy, just as they do in the United States. Indeed, as Colette Guillaumin suggests in this chapter's epigraph, they are fused together in our images of groups beyond our own.

Perceived Bases of Difference

To address our first main research question, we set out to investigate the place of culture and biology in Italian and American thinking about descent-based difference. What became apparent over the course of our comparative study, however, was that we also had to recognize two forms of difference that our respondents articulated less often and less clearly, but which nonetheless surfaced repeatedly. On the one hand was temperament or psychology, and on the other was socioeconomic status or structural position. Though interviewees often elided one or the other with either culture or biology, these two bases of differentiation have a conceptual distinctiveness that merits their exploration as well.

CULTURE

For Italian students, culture was generally the preferred framework for organizing knowledge about descent-based groups, recognizing sameness and difference, and making sense of others' behavior. In the guise of language, customs, or religion, culture was usually the most mentioned, salient, and emotion-laden feature attributed to populations. Ostensible cultural traits were granted prime explanatory value—for example, with respect to integration or the competitive presence of European and Asian athletes. And although our Italian interviewees usually defined their identity in terms of geographical belonging—referring to the country, region, or city of their birth—the traits they ascribed to themselves were mostly cultural ones. What made them feel attached to their birthplace was, along with affective ties, a particular outlook and way of life.

Culture also had a meaningful place in the U.S. interviews, but a different one. Unlike their Italian peers, the Americans strongly associated culture with race, often portraying racial identities as aligned with individuals' choices to perform certain cultural practices. They also invoked notions of "black culture" or "white culture" to explain sports outcomes.

The contrast between the two samples points to a certain commonality, however, in their usage of culture to describe and account for descent-based difference. Simply put, both Italians and Americans had no difficulty applying cultural explanations to themselves or to comparisons between themselves and others, but found it hard to ascribe them to others alone. When our young Italian interviewees were asked to describe who was Italian and how non-Italians differed from them, culture was far and away the distinction that was most salient to them. But when asked to define "race," which they associated much more strongly with Asian and African groups than with Europeans, culture vanished as a basis for differentiation. Culture also played little role in the Italian students' thinking about blacks' sports representation—but it resurged in their accounts of white athleticism; the same paradox held in the U.S. context.

Where the American interviewees differed from Italians was in the salience of whiteness as a race—no doubt due to the far-reaching institutionalization of racial categories in the United States—rather than as the invisible default signifier it was for their Italian counterparts. This was apparent in a greater tendency in the U.S. sample than in the Italian one to name whites as a racial group when asked for a list. The visibility of whiteness to American eyes led our largely white sample to bring culture to bear in their reflections on race in a way that did not happen in Italy. In both countries, the students associated cultural markers with a white "us," but in Italy, "race" was not about "us," whereas in the United States it was—and so culture was relevant to race in an American perspective but not an Italian one. The linkage of culture to whiteness in both countries, moreover, was also apparent in the students' depictions of human history as one of European cultural, scientific, and intellectual flourishing, compared to the timeless and unremarkable drudgery of life elsewhere.

BIOLOGY

Biology—whether in terms of surface phenotypic traits like skin color, physiognomic characteristics like musculature, constitutional properties like stamina, or genetic markers in DNA—indisputably figured in both American and Italian notions of descent-based difference. Indeed, our respondents from both countries were quite similar in their definitions of race as a matter of biology and in their certitude that blacks possessed unique physical qualities that led to disproportionate athletic success. The U.S. and Italian interviewees were also alike in being unable to fathom how whites' biological characteristics might account for their predominance in certain sports. Together, these results show both groups as tapping into a deep cache of classic Western thought linking race to stereotyped bodies.

The two samples diverged considerably, however, when it came to the ways in which they also challenged claims of descent-group physical difference. Our Italian interviewees were more likely than the Americans to reject a biological definition of—and express great hostility toward—the race concept. And although Morning did not pose a question to U.S. students about "Americanness" that could be compared to our question on *italianità*, it is notable that the Italian students rarely gave much weight to physical difference when contrasting Italians to non-Italians, reflecting on obstacles to integration, or for that matter, rating groups' likability. In these instances, biology was for the most part equated solely with skin color, which the Italian interviewees assured us was "unimportant," didn't "matter," and was something they "didn't even notice."

PSYCHOLOGY

Before conducting interviews in Italy, we had only a dim notion that beliefs about descent-based groups' temperaments or mentalities might emerge. The comments by students in Milan, Bologna, and Naples about both Italians and other descent-based groups, however, repeatedly referred to particular outlooks or dispositions, sometimes offering these as the cause for notable behaviors.

We use "psychology" as a broad umbrella term for capturing the range of mental characteristics that our Italian respondents attributed to various descent-based groups. We have often referred to one component as "temperament" when describing the students' claims about, for example, "open" and "friendly" Senegalese, "closed" and "severe" Chinese, or "violent" and "predatory" Moroccans in order to get at the emotive states or orientations they invoke. "Temperament" is also perhaps the closest link to the Western racial thinking of the eighteenth century, when Linnaeus and others ascribed humors such as being "sanguine" or "choleric" to human races, as well as other personality traits like stubbornness or gaiety.[5] At times, however, the Italian interviewees referred less to emotion and more to mentalities or outlooks, such as misogyny, criminality, "work ethic," "respect for others," "upright" character, and natural "rhythm" or musicality. Here we might add as well their American peers' rumination about blacks' physicality as contrasted with whites' cerebral orientation.

The difficulty of identifying exactly what kinds of psychological tendencies were imagined is compounded by the lack of clarity regarding their roots in culture or biology and, relatedly, the extent to which they were perceived as essential, primordial, or acquired dispositions. Both Italian and American students often chalked these tendencies up to culture, as in a Romani "culture of dishonesty." This framing suggests that primordial intergenerational transmission of values and norms leads to certain behaviors—in this case, criminality. Yet these mental habits were so often presented as monolithic and fixed that they seemed to take on the essential air of innate characteristics—a hardwired "aggressiveness" on the part of Muslims or African Americans, for example. The U.S. interviewees seem to have been less likely than their Italian counterparts to associate particular temperaments with particular descent-based groups, but perhaps only because they were not asked a similar set of questions juxtaposing Americans and non-Americans, or requiring a "thermometer" evaluation of specific groups. After all, the eighteenth-century notion of racial dispositions is alive and well in U.S. behavioral genetics and more broadly in U.S. society, where psychological traits related to violence, intelligence, sexuality, and more are routinely linked to an ostensible biology of race.[6]

SOCIETY

What we might call "societal" concepts of descent-based difference were in short supply among our interviewees, perhaps more so in Italy than in the United States. When contrasting Italians to non-Italians, for example, students paid relatively little attention to the many structural differences that might distinguish them, from citizenship and its attendant rights and privileges to differences in human capital (including language fluency) or vulnerability to discrimination. Moreover, the social constructivist perspective that racial groups are collective inventions was almost entirely absent from the Italian sample.

Social structure figured more prominently in the U.S. interviews, but as in Italy, it tended to be eclipsed by cultural and biological notions of difference.

Although almost one-fifth of the American students defined race as a social construct, for example, this definition was much less frequently voiced than biological and cultural definitions. Similarly, the U.S. interviewees were more likely than Italians to imagine ways in which socioeconomic inequalities might disproportionately channel members of some descent-based groups to a sport (or to sports in general). (This may have been an artifact, however, of their being posed a question comparing National Football League athletes within their own country, as opposed to the question about the international Olympics that we put to Italian subjects.) Yet, like their Italian peers, the U.S. respondents overwhelmingly gravitated to biological explanations for sports outcomes—at least when it came to black athletes.

In fact, as with culture, social structural explanations for group outcomes may have seemed relevant for the white "us," but not for nonwhite others. It is particularly curious that in Western Europe, where many seem to perceive class analyses as more powerful or appropriate than descent-based ones, our Italian interviewees were not more attuned to the structural inequalities that disadvantage newcomers and their offspring.[7] This paradox can be resolved, however, if we understand that, for our Italian respondents, social structure—like culture—was applicable to whites, not others. In Europe as well as the United States, the structure known as "class" (when acknowledged in the United States at all) is usually applied to intra-white divisions. It should not be surprising, then, that in our samples the idea of structural inequality was less available as a tool for social analysis when nonwhites or non-Europeans were being discussed.

Disentangling Rhetoric from Conceptualization

In chapter 1, the literature that we reviewed pointed to the difficulty of inferring concepts from discourse. There we focused on scholarship on two topics adjacent to the conceptualization of descent-based difference: speech norms regarding "race" and the social-scientific utility of the race concept. In both realms, we concluded that there might be more commonality between U.S. and Western European perspectives than is often thought. And our empirical investigation of American and Italian beliefs about difference underscores the need to factor in discursive norms in order to attempt comparisons of underlying concepts. Accordingly, we contend that indirect measures of conceptualization are crucial, rather than simply taking what is said at face value.

On the rhetorical surface, our respondents in both the United States and Italy grounded descent-based difference in multiple bases—cultural, psychological, biological, and social—and certain questions or scenarios were more likely to elicit one or another basis. When the same individual invoked different forms of difference depending on the question, as often happened, contradictions of the sort we highlighted in the last chapter would arise. It turned out to be entirely possible for an individual to fervently deny the existence of biological races in one breath, yet excitedly detail black musculature in the next.

How to account for such conflicts of logic? To some extent, the respondents were probably reproducing multiple discourses to which they had been exposed and compartmentalizing these into different domains—"sports," for example, or "integration"—where different speech norms prevailed. This compartmentalization obscured discrepancies between the arguments that interviewees made in different domains, and indeed, the students rarely seemed to notice the inconsistencies in their comments. As a result, they might sincerely intone, "There's just one human race," or "Race is socially constructed," even if they later portrayed race as a biological fault line in the human species.

At other times, however, their rhetoric seemed more strategic or disingenuous, or simply more aspirational. The claims that "people can choose their race" or "I don't even notice color" have the flavor of being "semantic moves" that are intended, consciously or not, to distance the speaker—or her society—from the immorality of racism.[8] By suggesting that racial distinctions are voluntarily chosen identities, as many U.S. interviewees did, or that color played no role in everyday life, as their Italian counterparts were wont to claim, the danger of being accused of complicity in an oppressive and unjust ideology could be kept at bay. Moreover, this moral imperative was hardly a hidden agenda; students frankly expressed their consternation, embarrassment, indignation, or outrage when asked to comment on the "ugly word" of race.

From such polyglot discourse about descent-based difference, then, what can we infer about underlying beliefs? First, it seems likely that a jumble of competing concepts of difference inhabited the interviewees' mental maps, without their being aware of the dissonances in some cases. But second, we can turn to indirect measures to gauge the relative weight of certain concepts. In particular, such indicators point to the enduring presence of a classic Western racial taxonomy; grounded in notions of biology and temperament, it has not been dislodged by competing understandings of group difference as cultural or structural. The casual use of color-coded labels like "white" and especially "black"; the resort to non-Europeans to epitomize racial or ethnic groups (or simply others, like non-Italians) and the concomitant invisibility of whiteness; the asymmetric application of biological, cultural, and structural reasoning to Europeans, Africans, and Asians; and finally, the flimsiness of the students' antibiological arguments—these were all ways in which American and Italian young people told us, without telling us, that the eighteenth-century race concept retained a meaningful place in their understandings of human difference.

Conclusion: Transatlantic Similarities

Our empirical research in Italy makes clear that it is far too soon to claim that biology-based concepts of descent-based difference have disappeared there. In conjunction with the U.S. findings of considerable culture-based conceptualization, this research concludes that the "new racism" hypothesis does not hold. It is not only the ascription of biological thought to the U.S. and cultural differentiation to Europe that is disproved, but more fundamentally, the assumption that Americans and Europeans are very different from each other when it comes to beliefs about descent groups. Of the many similarities that we encountered in their conceptualization of difference, perhaps the most important was their shared difficulty in adopting a sociological perspective. In both countries, the respondents largely pictured membership in descent-based groups as depending on individuals' static possession of certain biological, cultural, or psychological traits, rather than on a social system that creates and reinforces group boundaries.

Theorizing Concepts of Descent-Based Difference

If a "culture versus biology" binary not only fails to accurately capture distinctions between our Italian and U.S. interviewees but also cannot fully cover the conceptual variation within each sample, how might we better describe and compare their concepts of descent-based difference? This brings us to the second main question we pursue: What aspects of such conceptualization, beyond a cultural or biological grounding, should we pay attention to in our analyses? In this light, our findings regarding concepts of difference in Italy and the United States not only contribute empirical insights but also have theoretical and methodological implications. More specifically, they help us build an original analytical framework for the conceptualization of descent-based difference, which in turn can guide our methods for investigating—and comparing—such beliefs. Rather than rely on a handful of labels like "ethnicity" or "tribe," which are blunt instruments whose meaning varies from place to place, we need an alternative way of designating and describing concepts of descent-based difference that is more tailored and precise.

A New Framework for Analyzing Concepts of Difference

Accordingly, we argue that researchers should look at specific properties of a given concept in order to identify, distinguish, and analyze it. In other words, we propose to break concepts down into their constituent parts or elements. And based on our own findings, we theorize that there are six key characteristics of concepts of descent-based difference.

1. *A defining or constitutive basis of group membership:* Examples of such "grounds for difference" include genes, blood, culture, birthplace, temperament, and "soul."[9] Chandra would call these the "descent-based attributes [that] are necessary for membership" in ethnic identity categories.[10] Importantly, Chandra, like Weber, recognizes the role of subjectivity in such assessments of group membership: what counts is not necessarily any objective reality, but rather *belief in* and *perception of* an individual's possession of certain traits, whether a "Northern soul" or hooved feet.[11] It should also be noted that a broader set of characteristics can be attributed to descent-based groups than the ones that are thought to be strictly necessary for group membership. In other words, we can speak of a primary (constitutive) set of traits versus a secondary (descriptive) set—like blood (first order) versus dress (second order).

2. *Scope and reference group:* The very term "difference" implies that more than one entity is in play, so when we describe the perceived basis for difference, we have to ask: Difference from what? Concepts of difference necessarily have a certain scope: they apply to a set containing more than one constructed descent-based group, and usually these sets contain a clear if unspoken reference group. In Italy, this would be people descended from multiple generations of inhabitants of what is now recognized as Italian soil

and who are usually Catholic; in the United States today the unspoken reference group is European-descended, native-born individuals.[12]

To give an example of how a particular concept of difference thus obtains in a circumscribed system of recognized descent-based groups: in the United States, so-called whites, blacks, Asians, and American Indians populate a common set in which biological difference is imagined to distinguish each group from the others (and in which whites are the implicit reference group). It is less clear, however, whether or how this physically grounded concept of difference extends to Latinx or Middle Eastern people; they may be understood as people who are not physically distinct from the standard reference group so much as they are culturally different.[13] Their ambiguous position in the U.S. system illustrates, first, that the scope of a given concept of difference (here, the American biological "race" notion) is limited or circumscribed and doesn't apply to all recognized descent-based groups; and second, that more than one concept of descent-based difference can be operative in the same society. In this example, both biology- and culture-based concepts of difference simultaneously cohabit the national imaginary.

3. *Hierarchy:* Are the groups included within the scope of a particular concept of difference imagined as equal in worth, ability, and humanity, or are they arrayed along a vertical hierarchy? In the United States today, we find both a hierarchical, biology-based concept in which "races" continue to be measured against each other along every scale imaginable and an egalitarian "ethnic" conceptual system that is applied primarily to European-origin descent-based groups. Although the latter was a markedly vertical framework a century ago, when Celtic, Mediterranean, and other European "races" were stacked up against each other along a clear progression of inferiority to superiority, today Irish, Italian, German, or English ancestry, for example, no longer has such stark implications.[14]

4. *Origin or mechanism of difference:* How do people ostensibly come to acquire the attributes that are responsible for their being members of one descent-based group or another? We find that at least four mechanisms are imagined to be at work:

a. *Essential inheritance:* One's biological parents transmit certain inalienable, bodily, and group-constitutive characteristics to their offspring.[15] These intrinsic traits might be genetic, phenotypic (like skin color or blood), spiritual, or psychological.

b. *Primordial legacy:* People's early caregivers and surrounding social institutions transmit to them certain cultural attributes—practices, ideas, norms, values, outlooks—through passive socialization during their youth.[16]

c. *Deliberate acquisition:* Deliberate acquisition is perhaps the least-known route to becoming a member of a descent-based group, because purposive action by an individual to acquire the traits—whether cultural, physical, socioeconomic, or other—needed to "join" a descent-based group is likely to be seen as inauthentic or unnatural. After all, these groups are supposed to be objectively and incontrovertibly based on "descent"! But purposive self-refashioning has enough of an empirical footprint to warrant mentioning. Think, for example, of Morning's description of the "cosmetic" and "emotive" bids for racial group membership by individuals contending that their changed appearance, lifestyle, or simply feelings justified their claimed racial identities.[17] Other examples would be the Italians' claims in our interviews that respecting the law makes one Italian and the claims of some U.S. respondents that choosing to perform certain cultural practices can undergird one's racial membership.

d. *Social assignment (or construction):* In this view, individuals need not actually possess any particular shared traits to be assigned to an ostensibly descent-based group—or they need not be the only ones who possess them—because what is determinative is society's assignment of them, regardless of their personal characteristics. In other words, people's belonging in a particular group is driven not by the traits that inhere in them or that they objectively possess (like a certain height, hair color, or citizenship), but rather by a sociocultural process of classification that can operate independently of any such individual features. For example, the American star golfer Tiger Woods can be read as a textbook case of the social construction of race: despite his mixed African, Asian, European, and indigenous American ancestry, he is usually labeled as black. There is no objective or logical reason, biological or otherwise, that he could not be categorized differently, but there is a very strong social convention in the U.S. "one-drop rule" that determines his racial status.

As readers may have already realized, the typology of origins of difference that we have laid out here incorporates two important structural features.

One is a gradual diminution in the centrality of ancestry. Where biological kinship is the primary mechanism of *essential inheritance*, it is replaced by parenting in the *primordial legacy* scenario, and then the family becomes altogether irrelevant in *deliberate acquisition* and *social construction*. Yet all of these mechanisms can be invoked to justify or account for individuals' membership in groups that are largely understood to be communities of descent. The other structural feature of our typology is the progression in focus from the individual to society. The first three mechanisms presume that descent-group membership is driven by characteristics possessed or embodied by individuals, but the fourth, social assignment, allows that individual traits need not be determinative.

5. *The permanence of constitutive traits:* Closely related to the question of the origins or mechanisms for descent-based membership—yet not quite the same thing—is the issue of the fixity or fluidity of the traits believed to determine such belonging. More precisely, the perceived permanence of constitutive traits depends on which mechanism of membership acquisition is envisioned—and not on the type of trait itself.

At one end of our spectrum of the mechanisms of difference lies essential inheritance, which presumes the permanence of individual traits. After all, "essences" are intrinsic, inalienable and thus unchangeable qualities.[18] But individual characteristics acquired through the socialization process of primordial legacy may be seen as unlikely, but not impossible, to change. In even starker contrast, fluidity in individual traits is at the very heart of deliberate acquisition. This process, moreover, reminds us that malleability can be a feature of both a person's characteristics and the societal systems of classification that they navigate—and that these are distinct phenomena.[19] As Chinyere Osuji observed of racial categories in the United States and Brazil, social conventions may prevent people from being able to unilaterally choose their descent-based groups, even when they contend that they have refashioned themselves or their lives as ostensibly required.[20] This brings us squarely to our fourth mechanism for the generation of descent-based difference: social construction. Here plasticity is also the rule, but over a much slower, longer time scale than at the individual level. The historical record attests to fluidity both in the construction, recognition, and salience of particular groups (like Romani, Hispanics, whites, and so on) and in the "decision rules" about who belongs to which group (for example, South Asians in the United States cycling through the "Hindu," white, and now Asian racial categories).[21]

6. *The determinism of constitutive traits:* This phrase refers to the osten-sible consequences of primary traits, including their covariation with sec-ondary traits. What is the signature or primary trait of a descent-based group imagined to lead to, if anything? What about particular behaviors or outlooks (including identities)? Or reactions from others? Vincent Yzerbyt, Anouk Rogier, and Susan Fiske note, for example, that people make "social attributions" in which "shared enduring features" of a group are believed to be responsible for its members' behaviors.[22]

The taxonomy of key elements in the conceptualization of descent-based difference that we have presented here naturally implies that countless con-figurations might arise from the potential arrays of characteristics along these six dimensions. Yet our taxonomy also emphasizes the fundamental unity of any such variant concepts of descent-based difference, due not to their similarity but to their shared membership in a broad family. Regard-less of the local terminologies by which these conceptual variants might be called, they should be studied—and will be better understood—as mem-bers of an entire family of notions of descent-based difference.

It might be useful to think of this typology of key dimensions along which concepts of difference vary as a kind of structural assessment of the architecture or scaffolding of these ideas. What are the grounds they are built on? What is their scope—how far do they extend? Does the concept in question take on the vertical shape of hierarchy or a horizontal, egali-tarian form? What is the mechanism that supposedly pours the foundation of difference, and how durable is the resulting base expected to be? And finally, what are the other consequences of these fundamental character-istics ascribed to descent-based groups? Applying these questions to our inquiries into beliefs about difference will help us better assess the concep-tual houses we inhabit.

A Methodology for the Study of Descent-Based Difference

The theoretical framework to emerge from our empirical study also anchors a methodological approach. For the purposes of analysis and the compar-ison of concepts of descent-based difference, our research suggests the fol-lowing approaches:

Look beyond local conceptual vocabulary: The meaning of terms like "race," "caste," "ethnicity," "tribe," "clan," and so on, should not be assumed but rather investigated. To facilitate such inquiry, we adopt the generic analytic term "concept of descent-based difference," which not only sidesteps presumptions about the beliefs in play but also reminds us that the ideas we are examining are part of a wider range of notions found around the world.

Chart subjects' mental maps of descent-based difference: Groups that are particularly salient to them will be identified, and careful notes can be made of the forms and characteristics of difference they describe.

Use multiple measures: There is more than one way to explore the concepts of interest. As we have seen, asking varied interview questions (for example, "Who is Italian and who is not?," "How would you define 'ethnicity'?," or "How would you account for the predominance of European-origin athletes in certain Olympic sports?") sheds light on different facets of the conceptualization of difference. Mixed methods incorporating completely different types of data accomplish the same goal.

Reckon with the gap between discourse and belief: The disjuncture between what people think and what they say is well known.[23] Sometimes subjects' desire to provide what they believe is a socially desirable response is in play; other times they are unable to articulate what is consciously on their mind or to access implicit or unexamined ideas. And often people's ideas are simply confused, if not downright contradictory. Yet there is no substitute for listening to (or reading) their words in order to arrive at some understanding of how they make meaning of the world around them.

With these challenges in mind, we have found it useful to practice a selective and deliberate engagement with and disengagement from our interviewees' discourse. As the previous chapters show, we pay a great deal of attention to their words and the ideas they strive to convey. But we also listen to silences and gaps in their statements, wondering why, for example, an assertion made about one group is not applied to another. We track indirect measures of conceptualization, such as the examples they select to illustrate their claims. We also note the affect and emotion that interviewees bring to our conversations. And we draw contrasts throughout, asking why one group or domain is depicted differently than another in interviewees' detailing of the nature of descent-based difference. In short, we advocate paying close attention to both what is said and what goes unsaid—including what is expressed nonverbally—when attempting to trace the contours of beliefs about difference.

Break down and describe concepts of descent-based difference according to their fundamental components: In the previous section, we introduced a new framework for measuring, describing, and comparing concepts of difference. To subject such concepts to social-scientific analysis, we contend, we need a more precise language to capture their many dimensions. In particular, we suggest that a given system for conceptualizing descent-based difference can be more productively examined by decomposing it into the following elements of belief regarding: (1) constitutive traits, (2) scope, (3) hierarchy, (4) the origin or mechanism of difference, (5) the permanence of constitutive traits, and (6) the determinism or consequence attributed to constitutive traits. When studying individuals' beliefs about difference, then, we would do well to explore and document the forms that their working models of difference take on along each of these dimensions. We will illustrate this shortly in both the cases of Italy and the United States.

Use the components of conceptualization to also specify processes of differentiation: In delineating interwoven but distinct elements of the conceptualization of difference, from the ostensible bases of difference to their permanence or consequences, our framework also differentiates a series of phenomena that are often confused with each other. Processes or states like "racialization," "essentialization," and "biologization," for example, have been referred to interchangeably, but our taxonomy of conceptualization makes clear that these are not necessarily the same thing.

Biologization (characterization in terms of ostensibly bodily traits) is usually, but not always, a form of *essentialization* (depiction as embodying fixed, intrinsic qualities). And biologization is not the only form that essentialization can take: temperament or mindset, for example, can also be conceived as rooted in an essence that is passed down unfailingly from one generation to the next. In other words, our theoretical distinction between the traits that ostensibly dictate an individual's descent-based membership, on the one hand, and the imagined genesis of those traits, on the other, helps us understand that biologization is not synonymous with essentialization. Nor is *naturalization*, the presumption that a particular difference or grouping of people obtains "naturally," meaning independently of human will or agency. Naturalization is the opposite of a constructivist interpretation, yet not the same as essentialization. But like essentialization, naturalization can be linked to cultural, biological, or other characterizations of difference. After all, Barker perceived in British "new racism" an understanding of "human nature" as compelled to create and conserve cultural distinction.[24] Finally, readers will recall that we reserve the term *racialization* for groups coded in Linnaean color terms and arranged in a hierarchy, based on any kind of trait: temperamental, biological, cultural, or other.

As our interviews in both Italy and the United States make amply clear, the conceptualization of descent-based difference is a messy business: because people are not always able to articulate their ideas; because they can hold contradictory views with surprising ease; and because our understandings of difference are complex, multifaceted beliefs that extend along multiple dimensions. As analysts of such beliefs, we need a larger and more precise set of tools than the ones we have previously deployed. The theoretical framework we have presented here is an attempt to add that toolbox, drawing on what we have learned from our empirical research. In the next section, we put it into practice.

Rethinking Concepts of Descent-Based Difference in Italy and the United States

With the framework outlined here, we now have the tools we need to provide a comparison of descent-based conceptualization in the United States and Italy that moves beyond the inadequate culture-versus-biology dichotomy. We identify the principal concepts of descent-based difference that we encountered in the United States and Italy, detailing the ways in which they converge or diverge. To profile this series of concepts, we revisited the key constitutive bases documented in the first section of this chapter (such as culture and psychology), then built on them by adding what we learned about the other elements of conceptualization that we theorized in the following section, such as hierarchy and permanence.

In practical terms, we started with our Italian and American interviewees' depictions of a series of descent-based groups that were especially salient to them. Mining these portrayals for the conceptual elements highlighted by our theoretical framework, we then inferred varied types of notions of difference. To choose the descent-based groups whose imagery we would examine, we first looked for variety in their constitutive traits, selecting those whose signature characteristics were imagined by our respondents to be physical, cultural, or psychological. (Recall that descent-based groups were infrequently defined in terms of their structural position, an observation to which we will return shortly.) Second, we contrasted the imagined origins of the defining traits of these groups: Were their signature characteristics believed to be essential, primordial, or acquired? With these variations in mind, we identified four sets of groups, each of which we came to identify with a particular conceptual configuration of descent-based difference: biological essentialism; psychological essentialism; cultural primordialism; and cultural acquisition. Moreover, we concluded that some descent-based groups had a hybrid status: more than one notion of difference was firmly attached to them, and no one notion held clear primacy over others.

Before turning to the four configurations of difference that were most prevalent in our study, it is worth commenting on the absence of a social constructivist model from this list. As it turned out, our approach of working with the interviewees' descriptions of particular groups eliminated the constructivist model, because they did not identify any group as the product of a social process of invention. African Americans, for example, whose numbers had been bolstered by a patently arbitrary social convention—the "one-drop rule"—were instead seen as exhibit A for biological difference.[25] Similarly, the Roma—whose ranks are likely to have been fed over centuries by people from disparate geographic origins who practiced similar occupations—were strongly associated with fixed cultural and temperamental traits.[26] Even contemporary socioeconomic boundaries were likely to be recast as a matter of a group's work ethic or criminality. In other words, although there were many ways in which a structural, constructivist account could have been incorporated into the respondents' reasoning about descent-based groups—starting with "Americans" or "Italians," whose polyglot origins were well known to the students—it rarely was. This finding is consistent, moreover, with how infrequently our interviewees, especially the Italians, offered sociological or structural definitions of the term "race." Even when U.S. students invoked the idea that "race is a social construct," they were generally unable to elaborate on that notion or apply it to concrete instances. For all these reasons, we conclude that, at present, social constructivism is a perspective on descent-based difference with which few young Americans or Italians have a deep familiarity. At best, it is an idea that some have heard of, but few have been able to master or take truly to heart.

Biological Essentialism

One of the most prominent concepts of descent-based difference that surfaced in our interviews in both Italy and the United States was a belief in groups' *essential, fixed,* and *biological* characteristics.[27] Moreover, this shared notion was clearly grounded in a historical archive of classic Western racial thought whose *scope* included African/black, Asian/yellow, European/white, and Native American/red descent groups, with whites the implicit *reference group.*

The question of *hierarchy* in this conceptual system, however, is complex. For our Italian as well as our American respondents, the biologically essentialized category par excellence was the racialized figure of the black, and it was one to which superhuman physical prowess was ascribed. On the face of it, this might suggest a biological hierarchy with Afro-descendants at the top. Yet the ostensible physical superiority of blacks was also closely associated with primitiveness, animals, natural settings, poverty, slavery, and the general absence of culture, intellect, and civilization. These vestiges of the colonial imaginary that consolidated the Western race notion all marked Africans as decidedly inferior. In this light, the best indicator of hierarchy in this biologically essentialist conceptual regime was the implicit reference group position accorded to whites.

The one component of conceptualization we have not touched on yet, *determinism,* is the only element of the essentialist biological model on which our U.S. and Italian interviewees parted ways. Or more precisely, the Italians departed from the traditional race concept in that they did not seem to see biological traits as having meaningful consequences in other realms. What exactly does having the physical properties of blackness or yellowness supposedly entail in Italy? What outcomes (other than athletic achievement) do these ostensible defining characteristics produce or influence? The answers seemed to be: not much—at least not consciously—and very few. Recall, for example, that Italian interviewees did not see why *razza* would have anything to do with a group's integration into Italian society, because, in their eyes, it involved "only" skin color and nothing more. In contrast, American students easily linked race to all manner of outcomes and characteristics, such as educational attainment, health, values, and the experience of discrimination. Italians were clearly less accustomed to thinking about race or physical traits as a determining factor in individuals' life trajectories and in societal stratification.

Psychological Essentialism

Our interviews in both countries made amply clear that biology is not the only signal trait that can be associated with *essential* inheritance: the students also ascribed *temperaments* or *mentalities* to descent-based groups that appeared *fixed*, innate, and monolithic. This was particularly evident in our Italian respondents' commentary on two of the three "ancient others" we described in this book's introduction: the Muslim and above all the Romani. This belief that members of human descent-based groups—like animal breeds—inherit certain essential dispositions from their ancestors has a long pedigree. It hearkens back to very old European ideas about human behavior—including astrology, humoral theory, and animal husbandry—and to the race notion that drew on them all.²⁸ In this spirit, our Italian interviewees attributed dishonesty, laziness, and opportunism to the Roma and a penchant for violence and misogyny to Muslims, with such a sense of totality and permanence, that these characteristics could only be said to be essential or inborn. Tellingly, no one ever suggested that a Romani infant, adopted and raised by non-Romani parents, would be just like any other Italian child, even though several students made this claim for a hypothetical Asian or African child. That none of our interviewees voiced this possibility speaks, furthermore, to the *determinism* associated with psychological essentialism; the problematic temperaments that our Italian interviewees described were closely linked to outcomes—and above all to criminal behaviors like theft and assault.

Our U.S. interviewees were less likely than their Italian peers to articulate notions about group temperament, perhaps simply because Morning did not pose open-ended queries about their mental maps of difference or ask them to rate the likability of particular groups. Yet it seems likely that Linnaeus's attribution of distinct personality types to human races made its way to North America along with his color-coded taxonomy. After all, the racial stereotypes that circulate in the United States today often include imagined psychological traits. Intelligence and sexual proclivities are chief among these—think, for example, of the ostensibly hyposexual and intelligent Asian male versus the supposedly hypersexual and unintelligent black man. Violence, passivity, and other temperamental traits, however, are also recognizable in other stereotypes, including some that informed the American interviewees' comments on sport.

Such beliefs about inherited, fixed mental dispositions have not only different *scopes* in the United States and in Italy—that is, they are applied to different groups—but they also seem to have distinct *hierarchical* structures. With respect to Italy's "ancient others," we found dichotomies that contrasted an inferior "them" with a superior "us," the (often implicit) *reference group*. In our Italian respondents' eyes, the Roma were not simply one descent-based group among many, but a singular group against which all others could be favorably compared. Literally the least liked of all the groups we asked students to rate on our feeling thermometer, the Roma were in a class of their own at a full point below Muslims, the second least appreciated group.

In the classic racial framework that is institutionalized in the United States (and has deeply shaped the figures that we call "modern others" in Italy), the scope set is larger; not only does it include the original four Linnaean color-coded categories, but, it might be argued, it has been expanded in recent years to incorporate a "brown" category that includes Latinx, Middle Eastern and North African, South Asian, and other groups.[29] This expansion may make simple binary hierarchies unlikely (although note the U.S. census inclusion of an item that distinguishes "Hispanics or Latinos" from all others). Instead, psychological stereotypes may rely more on a continuum, with nonwhite groups representing the extremes between which whites, as the reference group, supposedly possess the optimal balance of mental qualities: neither hyposexual (like Asians) nor hypersexual (like blacks—or Latinos), neither unintelligent (like blacks or Latinos) nor purely cerebral (like Asians), whites are the Goldilocks of temperamental essentialism—always just right.[30] Here the superiority of the reference group operates by triangulation.[31]

Cultural Primordialism

An essentialist mechanism for producing fixed markers did not figure in the culture-based concept of descent-based difference we encountered in Italy as well as in the United States, but culture could be—and often was—the sign of alterity for what we might call "de-biologized" groups. In other words, descent-based groups, like Southern Italians and Eastern Europeans, who had been cast as physically distinct "races" a century ago—the former as *meridionali* in Italy and as "Mediterranean" in the United States, the latter as "Slavic" in both countries—were now seen as groups whose signature traits were the *cultural* products of *primordial* socialization, not biological inheritance.[32] This cultural model probably has the widest *scope* of any descent-based conceptualization in that it applies to the broadest range of groups, including both debiologized ones and ones that we could call "never-biologized" for never having been particularly salient, like Peruvians and Pakistanis. Cultural traditions, norms, and values are the presumptive basis for belonging to many communities of descent, and our interviewees routinely ascribed such practices and outlooks to immigrant groups and their descendants, though less often to regional minorities. These cultural depictions were often interlaced, however, with psychological essentialism; the criminalization of Eastern European groups offers an example of hybridization, which we will further explore shortly.

The broad array of descent-based groups to which our respondents applied a primordial culturalist lens might suggest that they were arranged in a flat, horizontal configuration rather than a vertical *hierarchy*. This might be the case in certain circumstances, such as the American students' recollections of their European immigrant ancestors' cultures.[33] At other times, however, a "good culture" versus "bad culture" hierarchy seemed to be in play—for example, in the U.S. interviewees' juxtaposition of a white "book culture" against a black "body culture" associated not just with physical pursuits but also with family dysfunction, drugs, and other forms of social deviance. Although the Italian respondents' attitudes toward culturalized groups did not follow the white-over-black racial ordering that colors attitudes in the United States, they did lionize an Italian culture to which newcomers should adapt, and they harshly criticized those groups they perceived as not doing so. In addition, the contrast between the Italians' positive remarks about European athletes' training and their disparagement of Asian competitors' regimes made clear that not all cultures were equal in their eyes.

Finally, a clear-cut divergence in Italian and American understandings of primordial cultural difference concerned its perceived *permanence* and, relatedly, its supposed *consequences*. There was a fixity and even at times an inevitability ascribed to cultural imprinting in Italy that veered toward essentialism. Not only did cultural markers seem to our Italian respondents to be harder to shake off or alter, but they were also perceived as having much more far-reaching and meaningful repercussions, such as forestalling integration. In their eyes, culture could be held responsible for anything from romantic discord to socioeconomic status. American students, in contrast, were more likely to expect that the customs and values of the immigrant generation would be all but lost by the second or third generation and would thus be of little consequence in the lives of its descendants. And as we will see next, the U.S. students were confident that individuals could and did make deliberate changes to their cultural habits at will.

Cultural Acquisition

A distinct, though less prominent, concept of descent-based difference that Italian as well as U.S. interviewees voiced was the idea that individuals could choose to adopt or *acquire* particular *cultural* practices, norms, or values that would warrant their membership in a particular descent-based group. This was a feature of the civic model of Italianness that we described in chapter 2, where some interviewees stated that anyone who obeyed the law, worked hard, assimilated Italian folkways, and contributed to the nation should be considered Italian. American respondents sometimes applied the same model to racial identity, observing that individuals should be free to choose their race and adopt the cultural practices they felt were consistent with that choice. This model was clearly based on a much more *fluid* understanding of descent-based difference than any of the others we have presented. Relatedly, its *scope* seemed limitless: a person might join any national, "racial," or "ethnic" group by dint of their cultural performance.[34] At the same time, no particular group was described as primarily composed of members who had deliberately acquired its defining traits, so it is difficult to say what *hierarchy*, if any, might obtain among such groups. The *determinism* of such traits also seems to be moot, or rather, the primary outcome of acquiring them was seen as simply gaining access to the desired descent group.

The cultural acquisition concept might be more of a rhetorical flight than a way of actually thinking about descent-based difference, much as social constructivism appeared to be in our two samples. It is unclear whether our U.S. interviewees really believed that a person could join the race of their choice based on their cultural consumption, for example, or whether their Italian counterparts truly felt that paying taxes and avoiding crime would turn immigrants into Italians. Instead, such claims may simply have been an appealing way of conveying an openness, inclusivity, and respect for individual autonomy that the students found morally desirable. Still, their observations about peers who were accepted in certain circles owing to behaviors that the respondents chalked up to culture—like the Romani coworker who was not really Romani because he did not "act like" other Roma, or the white roommate who dressed and talked like the black friends with whom he socialized—revealed that cultural acquisition was a possibility in their eyes, even if it was not one they entirely accepted or endorsed.

Hybrid Groups

Our interviews in Italy made clear that more than one conceptual regime could be brought to bear on a given descent-based group. Sometimes this was so thoroughly the case that it became difficult to distinguish primary or constitutive traits from secondary bases for group membership. In particular, Roma, Muslims, and Chinese seemed to have a hybrid status. And although the U.S. interviewees generally had less opportunity to discuss particular groups, we believe that current stereotypes in the United States routinely blend beliefs about varied bases of difference. We hypothesize, moreover, that any descent-based group that has been particularly salient or prominent in a society over time is likely to have become the object of multilayered beliefs about its defining characteristics.

Roma and Muslims in Italy, the "ancient others" with whom we associated the temperamental (psychological) essentialist concept of difference, were also frequently portrayed as bearers of primordial—and barbaric, highly objectionable—cultures. Romani people were accused of raising their children to steal and beg, and Muslims of inculcating misogyny and fanaticism. Indeed, it was the marriage of innate disposition and willful practice in the depictions of these two groups that seemed to provoke the unrepentant hostility of our Italian respondents. Both temperament and culture were thought to feed their supposedly outrageous, incomprehensible, and antisocial behaviors—and thus to justify the unparalleled hatred directed toward them. On the one hand, the human agency in cultural socialization holds individuals (and groups) responsible, leaving behavior open to moral judgment— hence the visceral condemnation to which our Italian interviewees subjected Roma and Muslims. On the other hand, an essentialist behavioral concept focused on innate dispositions warns that change is impossible, opening the door to subjugation, expulsion, or elimination.

Similarly, Italians' depictions of the Chinese revealed another hybrid essentialist-primordial concept of descent-based difference, but in this case it was biological (rather than psychological) traits that were most entwined with culture. As we saw throughout our conversations with Italian students, it was virtually impossible for them to speak of Chinese people without alluding to their perceived physical otherness. This was consistent with the students' tendency to use "Chinese" as an abstract proxy for "East Asian," recalling the large-scale racial category (*Homo asiaticus*) of Linnaeus. At other times, however, the Chinese were invoked more as an immigrant group of a distinct national origin, and in those instances the idea of a particular culture (and geopolitical status) came to the fore. The result was a recurring dual conceptualization of the Chinese as deeply physically marked (like blacks) as well as endowed with a recognizable, static, and threatening but impressive cultural repertory. Italian images of Chinese people exemplify Guillaumin's insight that where culture appears in descent-based conceptualization, biology is never far behind, and vice versa.[35]

These examples also reveal that hybrids may even involve three-way combinations, a configuration that is also relevant to the United States. Although the Roma were depicted in our Italian interviews as marked primarily by their temperamental and cultural orientations, they also have a history of being portrayed as physically distinct.[36] And the students' frequent description of the Chinese as "closed" verged on a psychological essentialism, adding to this group's perceived physical and cultural distinctiveness.

In the United States, where understandings of descent-based difference are anchored in the classic racial framework that is institutionalized in official U.S. categories, it should come as no surprise that descent-based groups are associated with the multiple forms of difference that were enumerated in eighteenth-century taxonomies.[37] In the same way that Linnaeus's descriptions of human races alluded to their physical, temperamental, and behavioral qualities, American stereotypes today often touch on all three of these realms. As in Italy, however, they place more weight on some types of traits than others. As De Genova has noted, indigenous, Asian, and Latinx Americans—but not African Americans—are strongly associated with cultural difference (from an implicit white reference group).[38] Blacks and Asians are perhaps most strongly linked to physical difference, as in Italy. And all of these nonwhite groups are typecast as having various psychological dispositions, from impassivity to passivity to passion, among others.

Our data from Italy as well as the United States underscore how multifaceted the conceptualization of descent-based difference is. More than one notion of such difference can inhabit the same society. An individual's perspective can be shaped by more than one model of difference, even if they contradict each other. And concepts of difference themselves are composed of multiple elements, giving rise to myriad potential variants; we have identified four as being particularly prominent in our samples of interviewees, but many other combinations might prevail in other times and places. Paying attention to the details that distinguish them, however, is especially important when making comparisons between two "cultural cousins" like the United States and Italy; contrary to the "new racism" hypothesis, there are so many similarities between these two countries that the divergences become particularly meaningful. The family resemblance and two-way traffic between their cultural products and imaginaries make a reflexive, subtle, and precise approach vital for facing the challenge of transatlantic comparison.

Renewing the Transatlantic Conversation on Race

European versus American arguments about the discursive and analytical uses of race stand to benefit from a careful examination and comparison of concepts of descent-based difference in both places. Simple claims about whether race exists or not on one side of the ocean or the other lump together distinct conceptual creations whose subtle (and not so subtle) variations are not only evident when we know where to look for them, but also tell us a great deal about the societies in which they have been spun together. To avoid eliding race with its conceptual similars (such as essentialisms without somatic markers), we will need more dedicated empirical research on the conceptualization of descent-based difference worldwide. Such new and finer-grained research will also help disentangle concepts of difference from the rhetoric in which they are couched. As our interviews with young Italians and Americans showed, striking discursive divergences can mask extensive conceptual convergences when it comes to thinking about difference. Treating concepts of difference as multifaceted complexes of belief, and distinguishing them from rhetoric, would help unknot the European versus American scholarly tangle over race in at least three ways.

First, the term "concept of descent-based difference" simply offers a more neutral, straightforward, and elastic linguistic alternative to "race." (In Romance languages, however, the expression might be more easily translated as "genealogical difference.") This is meaningful because some of the antagonism that arises when "race" is named—or not—is due to the fact that academics on either side of the Atlantic read different things into it. Writing "race," U.S. scholars in the humanities and social sciences today often mean "the construct of race": an idea about human difference that has become a social force in its own right. But European scholars read it to mean "the taxonomy of biological races," as if Americans were asserting, or taking for granted even, the matter-of-fact existence of biological sub-species called races and their objective effects in society. And to be fair, it is not always clear whether U.S. researchers—or journalists or politicians or doctors—are doing the former or the latter. Should Americans be careful to consistently specify "the idea," "the social construction," the "ideology," or the "social fact" of race? Perhaps, but for international social-scientific purposes, the language of "concepts of difference" leaves no doubt that we are referring to human beliefs, not taken-for-granted groupings.

In a related vein, we must recognize that the U.S.-European debate concerning race-blind versus race-conscious speech actually has little to do with concepts of difference per se; it is driven instead by clashing convictions about the impact of "racial" speech. In this arena, racial discourse can be likened to a double-edged sword, and the transatlantic conflict over its use is fundamentally a disagreement over whether the victories of one blade outweigh the devastation wrought by the other. Can race-conscious laws, programs, and speech further an agenda of social justice, even when they may simultaneously reify an ideology of difference that was born—and still displays the marks—of domination and inequality? Although this question is hotly debated within national boundaries—as shown by controversies over critical race theory in the United States, "Islamo-leftism" in France, or affirmative action in those countries and others—it can also be said to vary across them. Roughly put, Americans tend to believe in the potential for beating the sword of race into a plowshare, transforming it into an effective instrument of antidiscrimination policy.[39] Western Europeans, in contrast, have expressed more caution, often judging the sword of race as simply too dangerous to be wielded under any circumstance.

The risks and rewards associated with this powerful tool help explain both the heightened sensitivity around it and the difficulty of coming to a shared cross-national view regarding its use in policy, academic, and other public spheres, not to mention in the private discourse that our interviews explore. Both vantage points on the sword of race are deeply anchored in history and provoke real emotion, resulting in something of a transatlantic impasse that has made it hard to cross over and make sense of arguments on the other shore. The stalemate has dragged on, moreover, in the absence of empirical adjudication between them. This state of affairs cries out, then, for a serious social-scientific effort to examine the extent to which explicit references to race or other forms of descent-based difference actually facilitate or hinder attempts to build more just and inclusive societies.

Once we recognize that these debates about the utility of the race concept are fueled by a largely implicit or unspoken set of assumptions about the societal consequences of "race" language, we can also see what they overlook: namely, the crucial question of the actual state of descent-based conceptualization in society today, and not the wished-for normative condition. If we fully recognized that it is the existing system of beliefs about difference and its material reality—and not merely the desired one—that lends urgency to the matter of constitutional and census language, for example, we might embrace an agenda that has little preoccupied the opponents of "race" wording in law or social science but would no doubt be more far-reaching. Specifically, we would turn to the task of revising school curricula to ensure that children of all ages come to understand that the descent-based groups that populate our lives and, above all, our imaginations are ones that we make, remake, and unmake. Our interviews in Italy and the United States should serve as a wake-up call to equip young people with the conceptual tools they need to make sense of—and contribute to—the increasingly diverse societies in which they live. Truly comprehending the social construction of our categories would go a long way toward curbing their use for discrimination and domination.

The injunction against "race" mention makes sense in a society where essentialist beliefs about physical and behavioral group differences no longer circulate, and where there are no "whites" or "blacks" and no hierarchy of superiority, normativity, value, or desirability between them. Neither the United States nor Italy—nor France or the rest of the Western world—meet that standard at present, and no amount of linguistic policing—or for that matter, unthinking embrace—of "race" will suffice to reach it. Variants of the eighteenth-century European color taxonomy are alive and well in all of them, and it is of fundamental importance that we explore and document empirically just what these concepts are, in all their diversity, before deciding how policy and its language might best attend to that social reality.

Though aspirational and normative in nature, law and public policy must be firmly rooted in social fact.

A useful analogy, developed by Karen Fields and Barbara Fields, is between race and witchcraft.[40] It would surely be odd today to maintain a line in a Western constitution forbidding discrimination on the basis of being a witch; few believe in witches now, so they are no longer the socially salient, real, or persecuted category that they were just a few centuries ago.[41] One might reasonably fear, moreover, that including a mention of witches as a protected class under the law or in official documents might have the adverse effect of conjuring up belief in them where no such credence had previously existed. But if instead the conviction that witches existed were still widespread, it would be appropriate and useful to recognize the social reality of the concept—without going to the other extreme of reifying witches as natural phenomena—in order to use policy tools to eradicate the belief and its attendant prejudices and exclusions. As much as we might like to believe that race and its ilk belong to the category of bygone supernatural beliefs, the empirical data that we social scientists encounter tell us that it is too soon to consign them to the dustbin of history.

Instead, our shared beliefs about descent-based difference remain major forces behind diverse projects for gaining, bolstering, or rearranging power. And perhaps contrary to common assumption, it is not the grounds for difference per se—like culture or biology—that determines their utility for such political, economic, and social enterprises. Instead, it is the broader array of conceptual elements—including the ostensible mechanism for the production of group difference and its scope, as well as the degrees of hierarchy, permanence, and determinism—that make for the social functionality of a given notion of difference. Understanding these concepts in all their complexity, then, is a crucial first step before we enter into scholarly and policy debate about how to name, describe, manage, and perhaps even banish them.

APPENDIX A

Interview Data and Methodology

The Interview Samples

The Italian Sample

This book analyzes 106 semistructured interviews that we conducted with young Italians, most of them between the ages of nineteen and twenty-four, in order to explore their notions of descent-based difference.[1] Beginning with a few pilot interviews in 2010, we went on to complete the bulk of them from 2012 to 2013, focusing on three cities: Milan in the North, Bologna toward the center of Italy, and Naples in the South. In this way we prepared for the possibility that concepts of difference might vary depending on our interviewees' relationships to Italy's historical North-South divide.

Our objective of drawing comparisons to the sample of college students that Morning had interviewed in the United States placed certain constraints on our research design in Italy. For one thing, we needed to interview people in a similar age range, retaining the focus on college students and even the effort to include students in certain disciplines (namely, anthropology and biology) as well as to balance those in the social and natural sciences. We also expanded the Italian sample, however, relative to the American one. Not only is it twice as large (*n* = 106 compared to 52 in the United States), but it also includes students in educational institutions that are less elite than universities. Thirty-one of our Italian respondents were enrolled in *scuole professionali*; in these vocational training schools that are an alternative to high school, it was not hard to find interviewees of the same age as our college respondents. The Italian sample is also more geographically diverse, spanning North to South, whereas Morning's U.S. interviews were all conducted in one region of the country, the Northeast.

To identify potential interviewees, we first selected the major public universities of the cities that we were targeting: the University of Bologna (Università degli Studi di Bologna), the University of Naples (Università degli Studi di Napoli Federico II), and the two Universities of Milan (Università degli Studi di Milano), Bicocca and Statale. In Naples, we also recruited undergraduate students from the private Università degli Studi Suor Orsola Benincasa (University of Suor Orsola Benincasa) in order to include students from a wider range of majors than those at Federico II. At the universities, we aimed to recruit students from specific disciplines across the traditional divisions of science, social science, and humanities, namely: anthropology, biology, biotechnology, chemistry, history, psychology, sociology, and *beni culturali* (cultural heritage).

We also selected four vocational schools in Milan in order to add a non-university subset of interviews: Ferraris-Pacinotti Istituto Professionale per l'Industria e l'Artigianato and Istituto Professionale Bertarelli, two institutions now combined to specialize in mechanical trades like electronics and industrial chemistry; D. Marignoni Marco Polo Istituto Professionale di Stato per i Servizi Commerciali e Turistici, for students interested in business and the hospitality industry; and Istituto Superiore Marelli-Dudovich, where students can major in fashion design, health care, or web design, among other areas of study.

To solicit interviewees, we employed different approaches in line with the requirements of these varied institutions. For our pilot interviews at the University of Milan–Bicocca, Maneri made brief presentations in introductory courses, after which instructors passed around a sign-up sheet for interested potential respondents. In the vocational *scuole professionali* of Milan, administrators presented our project in classes and collected the names and contact information of interested students to pass on to us. At the University of Naples Federico II, departmental administrators selected and contacted undergraduate majors for us, asking them to reach out to us if they were interested in participating in our study. The other universities gave us

Table A.1 Selected Sample Characteristics

CHARACTERISTIC	PERCENTAGE OF SAMPLE (n = 106)
Gender	
Female	51
Male	49
Geographic origin and location	
Born and studying in the North of Italy	47
Born and studying in the North of Italy; parent(s) from the South	16
Born in the South; studying in the North of Italy	14
Born and studying in the South	23
Area: City of interview and institution type	
North: Milan (vocational school)	29
North: Milan (university)	27
North: Bologna (university)	21
South: Naples (university)	23
University major	
Anthropology or cultural heritage	19
History	19
Psychology	21
Sociology	8
Biology or biotechnology	21
Chemistry	12
Highest level of parental educational attainment	
University degree	26
High school (liceo)	19
High school (technical or magistrali)	31
Middle school	24

Source: Authors' tabulation.

the names and telephone numbers of students in the majors we selected; we used this information as frames for randomly sampling and then contacting potential interviewees. In general, when soliciting respondents, we described the project as focusing on "*italianità*—that is, what you think characterizes Italians and distinguishes them from other people," and we also noted that we would "ask for your views on immigration, ethnicity, and integration."

The resultant composition of our sample is described in table A.1. It is important to note, however, that we restricted it to native-born Italians, with the result that it was an entirely white sample.[2]

We did most of the interviews ourselves, with Maneri conducting thirty-four interviews across all three sites and Morning conducting twenty-eight in Milan and Bologna. We also benefited, however, from the help of three Italian research assistants. Gabriella Sarracino interviewed twenty undergraduates in Naples, while Roberta Marzorati and Daniela Cherubini interviewed thirteen and eleven vocational school students, respectively, in the Milanese periphery. On average, the interviews lasted ninety minutes and were usually conducted on school premises (in borrowed offices, empty classrooms, or meeting rooms). Afterwards, the interview audio recordings were professionally transcribed.

The U.S. Sample

The U.S. sample to which we compare our Italian data was collected by Morning from 2001 to 2002. Her study consisted of fifty-two open-ended interviews conducted with undergraduate students at four Northeastern universities, which she gave pseudonyms in order to protect the confidentiality of the faculty she also interviewed there. "Ivy" and "Pilot" were private, highly selective universities with undergraduate admissions rates around 10 percent, while "State" and "City" were public institutions that had admitted more than 60 percent of their undergraduate applicants for the 2001–2002 academic year.[3] The interview sample was stratified so that roughly one-third of the students at each school were randomly selected from the pool of anthropology majors, another third were selected randomly from biology majors, and the remaining third were chosen at random regardless of major. The sample was structured this way to investigate the understandings of race that are transmitted through formal education in the social and biological sciences that have the longest history of defining the nature of race. For more details about the study's research design and interviewee characteristics, please see *The Nature of Race: How Scientists Think and Teach about Human Difference.*[4]

The sample that resulted was 63 percent female and 73 percent non-Hispanic white. Nearly 60 percent of the interviewees hailed from the U.S. Northeast, while 12 percent were foreign-born. More than two-thirds reported having a father in a professional occupation, and over half said the same of their mothers. In other words, the U.S. sample was somewhat more female and definitely more diverse in its ancestral geographic origins than the larger Italian sample. Our U.S. interviewees were also from more privileged backgrounds, judging by parental occupation; this should not be surprising since the sample included only university undergraduates, whereas roughly one-third of the Italian sample was made up of vocational school students. (For this reason, we occasionally draw comparisons only between the university students in the two countries.) Finally, the decade separating the data collection for the two studies raises the question of whether any differences in their results might be attributed to the passage of time. As we show, however, a considerable amount of similarity characterizes the concepts of difference we encountered in the two national settings despite this time lag.

Comparative Sociology and the Challenges of Equivalence

Although we tailored our Italian sample to allow for comparisons to the college-focused interviews that Morning had conducted in the United States, the question protocol we constructed in Italian was very different from its American predecessor. This difference was due in part to disparate research questions: Morning's study focused on the role of formal education in transmitting scientists' views of race to the American public, whereas in Italy we aimed to take a broader measure of young Italians' views of descent-based difference.

A major reason for the difference between the two interview question-naires, however, was our sense that the term "race"—*razza* in Italian—could not be deployed as casually in the Italian context as in the American. Because *razza* is not as everyday or institutionalized a word in Italy as "race" is in the United States, its meanings are something to be explored rather than presumed. Although some scholars may be tempted to treat "race"—along with "ethnicity"—as etic terms that are universally used and understood similarly, we contend that these are emic concepts; employed in different ways, they are salient to varying degrees in varied societies, until proven otherwise. Our approach aligns with Frank Bovenkerk, Robert Miles, and Gilles Verbunt's call to "be prepared to inquire whether people are in fact referring to the same thing in different countries when they speak of immigration, ethnic minorities or racism."[5] Indeed, the general methodological challenge of cross-cultural equivalence that comparative analyses must confront—namely, how to find the equivalent terms and concepts across different national settings and languages—is at the heart of our project on imaginaries of difference.[6]

Three kinds of equivalence problem—contextual, conceptual, and measurement—prevented us from simply contrasting "racial" conceptualization in the United States and Italy.[7] Although there is a straightforward lexical translation of English "race" to Italian *razza*, with both words rooted in the same etymology, such facile "transcription" is no guarantee of a deeper equivalence.[8] "Theoretical '*faux amis*' ('false friends') based on a mere lexicological facsimile (minority for *minorité*, *profession* for liberal profession, etc.)" can obscure the fact that "these morphologically twinned words are separated by the whole set of differences between the social system in which they were produced and the new system in which they are introduced."[9] For one thing, contextual equivalence, which is based on the comparability of the uses to which terms are put, can be deceiving. The Italian word *razza*—like the Spanish *raza*—might seem to be a good contextual equivalent for "race" in English, to the extent that they can all be used to denote groups of human beings. But both *razza* and *raza* come with an additional association—that of a "breed" of animal—that makes them a problematic substitute for American English "race."[10] (Imagine being asked to fill out your "breed" on the U.S. census form!)

Even thornier is the issue of conceptual equivalence. We could not assume that *razza* conjured up for Italians the same groups, ascribed characteristics, or societal outcomes that "race" did for Americans; indeed, exploring just what these terms meant to our interviewees was at the heart of our research. These contextual and conceptual dissimilarities in turn had implications for measurement equivalence, or "whether the instruments used in separate societies in fact measure the same concept, regardless of whether the manifest content and procedures are identical or not."[11] In other words, what language or approach does a researcher use to convey or measure certain concepts across cultural settings?

The Interview Protocol

To get at people's concepts of difference, we chose to conduct semistructured, in-depth interviews as a way of obtaining rich, detailed data through a method that allowed for open-ended exploration as well as the possibility of follow-up probing. But as is well known, face-to-face interviews like ours come with the disadvantage that they can easily induce socially desirable responses that mask subjects' true ideas and feelings, especially on topics that may be perceived as sensitive, like group difference. As a result, we sequenced our questions to proceed from less delicate topics to ones that were more so at the end.

To avoid leading off with—or relying unduly on—a term like "race," which we feared could be highly problematic for our interviewees, we organized the Italian interview protocol as follows. (See appendix B for the questionnaire in both Italian and English.) First, after posing a few biographical questions, we asked respondents about their notions of *italianità* (Italianness): Who did they think of as Italian? Who in the country did they not consider Italian? What characteristics distinguished Italians from others? And could non-Italians become Italian? The goal here was to identify which descent-based groups were particularly salient for interviewees, and which characteristics tended to be ascribed to them, all without imposing terms like "race" and "ethnicity" or prompting respondents to think about specific groups. In short, following Michèle Lamont, we tried to elicit people's "mental maps" of Italy's communities of descent rather than make presumptions ourselves about which categories, groupings, or forms of difference would be salient for our respondents.[12]

Only after interviewees had had the opportunity to elaborate on their views of heterogeneity in Italy did we introduce the terms "ethnicity" and "race," respectively, by asking them to define these words, give examples of ethnic and racial groups, and describe the kinds of difference they associated with each. We also exhumed the older nomenclature of "Caucasoid," "Negroid," and "Mediterranean" races to see if they still had any purchase in contemporary Italy. (We found that they did not).[13]

Although the bulk of our questions allowed for open-ended responses, we used some closed scales as well. These were printed on a worksheet to which we asked respondents to turn at various points in the conversation; they were meant both to facilitate comparisons within the sample and to the U.S. interviewees and to provide a jumping-off point for open-ended discussions of our Italian respondents' beliefs. In this way, interviewees indicated numerically the degree of difference they perceived between Italians and others in terms of culture, nature, or social condition; expressed the extent of their agreement or disagreement with statements about biological races and about the potential for integration into Italian society of varied types of groups; positioned themselves along the political spectrum from left to right; and, above all, ranked a series of twenty groups (such as "Romanians" and "Chinese") in terms of their likability (being more or less *simpatico*).

Given the attention we paid to drawing up an Italian interview instrument that would elicit respondents' "mental maps" of descent-based difference without presuming or imposing the salience of race, some but not all of its items allow for direct comparison to Morning's results in the United States.[14] The definitional questions about the term "race" were used in both countries, as was the closed question about the existence of biological races. Moreover, a similar technique—if not exactly the same questioning—was used in two additional items we employed to understand interviewees' notions of difference. Specifically, we presented two empirical scenarios to be explained (regarding criminality and sports performance for Italian respondents; regarding a medical outcome and sports performance for U.S. respondents) in order to gauge how respondents used their concepts of descent-based difference concretely in reasoning about observed outcomes. For more detail on the interview protocol that Morning followed in the United States, see the questionnaire in appendix C.

Analysis and Writing

We began our analysis of the interview data during Morning's time as a 2014–2015 Visiting Scholar at the Russell Sage Foundation coupled with Maneri's sabbatical from the University of Milan–Bicocca. In general, we followed the iterative and cyclical techniques of open, axial, and systematic coding developed by Anselm Strauss, and we implemented them using Atlas.ti software.[15] First we divvied up different sections of the interview to be coded by one author or the other, but for each topic we collaborated on establishing the initial list of inductive codes to be applied. We began by separately "open coding"—that is, generating codes inductively—within the topic-relevant passages in a subset of interviews and then comparing notes on the codes we each thought important to use; the result was a jointly developed starting list of codes. Next, each of us sought separately to apply these codes systematically to the selected passages in our trial subset of interviews, in order to ensure intercoder reliability. In this way we arrived at a consensus about key codes to apply and about when and where to apply them. Once we had established these basic rules, each of us focused on applying the codes for our assigned topics to all the interviews in our sample and on further developing and adding to them in the interpretive and analytical process that Strauss labels "axial coding."[16]

Throughout the process of coding and its concomitant analytical work, we relied extensively on the annotation of our codes (using Atlas.ti's "comment" feature for codes) and on the writing of dozens of memos regarding each phase of coding. Not only did these notes provide us with a ready "dictionary" for the meanings of the hundreds of codes we generated and the motives for their development, but our memos in particular documented the observations, questions, hypotheses, and findings that emerged.

Although qualitative analysis was central to our attempt to understand the subtleties of the ideas that our interviewees expressed, we also used quantitative tools at times. Simple descriptive statistics such as frequencies of the mentions of certain ideas, shares of interviewees expressing a particular belief, or the prevalence of co-occurring mentions (for example, pairing "Muslims" with "non-Italians") all helped to convey a sense of the patterns we identified. However, we relied on the texture and contours of respondents' language to delve most deeply into their cosmologies of descent-based difference. Here, Atlas.ti's capacity to pull up subsets of quotations or passages that we wanted to scrutinize together, or to compare and contrast, significantly facilitated our work.

The likelihood of some socially desirable commentary on the topic of descent-based difference also led us to pay considerable attention to aspects of the respondents' language beyond their overt declarations. For one thing, we kept track of expressions of uncertainty, ambivalence, embarrassment, and so on, effectively heeding Bonnet's call for treating social desirability as worthy of study in itself, rather than as simply a research flaw to be remedied.[17] For another, we took careful note of what was only hinted at, or what was simply left unsaid.[18] We noted, for instance, that certain descent-based groups were referenced for certain kinds of arguments but not others.

Despite the limits to any claims we might make about having fully unveiled our respondents' most deeply held worldviews, we contend that their words nonetheless brought to light a fabric of widespread and subtly textured ideas— "a slow accumulation of images, commonplaces, set phrases and cultural schema" and "locally available social categories"—that can fruitfully be compared across national settings.[19] Like Lamont and her colleagues, we understand the interviews as "significant expressions of intersubjectively shared classification systems or collective representations as they manifest and are captured at one point in time"—sometimes in a cavernous, empty lecture hall in Milan in front of a female U.S. professor of color, and perhaps at others in a cramped, sunlit office in Bologna with a white male Italian sociologist.[20] Although we found surprisingly little difference in the gist of what our interviewees told either Ann, the "naive American outsider," or Marcello, the "native Italian insider," the binational cooperation behind the project seemed to leave an impression on many of them and channeled some of their reflections toward U.S.-Italy comparisons.

Drafting the book manuscript was also a multilayered process, and one that was more of a cross-national struggle than either of us had anticipated. Each of us wrote separate chapters in our native languages, later translating Maneri's Italian into English. Naively assuming that a good translator would produce texts that could be seamlessly interspersed with Morning's English chapters, we were taken aback when we realized that our very good translator had delivered nominally English text that was so faithful to the Italian original that it often preserved a Latin vocabulary that sounded stiff to American ears. Most of all, the translations left intact a style that flowed in Italian but seemed meandering to a U.S. social scientist of the hyperstructured and formulaic *Craft of Research* school of writing: "topic sentence"–claim-warrant-evidence.[21] The final steps, then, in putting together a monograph that spoke with one voice were to (a) structure the exposition of each chapter's argument in a more uniform (and admittedly U.S.-centric) style; and (b) enlist an American editor to smooth over the translated language. In other words, true to an inquiry focused on concepts and discourse about descent-based difference, we vividly experienced and had to work through national differences in not just our own worldviews, but in our very ways of expressing them.[22]

Italian Interview Questionnaire and Worksheet with English Translations

OUR INTERVIEWS in Italy were based on both a protocol of largely open-ended questions that an interviewer posed to respondents in person and a worksheet that the interviewee filled out during the course of the conversation. The questionnaire and worksheet appear here in the original Italian, followed by our translations into English.

Questionnaire: Italian Original

Intervista #: _____ Data: _____

Intervistato/a da: _____

Luogo: _____ Corso: _____

M / F _____

A. Background

Vorrei cominciare la nostra intervista con alcune domande su di te e la tua famiglia.

   1. Quanti anni hai?
   2. Dove abiti? Sei cresciuto/a lì?

3. I tuoi genitori sono nati lì o da un'altra parte?
4. E che lavoro fanno?
   Padre: _____ Madre: _____
5. Cosa hanno studiato? Quale titolo di studio hanno?
   Padre: _____ Madre: _____
6. Tu cosa hai studiato alle superiori?

B. *Definizione delle Differenze tra Gruppi*

Adesso ti vorrei invitare a riflettere un po' sugli italiani e gli altri.

7. Se dovessi spiegare *chi* dovrebbe essere considerato come parte del popolo italiano, cosa diresti?
8. Al giorno di oggi vivono anche *in Italia* molte persone che non sono considerate italiane. Quali sono i gruppi che ti vengono in mente per primi?
9. In generale, secondo te quali sono le differenze principali tra italiani e non-italiani *in Italia*?
10. Possono i non-italiani *in Italia* diventare italiani?
11. *(Se la risposta a [10] è "Sì," chiedi: "Come?" Se invece la risposta a [10] è "No," chiedi: "Perché no?")*

Passiamo adesso a un altro genere di domande. Ti chiederò di darmi delle definizioni di due termini.

12. Come definiresti il termine "etnia"?
13. Puoi dare degli esempi di gruppi etnici?
14. E quindi, in generale, quali sono le caratteristiche che distinguono un gruppo etnico da un altro?
15. Come definiresti il termine "razza"? *(Se la risposta è che le razze non esistono, chiedi: "Su quale tipo di differenza si fonda allora il razzismo?")*
16. Puoi dare degli esempi di gruppi razziali?
17. È questo un elenco completo delle razze?
18. E invece il gruppo "caucasoide" è una razza secondo te?
19. E il gruppo "negroide"?
20. E il gruppo "mediterraneo"?
21. E quindi, in generale, quali sono le caratteristiche che distinguono un gruppo razziale da un altro?

22. Le tue definizioni di razza o etnia sono state influenzate da quello che hai studiato a scuola o all'università? Avete mai toccato questi argomenti? Cosa vi hanno insegnato?

23. E sempre parlando delle tue definizioni credi che siano state influenzate da altre fonti di conoscenza? Letture, conversazioni, media, genitori, amici?

24. A proposito delle differenze tra gruppi, vorremmo sapere come vedi le differenze tra italiani ed extracomunitari *in Italia*. Ti sembra di poter dire che le loro differenze sono di tipo culturale (usanze, religioni), sociale (cittadinanza, reddito, istruzione), o biologiche (somatiche, genetiche)?

25. *(Mostrare il worksheet, section A, "Scale di Differenza")* Per riassumere, dove collocheresti il grado di differenza tra italiani ed extracomunitari in Italia in queste tre scale? *(Controllare che le risposte siano coerenti con quanto detto nelle domande precedenti, altrimenti chiedere spiegazioni.)*

26. *(Sempre sul worksheet, section A, "Scale di Differenza")* Adesso ti chiederei di esprimere il tuo grado di accordo/disaccordo con la seguente affermazione, usando questa scala: "Ci sono razze biologiche nella specie *Homo sapiens*."

   1. Per niente d'accordo
   2. Poco d'accordo
   3. Né d'accordo né in disaccordo
   4. Abbastanza d'accordo
   5. Molto d'accordo

27. Perché sei d'accordo/in disaccordo?

C. Spiegazioni delle Differenze

Adesso ti descrivo due fenomeni attuali dove sono state osservate delle differenze tra gruppi. Nei due casi ti chiederò di provare a fornire delle possibili spiegazioni di queste differenze. Non mi interessa che tu dia la spiegazione "giusta," ammesso che esista, ma di fornire una o più spiegazioni plausibili.

28. La prima problematica ha a che vedere con la criminalità. Secondo alcuni dati gli immigrati in Italia hanno proporzionalmente un

maggiore coinvolgimento in attività illegali. Secondo te quali sono le possibili spiegazioni? Ti sembra ci siano altre possibili spiegazioni?

29. Quale spiegazione ti sembra la più plausibile? Perché?

30. La seconda osservazione ha a che fare con lo sport: Ai mondiali o alle olimpiadi certi sport sono dominati da particolari gruppi di popolazione. Ad esempio gli atleti di origine africana ("neri") dominano da molti anni le gare di velocità su pista. Ma invece non si trovano quasi mai in altri sport come il nuoto. Secondo te quali sono le possibili spiegazioni? Ti sembra ci siano altre possibili spiegazioni?

31. Quale spiegazione ti sembra la più plausibile? Perché?

32. *(Se vengono menzionate differenze fisiche o biologiche tra razze)* Da dove vengono, come si spiegano queste differenze?

33. *(Se vengono menzionate solo differenze che attribuiscono una superiorità fisica agli atleti di origine africana)* Come spiegheresti allora il dominio di atleti di origine europea ("bianchi") in sport come il nuoto?

D. Domande a Risposta Chiusa

(Mostrare il worksheet, section B, "Affermazioni") Ora ti presento alcune affermazioni. Puoi esprimere il tuo grado di accordo/disaccordo usando la scala che ti mostriamo?

1. Per niente d'accordo
2. Poco d'accordo
3. Né d'accordo né in disaccordo
4. Abbastanza d'accordo
5. Molto d'accordo

34. "Alcune culture non sono integrabili nella società italiana." (1, 2, 3, 4, 5)

35. "Alcune etnie non sono integrabili nella società italiana." (1, 2, 3, 4, 5)

36. "Alcune razze non sono integrabili nella società italiana." (1, 2, 3, 4, 5)

37. "Un figlio di immigrati, nato e cresciuto in Italia, sarà in tutto e per tutto come un italiano." (1, 2, 3, 4, 5)

38. "Un figlio di meridionali, nato e cresciuto nel nord d'Italia, sarà in tutto e per tutto come un settentrionale." (1, 2, 3, 4, 5)

39. Puoi dire *perché* sei d'accordo/in disaccordo con le affermazioni su culture/etnie/razze non integrabili?

- Culture
- Etnie
- Razze

40. Puoi dire *perché* sei d'accordo/in disaccordo con le affermazioni sui nati e cresciuti in Italia?

- Immigrati
- Meridionali

E. Identità e Atteggiamenti

Adesso ti vorrei fare alcune domande sulle tue esperienze personali in termini di etnia, di razza, o di nazionalità.

41. Abbiamo parlato di vari gruppi che si possono distinguere in base alle proprie origini. Pensando alle tue origini tu come ti definiresti?
42. Perché?
43. Hai o hai avuto contatti con persone di origine straniera? *(Se "sì": "Me li puoi descrivere?")*
44. Spesso abbiamo maggiori simpatie o antipatie personali verso questo o quel gruppo. Potresti dire, per ciascuno dei seguenti gruppi, se ti è più o meno simpatico? *(Mostrare il worksheet, section C, "Termometro di Simpatia")*

Italiani	Cattolici	Albanesi
Extracomunitari	Ebrei	Marocchini
Europei	Musulmani	Senegalesi
Immigrati	Settentrionali	Nigeriani
Clandestini	Meridionali	Cinesi
Rom	Rumeni	Pakistani
		Peruviani

45. Potresti spiegare le scelte che hai fatto?

46. Queste scelte derivano da esperienze dirette, cose che hai sentito da altre persone, insegnanti/docenti, media? *(Porre questa domanda per ogni affermazione data nella risposta precedente.)*

F. Politiche

Chiuderemo l'intervista con una serie di domande di natura politica.

47. In alcuni paesi europei per ottenere la cittadinanza bisogna superare un test di conoscenza della lingua, delle norme, della storia o della cultura del paese di arrivo. Secondo te la concessione della cittadinanza italiana dovrebbe essere basata su uno o più di questi criteri? *(Se la risposta è "Sì," chiedi: "Quali? E dunque, chi non passasse il test dovrebbe essere escluso dalla cittadinanza?")*

48. In alcune classi nelle scuole italiane gli studenti di origine straniera sono la maggioranza. Secondo alcuni questo ha delle conseguenze negative. Secondo te la percentuale di stranieri nelle classi dovrebbe essere limitata entro una certa quota? (Sì/No) Perché?

49. In alcuni paesi in occasione del censimento viene chiesto agli intervistati a che razza appartengono. In altri invece quale sia l'etnia di provenienza. In altri ancora vengono fatte domande sul paese di origine proprio o dei propri genitori. Secondo te sarebbe utile introdurre anche da noi alcune di queste domande? (Sì/No) Perché?

50. *(Se la risposta a [49] è "Sì," chiedi: "Quali?" Se la risposta è "No" chiedi: "Nemmeno per indagare l'esistenza della discriminazione?")*

51. *(Mostrare il worksheet, section D, "Politica")* Alcuni si definiscono di centro, altri di destra o di sinistra. Potresti dirmi in una scala da 1 a 10 la posizione che corrisponde alle tue idee/valori politici, considerando che 1 = estrema sinistra, 5 e 6 = centro, e 10 = estrema destra?

Sinistra				Centro				Destra	
1	2	3	4	5	6	7	8	9	10

52. Ti ringrazio molto per le tue risposte. C'è qualcos'altro che vorresti aggiungere—ad esempio su qualcosa che non ho chiesto?
53. Ci sono delle domande che vorresti farmi?

Grazie!

Note

Worksheet: Italian Original

A. Scale di Differenza

1. Dove collocheresti il grado di differenza tra italiani ed extracomunitari in Italia in queste tre scale?

Cultura

Uguali				Diversi
I	2	3	4	5

Natura

Uguali				Diversi
I	2	3	4	5

Condizione sociale

Uguali				Diversi
I	2	3	4	5

2. Puoi esprimere il tuo grado di accordo o disaccordo con la seguente affermazione? "Ci sono razze biologiche nella specie *Homo sapiens*."

1. Per niente d'accordo
2. Poco d'accordo
3. Né d'accordo né in disaccordo
4. Abbastanza d'accordo
5. Molto d'accordo

B. Affermazioni

Qui di seguito trovi alcune affermazioni. Puoi esprimere il tuo grado di accordo/disaccordo usando la scala che ti mostriamo?

1. Per niente d'accordo
2. Poco d'accordo
3. Né d'accordo né in disaccordo
4. Abbastanza d'accordo
5. Molto d'accordo

3. "Alcune culture non sono integrabili nella società italiana." (1, 2, 3, 4, 5)
4. "Alcune etnie non sono integrabili nella società italiana." (1, 2, 3, 4, 5)
5. "Alcune razze non sono integrabili nella società italiana." (1, 2, 3, 4, 5)
6. "Un figlio di immigrati, nato e cresciuto in Italia, sarà in tutto e per tutto come un italiano." (1, 2, 3, 4, 5)
7. "Un figlio di meridionali, nato e cresciuto in Italia, sarà in tutto e per tutto come un settentrionale." (1, 2, 3, 4, 5)

C. Termometro di Simpatia

8. Potresti indicare, per ciascuno dei seguenti gruppi, se ti è più o meno simpatico?

Meno simpatico   Più simpatico

1   2   3   4   5   6   7   8   9   10

Italiani (1, 2, 3, 4, 5, 6, 7, 8, 9, 10)
Extracomunitari (1, 2, 3, 4, 5, 6, 7, 8, 9, 10)
Europei (1, 2, 3, 4, 5, 6, 7, 8, 9, 10)
Immigrati (1, 2, 3, 4, 5, 6, 7, 8, 9, 10)
Clandestini (1, 2, 3, 4, 5, 6, 7, 8, 9, 10)
Rom (1, 2, 3, 4, 5, 6, 7, 8, 9, 10)
Cattolici (1, 2, 3, 4, 5, 6, 7, 8, 9, 10)
Ebrei (1, 2, 3, 4, 5, 6, 7, 8, 9, 10)
Musulmani (1, 2, 3, 4, 5, 6, 7, 8, 9, 10)
Settentrionali (1, 2, 3, 4, 5, 6, 7, 8, 9, 10)

Meridionali (1, 2, 3, 4, 5, 6, 7, 8, 9, 10)
Rumeni (1, 2, 3, 4, 5, 6, 7, 8, 9, 10)
Albanesi (1, 2, 3, 4, 5, 6, 7, 8, 9, 10)
Marocchini (1, 2, 3, 4, 5, 6, 7, 8, 9, 10)
Senegalesi (1, 2, 3, 4, 5, 6, 7, 8, 9, 10)
Nigeriani (1, 2, 3, 4, 5, 6, 7, 8, 9, 10)
Cinesi (1, 2, 3, 4, 5, 6, 7, 8, 9, 10)
Pakistani (1, 2, 3, 4, 5, 6, 7, 8, 9, 10)
Peruviani (1, 2, 3, 4, 5, 6, 7, 8, 9, 10)

D. Politica

9. Potresti dirmi in una scala da 1 a 10 la posizione che corrisponde alle tue idee/valori politici, mettendo che 1 = estrema sinistra, 5 e 6 = centro, e 10 = estrema destra?

Sinistra   Centro   Destra

1   2   3   4   5   6   7   8   9   10

Questionnaire: English Translation

Interview #: _____ *Date:* _____   *Interviewed by:* _____   *University:* _____ *Major/Track:* _____   *M / F* _____

A. Background

I'd like to begin our interview with some questions about you and your family.

1. How old are you?
2. Where do you live? Did you grow up there?
3. Were your parents born there or elsewhere?

4. And what kind of work do your parents do?
   Father: _____ Mother: _____
5. What did your parents study? What degrees did they earn?
   Father: _____ Mother: _____
6. What did you study in high school?

B. Definition of Group Differences

Now I'd like to invite you to reflect a bit on Italians and others.

7. If you had to explain *who* should be considered Italian ["part of the Italian people"], what would you say?
8. Today many people live *in Italy* who are not considered Italian. Which groups come to mind first for you?
9. In general, what in your view are the main differences between Italians and non-Italians in Italy?
10. Can non-Italians *in Italy* become Italian?
11. *(If the answer to [10] is "Yes," ask: "How?" If instead the reply to [10] is "No," ask: "Why not?")*

   Now let's move to another kind of question. I'll ask you to give me definitions of two terms.

12. How would you define the term "ethnicity"?
13. Can you give examples of ethnic groups?
14. And therefore, in general, what are the characteristics that distinguish one ethnic group from another?
15. How would you define the term "race"? *(If the answer is that races do not exist, ask: "So on what kind of difference is racism based?")*
16. Can you give examples of racial groups?
17. Is this a complete list of races?
18. And do you think the Caucasoid group is a race?
19. And the "Negroid" group?
20. And the "Mediterranean" group?
21. And therefore, in general, what are the characteristics that distinguish one racial group from another?
22. Have your definitions of race or ethnicity been influenced by what you've studied at school or college? Did you ever cover this topic? What did they teach you?

23. And again, on your definitions: Do you think they have been influenced by other sources of information? Reading, conversations, media, parents, friends?

24. With respect to the differences between groups, we would like to know how you see the differences between Italians and *extracomunitari* (people from outside the European Union) *in Italy*. Do you think you could say that their differences are cultural (customs, religions), structural (having to do with citizenship, income, education), or biological (somatic, genetic)?

25. *(Show section A, "Difference Scales," of the worksheet)* To recap, where would you put the degree of difference between Italians and *extracomunitari* in Italy on these three scales? *(Check that the responses are consistent with what has been said previously; if not, ask for explanation.)*

26. *(Still on the worksheet, section A, "Difference Scales")* Now I'd ask you to indicate the degree of your agreement/disagreement with the following statement, using this scale: "There are biological races in the species *Homo sapiens*."

    1. Strongly disagree
    2. Disagree somewhat
    3. Neither agree nor disagree
    4. Agree somewhat
    5. Strongly agree

27. Why do you agree/disagree?

C. Explanations of Differences

Now I will describe to you two contemporary situations in which differences between groups have been observed. In both cases, I'll ask you to offer some possible explanations for these differences. I'm not concerned with your giving the "right" answer, if there even is one, but rather with your giving one or more plausible explanations.

28. The first issue has to do with crime. According to some data, immigrants in Italy are disproportionately involved in illegal activities.

In your opinion, what are possible explanations? Do you think there are other possible explanations?

29. Which explanation seems the most plausible to you? Why?

30. The second issue has to do sports: In world or Olympic competition, certain sports are dominated by particular population groups. For example, athletes of African origin ("blacks") have dominated speed events in track for many years. Yet they are rarely found in other sports like swimming. In your opinion, what are possible explanations? Do you think there are other possible explanations?

31. Which explanation seems the most plausible to you? Why?

32. *(If physical or biological differences between races are mentioned)* Where do they come from—how to explain—these differences?

33. *(If physical superiority is attributed to athletes of African origin)* How would you explain, then, the predominance of athletes of European origin ("whites") in sports like swimming?

D. Closed-Ended Questions

(Show section B, "Statements," of the worksheet) Now I'll give you a series of written statements. Can you indicate your degree of agreement or disagreement using the scale we give you?

1. Strongly disagree
2. Disagree somewhat
3. Neither agree nor disagree
4. Agree somewhat
5. Strongly agree

34. "Some cultures cannot be integrated into Italian society." (1, 2, 3, 4, 5)

35. "Some ethnic groups cannot be integrated into Italian society." (1, 2, 3, 4, 5)

36. "Some races cannot be integrated into Italian society." (1, 2, 3, 4, 5)

37. "A child of immigrants who is born and raised in Italy will be for all intents and purposes like an Italian." (1, 2, 3, 4, 5)

38. "A child of Southerners who is born and raised in the north will be for all intents and purposes like a Northerner." (1, 2, 3, 4, 5)

39. Can you say *why* you agree/disagree with the statements about the integration of certain cultures, ethnic groups, and races?

    · Culture
    · Ethnicity
    · Races

40. Can you say *why* you agree/disagree with the statements about the children of immigrants and Southerners?

    · Immigrants
    · Southerners

E. Identity and Attitudes

Now I'd like to ask you some questions about your personal experiences in terms of ethnicity, race, or nationality.

41. We've talked about various groups that can be distinguished on the basis of their origins. Thinking of your own origins, how would you define (or identify) yourself?
42. Why?
43. Do you have, or have you had, contacts with people of foreign background? *(If "Yes," ask: "Can you describe them for me?")*
44. Often we have more or less positive sentiments [*maggiori simpatie o antipatie*] toward this or that group. Could you say, for each of the following groups, whether you view it more or less positively? *(Show section C, "Likability Thermometer," of worksheet)*

Italians	Catholics	Albanians
Extracomunitari	Jews	Moroccans
Europeans	Muslims	Senegalese
Immigrants	Northerners	Nigerians
Undocumented	Southerners	Chinese
Roma	Romanians	Pakistanis
		Peruvians

45. Could you explain the choices you made?

46. Are these choices derived from personal experience, things you've heard other people say, teachers/professors, the media? *(Ask for each statement given in the previous response.)*

F. Politics

We'll end the interview with a series of questions that are political in nature.

47. In some European countries, the granting of citizenship is based on a test of one's knowledge of the language, norms, history, or culture of the host country. In your view, should the granting of Italian citizenship be based on one or more of these criteria? *(If the response is "Yes," ask: "Which? And so someone who does not pass the test should be denied citizenship?")*

48. In some classrooms in Italian schools, students of immigrant origin are in the majority. According to some, this has negative consequences. In your opinion, should the percentage of foreigners [*includes immigrants and their children*] in the classroom be limited to a certain quota? (Yes/No) Why?

49. In some countries, the census asks respondents which race they belong to. In others, they are asked for their ethnic origin. Still others ask about the country of origin of the respondent or their parents. In your opinion, would it be useful to introduce some of these questions here [*da noi*]? (Yes/No) Why?

50. *(If the answer to [49] is "Yes," ask: "Which ones?" If the answer is "No," ask: "Not even for investigating the existence of discrimination?")*

51. *(Show section D, "Politics," of the worksheet, p. 4)* Some people define themselves as centrist, others as on the right or the left. Could you tell me, on a scale from 1 to 10, the position that corresponds to your political ideas or values, where 1 = the extreme left, 5 and 6 = the center, and 10 = the extreme right?

Left				Center					Right
1	2	3	4	5	6	7	8	9	10

52. Thank you very much for your answers. Is there anything else you'd like to add—for example, on something I didn't ask?
53. Are there any questions you'd like to ask me?

Thank you!

Notes

Worksheet: English Translation

A. Difference Scales

1. Where would you put the degree of difference between Italians and *extracomunitari* in Italy on these three scales?

Culture

Same				Different
I	2	3	4	5

Nature

Same				Different
I	2	3	4	5

Social Condition

Same				Different
I	2	3	4	5

2. Can you indicate the degree of your agreement/disagreement with the following statement? "There are biological races in the species *Homo sapiens*."

   1. Strongly disagree
   2. Disagree somewhat
   3. Neither agree nor disagree
   4. Agree somewhat
   5. Strongly agree

B. Statements

Below are some statements. Can you indicate your degree of agreement or disagreement using the scale below?

1. Strongly disagree
2. Disagree somewhat
3. Neither agree nor disagree
4. Agree somewhat
5. Strongly agree

3. "Some cultures cannot be integrated into Italian society." (1, 2, 3, 4, 5)
4. "Some ethnic groups cannot be integrated into Italian society." (1, 2, 3, 4, 5)
5. "Some races cannot be integrated into Italian society." (1, 2, 3, 4, 5)
6. "A child of immigrants who is born and raised in Italy will be for all intents and purposes like an Italian." (1, 2, 3, 4, 5)
7. "A child of Southerners who is born and raised in the North will be for all intents and purposes like a Northerner." (1, 2, 3, 4, 5)

C. Likability Thermometer

8. Could you indicate, for each of the following groups, whether you view it more or less positively?

View less positively								View more positively	
1	2	3	4	5	6	7	8	9	10

Italians (1, 2, 3, 4, 5, 6, 7, 8, 9, 10)
Extracomunitari [people from outside the European Union] (1, 2, 3, 4, 5, 6, 7, 8, 9, 10)
Europeans (1, 2, 3, 4, 5, 6, 7, 8, 9, 10)
Immigrants (1, 2, 3, 4, 5, 6, 7, 8, 9, 10)
Clandestini [undocumented migrants] (1, 2, 3, 4, 5, 6, 7, 8, 9, 10)
Roma (1, 2, 3, 4, 5, 6, 7, 8, 9, 10)
Catholics (1, 2, 3, 4, 5, 6, 7, 8, 9, 10)
Jews (1, 2, 3, 4, 5, 6, 7, 8, 9, 10)

Muslims (1, 2, 3, 4, 5, 6, 7, 8, 9, 10)
Northerners (1, 2, 3, 4, 5, 6, 7, 8, 9, 10)
Southerners (1, 2, 3, 4, 5, 6, 7, 8, 9, 10)
Romanians (1, 2, 3, 4, 5, 6, 7, 8, 9, 10)
Albanians (1, 2, 3, 4, 5, 6, 7, 8, 9, 10)
Moroccans (1, 2, 3, 4, 5, 6, 7, 8, 9, 10)
Senegalese (1, 2, 3, 4, 5, 6, 7, 8, 9, 10)
Nigerians (1, 2, 3, 4, 5, 6, 7, 8, 9, 10)
Chinese (1, 2, 3, 4, 5, 6, 7, 8, 9, 10)
Pakistanis (1, 2, 3, 4, 5, 6, 7, 8, 9, 10)
Peruvians (1, 2, 3, 4, 5, 6, 7, 8, 9, 10)

D. *Politics*

9. Could you tell me on a scale from 1 to 10 the position that corresponds to your political ideas or values, where 1 = the extreme left, 5 and 6 = the center, and 10 = the extreme right?

Left				Center					Right
1	2	3	4	5	6	7	8	9	10

U.S. Interview Questionnaire

THE FOLLOWING questionnaire was used by Morning in interviews with university undergraduate students at four Northeast campuses in the United States in 2001–2002. Further information about the data collection and results can be found in Morning's book, *The Nature of Race: How Scientists Think and Teach about Human Difference* (2011).

> *Interview #:* _____ *Date:* _____
> *University:* _____
> *Dept./Major:* _____ *M / F* _____

A. Background

1. I know I checked that you are eighteen or older, but please remind me how old you are?
2. So you are a senior or a junior here at the university?
3. What part of the country are you from originally?
4. Is that where you spent most of your childhood?
5. What are your parents' occupations?
   Father: _____ Mother: _____

6. Do you know how much education your parents have completed?
   Father: _____ Mother: _____

7. A lot of the questions I'll ask you today will have to do with how race might come up in the classroom here. But before we get to that, I'm curious to know a little about the racial makeup of the community where you grew up—how would you characterize it?

8. Are ethnic or religious identities important to people in your home community?

9. Did your elementary and secondary schools tend to have the same racial and ethnic makeup as your home community?

10. How do you usually describe yourself in terms of race?

11. Would you say you have any religious affiliation? If so, what is it?

12. How would you describe your political leanings—for example, in terms of political party affiliation or a liberal-to-conservative spectrum?

B. Education

13. You are majoring in (*name major*). Do you have a second major as well?

14. How would you characterize your academic experience here at (*name university*): positive, negative, or somewhere in between?

15. Why do you characterize it that way?

16. Here I have a list of all the undergraduate majors here at the university. Would you please check off all the areas in which you can recall having completed at least one class so far?

17. As I mentioned, I'm interested in exploring with you today the ways in which the topic of race may come up in the classroom setting. Would you say that the topic of race has come up much in the classes you have taken here?

18. Is race more likely to be a topic of discussion in certain subject areas than others? To answer, you might want to look back at the list of departments in which you've taken classes.

19. What kinds of issues is race usually connected to in each of these subject areas?

20. Now let's turn to your department (*name department field*) in partic-
    ular. In the undergraduate courses offered by your department, does
    the topic of race (or race-related issues) come up much?
21. When race is discussed in (*name department*) classes, what kinds of
    issues is it usually connected to?
22. In addition to your academic work, I'm also interested in discussions
    about race that students might have *outside* the classroom. In general,
    would you say the topic of race comes up often at this university?
23. In connection with what kinds of topics is race usually brought up?

C. Conceptualizations of Race

So far I've asked you several questions related to race and how people
talk about it, but I haven't asked you how you define the meaning of the
word "race." This might seem like a strange question, since race is such an
everyday idea in the United States that we generally don't think very often
about how it is defined. But research has shown that different people have
different ideas about things like what determines a person's race, or which
groups should be considered races.

24. First of all, if you had to give a definition of the word "race," or
    explain what it was, what would you say?
25. What kind of information or facts would you use to support that
    definition?
26. What are the main kinds of differences that exist between racial
    groups; that is, what kinds of things make racial groups different
    from each other?
27. Do you think there are biological differences between different races?
    Why or why not?
28. How would you say racial differences come about—what causes them?

At this point, I'd like to ask you how you think some other groups of
people would define the concept of race. I'll do this by showing you a
printed statement, and then asking you first for your opinion about it, and
then I'll ask you how you think some other people would react to it.

29. First, I'm going to give you a card with a short statement printed on it; this sentence is taken from a survey that was conducted in the 1980s.[1] After you've read the statement, I'd like to know whether you agree or disagree with it. *(Hand over the card, which reads: "There are biological races within the species* Homo sapiens. *")* Now, how would you describe your reaction to this statement: Do you agree or disagree?

30. *Why* do you [agree/disagree]?

31. Let's stick with this statement for a minute. How do you think that most of your peers—other students here at *(university name)*— would react to it? In general, do you think other students would agree or disagree? Why?

32. What about Americans in general, the public? Do you think most Americans would agree or disagree with the statement I showed you? Why?

Now I'm going to describe to you two scenarios—taken from real life— where racial groups differ in terms of some outcome or phenomenon. In each case, I'll describe the facts of the situation to you, and then ask you to give me a couple of possible explanations for the differences in the experiences of different racial groups. That is, I'd like you to give a couple of plausible reasons that might explain the situations I'll describe to you.

33. The first scenario I'll describe refers to a biomedical outcome, namely, the weight of babies at birth. Researchers have discovered that at birth, babies of different racial groups tend to have different weights.[2] For example, white babies have among the highest median weight, black babies among the lowest, and Asian babies' weights tend to be in the middle. In your opinion, what are some possible explanations for this finding?

34. Which do you think is the most likely explanation? Why?

35. The second scenario I'll describe has to do with sports, and the over-representation, or underrepresentation, of certain racial groups in certain sports, compared to their share of the total population of the country. To give you an example from football: in the NFL, blacks make up 67 percent of the players and white athletes are in the minority. But in the total population of the United States as a whole, whites make up the majority and blacks count for only 12 percent

of the population.[3] In your opinion, what could be some plausible explanations for why the racial composition of the National Football League is so different from the racial makeup of the country as a whole?

36. Which explanation do you think is the most likely one? Why?

37. Those are all the questions I have for you. Is there anything else that you'd like to add—maybe a comment on a related topic I didn't think to ask you about?

38. And are there any questions that you'd like to ask me?

NOTES

Introduction: Thinking and Talking about Difference

1. In the original Italian: "Tutti i cittadini hanno pari dignità sociale e sono eguali davanti alla legge, senza distinzione di sesso, di razza, di lingua, di religione, di opinioni politiche, di condizioni personali e sociali." See Senato della Repubblica, *Costituzione della Repubblica Regolamento del Senato*, updated April 20, 2012, https://www.senato.it /documenti/repository/istituzione/costituzione.pdf (accessed January 28, 2020). All translations are by the authors.
2. Mattioli 2018.
3. Cremonesi 2018.
4. Mosca 2018.
5. Rizzuti 2018.
6. Santerini 2017.
7. AgenPress.it 2018.
8. Maneri and Quassoli 2020.
9. AgenPress.it 2018.
10. "Young people have to know what truly happened: it's the only way to build a bulwark against present and future violence," Senator Segre stated; see ibid.
11. *France 24* 2013, 2018.
12. *France 24* 2013.
13. Möschel 2011, 2014.
14. Rickards and Biondi 2014.
15. Capasso and Fantini 2016; *ImolaOggi* 2018; Piccaluga 2017.
16. See, for example, Loïc Wacquant's 1997 review of Stoler 1997; Pierre Bourdieu and Wacquant's 1999 critique of Hanchard 1994; Andreas Wimmer's 2015 denunciation of "race-centrism" in Omi and Winant 2014 and Bonilla-Silva 2013; Adrian Favell's 2016 reply to Alba and Foner 2015; and Beaud and Noiriel 2020.

17. Beaman 2017; Fleming 2017; Hanchard 2003; Winant 2015.
18. Favell 2016, 2352.
19. Wacquant 1997, 232; Green 1999; Lamont and Thévenot 2000a.
20. On Latin America, see Bailey, Fialho, and Penner 2016; Golash-Boza 2011; Hartigan 2013; Loveman 2014; and Telles 2004. On Asia, see Dikötter 1997 and Takezawa 2011. On Africa and the Middle East, see Glassman 2011; Hall 2011; and Hopper 2015.
21. Barker 1981.
22. On the United Kingdom, see Gilroy 1987; Sivanandan 1988; and Solomos 1991.
23. Wieviorka 1993, 64; Balibar 1991, 22. See also Taguieff 1988 and Wieviorka 1992.
24. Bobo, Kluegel, and Smith 1997; Bonilla-Silva 2003; Gaertner and Dovidio 1986; Schofield 1986; Sears 1988; Sniderman et al. 1991. For an overview, see Sears, Sidanius, and Bobo 2000.
25. Balibar and Wallerstein 1991; Bovenkerk, Miles, and Verbunt 1990; Calavita 2005; Essed 1991; Kastoryano 2005; Modood 2001; Stolcke 1995.
26. Balibar 1991, 26.
27. Kastoryano 2005.
28. Essed 1991; Lamont 2000a, 171, 178, 181.
29. Lamont 2000a, 321.
30. El-Tayeb 2011a, 181; Bonilla-Silva 2000.
31. Duster 1990; Nelkin and Lindee 1995.
32. Bonilla-Silva 1996; Reskin 2012.
33. Morning 2009.
34. Brubaker 2013.
35. Loveman 1999; Miles 1999; Wimmer 2012.
36. For a global comparison of national census questions on ethnicity and race, see Morning 2008.
37. Hattam 2004; Wilkerson 2020; Wimmer 2012.
38. Loveman 2014, 37.
39. Brubaker, Loveman, and Stamatov 2004, 47.
40. Loveman 1999, 896.
41. We use the terms "Roma" (proper noun) or "Romani" (adjective) as umbrellas to include varied groups previously labeled as "gypsies," even if they identify as Sinti, Kalé, and so on, rather than as Romani. The contemporary Italian counterpart to this use of "Roma" would be *zigani*, which is intended to be a comprehensive alternative to the pejorative *zingari*; see, for example, Vitale 2009.
42. Hollinger 1998.
43. In Romance languages, "descent-based difference" might be translated as "difference based on descent" or even "genealogical difference."
44. Chandra 2012, 9, 11, 14.
45. Weber 1978[1956]; Zerubavel 2012.
46. Brubaker 2013.
47. Marks 1995.
48. Fredrickson 2002.

49. Although these are technically secondary schools, they frequently enroll students age eighteen and over, who are comparable in age to college students.

50. Morning 2011; Roberts 2011. For a comparative historical view, see Skarpelis 2021.

51. Davis 1991; Katzew 2004; Wolfe 2001.

52. Lamont and Thévenot 2000b; Taylor 1985, 129.

53. El-Tayeb 2011a; Essed 1991; Smedley and Smedley 2012; Wilder 2013.

54. Winant 2015, 2180.

55. Alba 2005; Alba and Foner 2015; Crul and Mollenkopf 2012; Crul and Vermeulen 2003; Foner and Simon 2015.

56. Coleman 2006, 401.

57. Ibid., 402.

58. Domingo 2008; Rodríguez-Muñiz 2021.

59. Smedley and Smedley 2012.

60. De Genova 2006.

61. See Kastoryano's 2002 prediction that other forms of convergence—political, economic, legal, and cultural—will also spur comparative analyses across clusters of nations.

62. Alba and Foner 2015; Foner and Simon 2015; Kastoryano 2002; Small 1993.

63. Van den Berghe 1970; see also Suzuki 2017. Our intellectual agenda is in line with Mara Loveman's (1999, 896) call for a "comparative sociology of group-making" and Stephen Small's (1993, 245) "racialisation problematic," a paradigm for "understanding and explanation of the creation and variations in 'racialised' group boundaries and identities in various socio-historical contexts."

64. See, for example, Arystanbek 2020; Pesarini 2020.

65. Snyder 2021.

66. Originally a literary reference from Dante and Petrarch, *il bel paese* has become a synonym for Italy.

67. Organization for Economic Cooperation and Development 2020.

68. Fondazione ISMU 2018.

69. Gonzalez-Barrera and Connor 2019.

70. It is always risky to describe something as "undisputed," and especially so in this instance, when many American readers are likely to be quite aware that Italians' "Europeanness," as Maxim Silverman 1992 put it—or more precisely, their whiteness—has been far from assured in the United States or even in their own post-Unification narratives; see Guglielmo and Salerno 2003 and Welch 2016. However, we intend here simply to signal that Italy and its political forerunners play a starring role in any historical account of Western Europe.

71. We use the word "gypsy" here to refer to the stereotypical figure as it has been imagined negatively in the West. When referring to actual people, we use the terms "Roma" or "Romani."

72. Hannaford 1996; MacMaster 2001.

73. Ferber 1999; MacMaster 2001.

74. Allievi 2002; Castles 1993; Cousin and Vitale 2002; Lamont 2000a; Lewis 2008; Mack 2001.

75. Lucassen, Willems, and Cottaar 1998.
76. Byron 2002; Carter 2008; Fredrickson 2002; Hannaford 1996; Petrovich Njegosh 2012; Scacchi 2012.
77. Hannaford 1996; Welch 2016.
78. Gibson 1998, 2002.
79. Bonavita 2009; Castelli 2000; Deplano 2015; Deplano and Pes 2014; Finaldi 2009; Gabrielli 2019; Labanca 2002; Podestà 2014; Re 2010.
80. Bernhard 2019; De Donno 2006; Gillette 2002. On the contributions of U.S., British, and Scandinavian scientists to German eugenic notions, see Kevles 1995[1985] and Whitman 2017.
81. Cousin and Vitale 2014; Fallaci 2004.
82. Carr 2012; Merrill 2011; Möschel 2007, 124; Proglio and Odasso 2017. Although *extracomunitari* technically include citizens of European nations like Switzerland and Norway who are not members of the European Union (EU), as well as citizens of non-European countries like the United States and Australia, in practice the term is used overwhelmingly to denote nationals of African, Asian, or Latin American countries. The particularity of this Italian term can be traced to Italy's late entry into the Schengen Area, the zone of European nations that have done away with internal border controls. At that time in the 1990s, immigration was on the rise, and the depiction of Italy as the weak link in Fortress Europe impressed upon its inhabitants the need to tighten control of its territorial boundaries against interlopers.
83. Essed 1990; Lamont and Thévenot 2000a.
84. "Italian occupation will be kinder and gentler than past, non-European occupations and . . . local populations will be grateful to the Italian state for improving their living conditions," opined the nineteenth-century statesman Leopoldo Franchetti, quoted in Welch 2016, 53; see also Bidussa 1994 and Labanca 2002.
85. Lombardi-Diop and Romeo 2012.
86. Guglielmo and Salerno 2003.
87. Lamont 2000a, 2000b.
88. Morning 2011.
89. See, for example, monographs by Beaman 2017; Fleming 2017; Glassman 2011; Golash-Boza 2011; Hall 2011; Kim 2008; Loveman 2014.
90. Alba and Waters 2011; Antonsich 2012.
91. Crul and Mollenkopf 2012; Hochschild and Mollenkopf 2009; Schneider et al. 2012.
92. Alba and Foner 2015; Foner 2015.
93. Alba and Holdaway 2014; Crul and Mollenkopf 2012.
94. As in the work of Banton 1977; Guillaumin 2002[1972]; Miles 1993; and Taguieff 1988.
95. Welch 2016. For notable, if not recent, exceptions, see Carter 1997; Cole 1997; and Sniderman and Piazza 1993.
96. Danewid et al. 2021; Forgacs 2014; Giuliani 2019; Giuliani and Lombardi-Diop 2013; Hawthorne 2017; Hawthorne Forthcoming; Mellino 2011; Merrill 2013; Pesarini 2014; Proglio and Odasso 2017; Welch 2016.
97. Crul and Mollenkopf 2012, 9; Schneider et al. 2012, 232.

98. Favell 2016, 2352; Lamont and Thévenot 2000a; Foner and Simon 2015; Crul and Mollenkopf 2012.
99. Lamont and Thévenot 2000a, 17.

Chapter 1: Debating "Race" in Europe and the United States

1. Tabet 1997, 8.
2. Ibid., 40.
3. Ibid., 57.
4. Ibid., 189.
5. Ibid., 190.
6. Ibid., 191.
7. We translate the children's use of *negro* here as English "negro" in order to distinguish this older, more pejorative word from the contemporary Italian color term *nero* ("black"), which is also used as a group label. Note, however, that when used by adults in hostile discourse—for example, in racist stadium chants—we translate *negro* as "n*gg*r," following examples like Möschel 2014, 133.
8. Tabet 1997, 151.
9. Ibid., xxxii.
10. Morning 2011; Winant 2007.
11. For an eclectic sample of studies of European stereotypes, see Blanchard and Bancel 1998; Bontempelli 2015; and Gullestad 2006. For some continental theorists of race and racism, see Balibar 1991; El-Tayeb 2011a; Goldberg 1990; Guillaumin 2002[1972]; Kastoryano 2005; and Taguieff 1988. Important empirical contributions can be found in Essed 1990, 1991; and Wieviorka 1992. We also note Christopher Bail's 2008 analysis of data from twenty-one European countries concerning the symbolic boundaries drawn against immigrants; he finds that race and religion are relatively salient in countries on the "periphery" and in new immigration destinations: Southern Europe (Spain, Portugal, and Italy), Eastern Europe (Poland, Czech Republic), Finland, and Ireland. But these survey data do not offer fine-grained information about the notions of difference that respondents associated with race or other groupings.
12. Alim and Reyes 2011.
13. Morning 2008; Simon 2013.
14. Möschel 2007, 74–75.
15. Quoted in Möschel 2011, 1651–52.
16. Grigolo, Hermanin, and Möschel 2011, 1639.
17. Ibid., 1635.
18. Curcio and Mellino 2010.
19. Lombardi-Diop 2012, 175.
20. Simon 2017, 2330.
21. Cohen 2018, 4.
22. Bonnet 2014; Pollock 2004.
23. Skarpelis 2021, 13.

24. As Grigolo, Hermanin, and Möschel (2011, 1638) aptly put it, "How to respond to the argument and uneasy feeling that even liberal democracies cannot be trusted once racial or ethnic categorizations are introduced and how to prevent them from using race and ethnic origin for purposes other than the fight against discrimination?" See also Möschel 2014, 119; and de Schutter and Ringelheim 2010.
25. Möschel 2014, 115.
26. Banton 2012, 1129.
27. Goldberg 2009, 154; see also Möschel 2014 and Suk 2007.
28. Giuliani 2015.
29. Goldberg 2009, 158, 155.
30. Solomos and Wrench 1993, 5; see also Bovenkerk, Miles, and Verbunt 1990 and Simon 2017.
31. Bonnet and Caillault 2015, 1192.
32. Möschel 2011, 1611.
33. Hermanin 2011.
34. Möschel 2014, 119.
35. Saada 2012; Silverman 1992; Simon 2017; Stoler 2002.
36. Cohen 2018, 47.
37. Fleming 2017; Vincent 2014. For more, see Onishi 2020.
38. Bonnet 2014, 1288; Cohen 2018.
39. Simon 2017, 2331; Simon and Clément 2006.
40. Scacchi 2012.
41. Cole 1997.
42. Angel-Ajani 2000, 339; Maher 1996a.
43. Rivera 2014; see also Kyeremeh 2017 and Valeri 2006, 2010.
44. Bubola and Pianigiani 2020; Cousin and Vitale 2014; Lombardi-Diop 2012; Maheshwari 2019; Povoledo 2021.
45. Bonnet 2014, 1289.
46. Sulmont and Callirgos 2014, 141–42.
47. Quillian 2006.
48. For example, by gender, age, and class. See Bonilla-Silva 2002; Frankenberg 1993; and Goldberg 2009.
49. Foldy and Buckley 2014; Frankenberg 1993; Perry 2002; Pierce 2012; Pollock 2004.
50. Bonilla-Silva 2002, 42 (emphasis in original).
51. Frankenberg 1993; Obasogie 2014.
52. Hartigan 2013, 33.
53. Durupt 2017. The minister was also incensed that the teachers were reserving two sessions for discussion among minority-group members only; he condemned the plan as "unconstitutional and unacceptable."
54. *Franceinfo* 2020, 2021; Onishi 2021b; Onishi and Méheut 2021; Skarpelis 2021.
55. Fuchs 2020.
56. Crowley and Schuessler 2021.

57. DeMillo 2021.

58. Edmondson 2021.

59. Omi and Winant 2014, 56; see also Vertovec 2021.

60. Edmondson 2021.

61. America First Caucus, "America First Caucus Policy Platform," https://punchbowl .news/wp-content/uploads/America-First-Caucus-Policy-Platform-FINAL-2.pdf; see also Asmelash 2021. These expressions seek to preserve "white democracy"; see Beltrán 2020 and Olson 2004. On memory laws in the United States and Russia, see Snyder 2021. For a parallel in white British "racialism," see St. Louis 2021.

62. Observatoire du décolonialisme et des idéologies identitaires 2021; see also Skarpelis 2021.

63. Note this use of "racial realism" is diametrically opposed to the essentialist reading of race that white supremacists have embraced under the same name; see Saini 2019.

64. Morning 2011; Bobo, Kluegel, and Smith 1997, 41. On the American Dream, see Hochschild 1995.

65. Gonyea 2017; White 2018.

66. Winant 2007.

67. Fassin and Fassin 2006; Saada 2012; Ndiaye 2009. For earlier work, see, for example, Guillaumin 2002[1972] and Taguieff 1988. For later work, see Bessone 2013; Fassin and Fassin 2006; Mazouz 2020; Ndiaye 2009; Saada 2007, 2012; and Schaub 2015. French scholars have also produced searching investigations of race in the U.S. context; see Sabbagh 2003, 2007, and Schor 2009, 2017.

68. Curcio and Mellino 2010. On racism, see Balbo 1989; Balbo and Manconi 1990, 1992. On Italian imperialism, see Del Boca 1976–1984, 1986, and Labanca 1996, 2002.

69. Giuliani and Lombardi-Diop 2013; Petrovich Njegosh and Scacchi 2012; Picker 2017; Danewid et al. 2021; Hawthorne Forthcoming.

70. El-Tayeb 2011a, xv. The irony of race being perceived as foreign on the continent whose languages gave form to it has a parallel in Ann Stoler's (2011) observations about the paradox of the colonial and racial aphasia of French intellectuals with direct personal experience of France's empire. Reflecting on the biographies of Pierre Bourdieu, Jacques Derrida, and Pierre Nora, all of whom had lived in French-ruled Algeria, she comments that "there is something in all of these left luminaries that seems to refuse a more intimate colonial history, to resist the colonial entanglements that so closely touched on the subjects of their intellectual lives." More broadly, she raises the question of "why one of the global heartlands of critical social theory and the philosophies of difference has so rarely turned its acute analytic tools to the deep structural coordinates of race in France" (128–29).

71. Essed 1991, 287.

72. Simon 2017.

73. Bail 2008; Quillian 1995; Semyonov, Raijman, and Gorodzeisky 2006; Sniderman et al. 2000; Wieviorka 1992.

74. Foner and Simon 2015, 11; Crul and Mollenkopf 2012.

75. Beauchemin, Hamel, and Simon 2015, 23.

76. On prejudice in political and media discourse, see Dal Lago 1999; Maneri 1998a, 2003, 2011; and Maneri and Quassoli 2020. On anti-Roma attitudes and exclusion, see Clough Marinaro and Sigona 2011; Hermanin 2011; Piasere 2015; and Vitale 2008. For other forms of prejudice and discrimination, see, for example, Ambrosini 2013; Balbo and Manconi 1993; Calavita 2005; Carter 1997; Cole 1997; Cousin and Vitale 2006; Daly 1999; Hawthorne 2019; Kyeremeh 2017; Pesarini and Tintori 2020; Sniderman et al. 2000; and Vasta 1993.
77. Goldberg 2009, 185.
78. See, for example, Boulila 2018 on Switzerland.
79. Lentin 2014, 1275.
80. Goldberg 2009, 154; see also Möschel 2014.
81. Goldberg 2009, 155.
82. Grigolo, Hermanin, and Möschel 2011, 1637; Mellino 2011; Skarpelis 2021.
83. Lombardi-Diop 2012, 175; Picker 2017; Simon 2017, 2329. El-Tayeb (2011b, 228) describes an "invisible racialization" that coincides with race-blind speech norms: "This dialectic of memory and amnesia, in the shape of an easily activated archive of racial images whose presence is steadfastly denied, is fundamentally European, I argue, in part constituting dominant notions of what Europe means: though rarely mentioned, race is present whenever Europe is thought."
84. Giuliani 2015; Mazouz 2020.
85. Simon 2017, 2329; see also El-Tayeb 2011b, 233.
86. Möschel 2014, 135–36.
87. Goldberg 2009, 152, 154.
88. Hartigan 2013, 30–31; Telles 2004; Twine 1997.
89. Although data about "ethnicity" is collected by a majority of countries, and possibly used for similar purposes; see Morning 2008.
90. Brubaker 2013.
91. Montagu 1942.
92. See the United Nations Educational, Scientific, and Cultural Organization (UNESCO) statements on race in Reardon 2005.
93. For an account of racial constructivism getting "lost in transmission" in the United States, see Morning 2011. On the Italian case, see Barbujani 2006 and Grossi 2012.
94. Lentin 2014, 1274.
95. On "racism without races," see Balibar 1991, 22.
96. Miles 1993, 42.
97. Wacquant 1997, 222 (emphasis in original).
98. Wimmer 2012, 5; Wimmer 2015.
99. Möschel 2014, 116; see also Beaud and Noiriel 2020; El-Tayeb 2011a, xvi; Fassin and Fassin 2006.
100. Wimmer 2012; for a similar finding in Germany, see Schaeffer 2013.
101. Alba and Foner 2015; Favell 2016, 2355.
102. Wimmer 2012, 6.
103. Wilson 1978. Detractors see this brand of skepticism as exculpatory; in the European context, Lentin (2014, 1274) portrays it as an "anything but race" position: "For an

act to be considered racist it would appear that it must be provable that the victim did nothing nor possessed any attribute other than a dark(er) skin colour. As soon as the victim can be found to follow practices or have other characteristics that set him/her apart from the society in which he/she lives, any negative reaction he or she is met with may be considered something other than racist."

104. Möschel 2014, 2, 114, 115.
105. See interview examples in Morning 2011; see also Pierce 2012.
106. Möschel 2014, 114.
107. Stoler 2011, 146; El-Tayeb 2011a, xvi.
108. Abend 2006; Jasanoff 2004.
109. Wacquant 1997, 223–24 (emphasis in original).
110. Ibid., 224; Wagley 1965.
111. Loveman 1999; Wimmer 2012, 10.
112. Wacquant 1997, 225.
113. Cole 1997, 14.
114. Ibid.
115. Calavita 2005, 164, 155.
116. Carter 1997. See also Merrill 2006 on gender and migration to Italy, as well as the reflections—from a privileged class position—of the writer Jhumpa Lahiri 2016 on fluency and Italians' interactions with foreigners of color.
117. Angel-Ajani 2000; Calavita 2005; De Genova 2018; Kim 2012; Soggia 2012.
118. De Genova 2018, 1772.
119. Möschel 2014.
120. Bird 2000; Bleich 2011; Brubaker 1992; Kastoryano 2002, 2005; Lamont et al. 2016; Stoler 1997.
121. Bonnet and Caillault 2015, 1197; Frankenberg 1993; Pierce 2012; Bonilla-Silva 2002; Cohen 2018.
122. Bonnet 2014, 1288; see also Simon 2017, 2329; Alba and Foner 2015, 101.
123. El-Tayeb 2011a, xxiv. Goldberg calls this paradox "antiracialism," meaning "to take a stand . . . against a concept, a name, a category [which] does not itself involve standing (up) against (a set of) conditions of being or living" (quoted in Lentin 2014, 1275). Taguieff calls it "a 'lexicocentrical' illusion based on primitive cognitive assumptions, according to which the simple removal of race from a language also removes the substantive underlying relationships or interactions" (quoted in Möschel 2014, 115). It is striking that in 2021 Taguieff came out in support of the French government's condemnation of scholarship on race and helped found the Observatoire du décolonialisme et des idéologies identitaires (see Onishi 2021a).

Chapter 2: Italian Mental Maps of Difference

1. ABC News 2013; on the historical roots of Europeans' likening of Africans to primates, see Schiebinger 1993.
2. *La Repubblica* 2013.
3. Kendi 2019; Phillips 2017.

4. On "mental maps," especially in comparative perspective, see Lamont 2000a.

5. Colombo and Sciortino 2004.

6. United Nations High Commissioner for Refugees 2019.

7. Data accessed August 5, 2019 using the Istituto Nazionale di Statistica's *demo* interface at www.istat.it.

8. Fondazione ISMU 2018, 1.

9. With respect to "the popular idea that [Romani people] are not Italians and do not 'belong' to Italy," Nando Sigona (2011, 591) notes Italy's local state agencies for "Nomads and Non-Europeans." As for Italian-born children of immigrants, who would be considered "second-generation Italians" from an American point of view, they—like Rom, Sinti, and Camminanti—are counted among the "foreign" student population in Italy's official educational statistics (Ministero dell'Istruzione 2014).

10. Balbo and Manconi 1990; Curcio 2011; Gallini 1996; Maneri 1998b; Vimercati 1990.

11. Maneri 1998b; Dal Lago 1999; Quassoli 1999.

12. Maneri 2011; Palidda 2000.

13. Calavita 2005; Cole 1997; Hargreaves 1995.

14. Maher 1996a. Similarly, a 1994 survey found that Central and North Africans were more likely than Eastern Europeans to be perceived as "inferior by nature"; see Sniderman et al. 2000.

15. Jordan 1968; Sniderman et al. 2000.

16. Istituto Nazionale Previdenza Sociale 2018; Calavita 2005, 128.

17. Ambrosetti and Cela 2015; Colombo and Sciortino 2004; De Genova 2013.

18. MacMaster 2001, 216.

19. Balibar 1991, 22; see also Bonilla-Silva 2000; Bonnet 2014; Calavita 2005, 158.

20. Bail 2008; Calavita 2005; Cousin and Vitale 2014; European Commission 2007, 123.

21. European Commission 2012, 114, 116; Pew Research Center 2014, 26, 28.

22. Poushter and Fetterolf 2019, 15.

23. Pew Research Center 2018, 75.

24. Essed 1990; Balbo and Manconi 1993.

25. Ambrosini 2013.

26. Sigona 2011, 603; Hermanin 2011.

27. Piasere 2015, 66–67; Tosi-Cambini 2008; see also Clough Marinaro and Sigona 2011, 583; and Vitale 2008, 10.

28. Möschel 2014, 145; Breviglieri and Vitale 2008; Hermanin 2011.

29. Organization for Security and Co-operation in Europe, "Hate Crime Reporting: Italy," https://hatecrime.osce.org/italy (accessed August 9, 2019).

30. Cronache di ordinario Razzismo, "Il razzismo quotidiano," http://www.cronachedi ordinariorazzismo.org/il-razzismo-quotidiano/ (accessed August 9, 2019.

31. "Aggressioni razziste dall'1 giugno 2018," https://www.google.com/maps/d/viewer?mid =1kjmhct5NVKjSwAfo9OndqprhgQ6OEr8A&ll=45.566356230681386%2C9.8494840 62499977&z=5 (accessed August 9, 2019).

32. Balbo and Manconi 1993; on stigma or disrespect, see Lamont et al. 2016.

33. Daly 1999.

34. Khouma 2009, 2010; Kuti 2019. See also Scego 2020 for the first anthology by black Italian women; Di Maio 2009 on the "autobiographical fiction" of Italian-language writers of African descent; and Zhang 2013 on Italian novels centered on Chinese immigration.

35. Piasere 2015, 75; see also Petruzzelli 2008.

36. Since Hans Kohn's contribution (1994[1944]), a wide-ranging body of literature has described two visions of nation and citizenship, termed "civic" and "ethnic"; see Brubaker 1992; Noiriel 1988; Smith 1991; and Todorov 1989. The first of these perspectives, often associated with the French experience, is informed by a liberal Enlightenment tradition. In the second perspective, advocated by exponents of German Romanticism and the Prussian Reform Movement, the nation is a natural entity, with prehistoric origins, to which people belong by virtue of their history, ancestry, language, religion, customs, and folklore.

37. See similar findings in Colombo 2010.

38. We adopt the term "primordialism" from the discussion in Cornell and Hartmann 2007 of work by scholars such as Harold Isaacs, Clifford Geertz, and Edward Shils. In their overview, primordial accounts of race and ethnicity stress the powerful affective ties that are largely rooted in circumstances of birth, such as language, name, nationality, religion, and locale.

39. Our deliberate use of the term *extracomunitari*, meaning "non-EU nationals," in place of "foreigners" or "immigrants" might well be questioned, insofar as this is the most general category that has been constructed and objectified as "other" in public discourse and is fairly widespread. Some respondents understandably expressed doubts about the meaning and appropriateness of this term.

40. We thank Mary Waters for the observation that the students unwittingly reproduced Milton Gordon's (1964) stages of assimilation, emphasizing particular sites and practices as crucial for integration.

41. Ethnicity occupied a middle ground probably because some interviewees equated it with culture and others with race, as we will explore further in the next chapter.

42. Lamont and Molnár 2002.

43. Nelson 2008.

44. Similar to findings previously discussed from Calavita 2005 and Sniderman et al. 2000.

45. Fiske 2002; Fiske, Cuddy, and Glick 2007.

46. Blanchard and Bancel 1998.

47. On the image of the Moroccans at the beginning of the 1990s, see Maher 1996b. For further background on criminalizing representations of Albanians and Romanians, see Maneri 2011, 2018; Dal Lago 1999; and Binotto, Bruno, and Lai 2016. On photographic representations, see Gariglio, Pogliano, and Zanini 2010.

48. Binotto, Bruno, and Lai 2016.

49. Sniderman et al. 2000; see also Saini 2019.

50. According to the CIA World Factbook, Muslims make up 53.5 percent of Nigeria's population and 95.9 percent of Senegal's. See https://www.cia.gov/the-world-factbook/ (accessed December 5, 2021).

51. There are many different estimates of the size and citizenship of the Roma population (usually counted together with the much less numerous Sinti and Camminanti) in Italy. Accurate estimation is difficult because of both a lack of official data and a tendency among the Roma to conceal their identity, given the level of prejudice against them. The data provided by international organizations, associations, and commissions of inquiry tend to converge but may not be reliable. For this study, we came up with our estimate by drawing on the estimates provided in a report of the Commission for the Protection and Promotion of Human Rights to the Italian Senate (Senato della Repubblica 2011) and in Enwereuzor and Pasquale 2009.
52. Patriarca 2015.
53. Guillaumin 2002[1972], 96.

Chapter 3: "Race" Talk

1. Taken from Lieberman 1997.
2. The datedness of the term "mulatto" is evident from its usage on the U.S. decennial census from 1850 through 1920 (with one exception); see Davis 1991 and Nobles 2000.
3. We also identified some "geographic" concepts of race—as well as a few "ambiguous" ones—but we touch on them only briefly.
4. See chapter 1 for examples of scholarly work (for example, Balibar 1991; Bovenkerk, Miles, and Verbunt 1990; Calavita 2005; Kastoryano 2005) that puts Martin Barker's 1981 notion of "new racism" in comparative perspective.
5. The U.S. descriptive statistics presented here differ from those published in Morning 2011 because here we focus only on definitions of the word "race." In contrast, Morning 2011 categorized the American respondents' racial concepts based on their combined answers to a series of questions. Here we disaggregate and report separately on interviewees' comments on racial definition, difference, and taxonomy.
6. Overall, however, the conceptual range of the Italian university students was fairly close to that of their peers in vocational schools, so we generally do not provide separate breakdowns on the conceptual categorization of their race definitions.
7. Lieberman 1997.
8. In accordance with the institutional review board provisions for the American interviews, we use pseudonyms for both individuals and universities in the United States. For the Italian sample, we use pseudonyms for the student interviewees but provide the real names of their educational institutions.
9. Timmermans and Tavory 2020.
10. Bonnet 2014, 1276.
11. Pollock 2004.
12. Bonnet 2014, 1283–84.
13. Lamont 2000a.
14. Morning (2011) did not ask U.S. interviewees for definitions of "ethnicity," and so we cannot make a direct comparison here.

15. Comparing university to vocational students overall, however, showed the two groups to be quite similar on average in their embrace of biological or cultural definitions of ethnicity.

16. Cornell and Hartmann 2007.

17. Bonavita (2009) furnishes dramatic examples of such racial logic in his study of Fascist-era Italian literature.

18. Faso 2008, 63.

19. Morning 2011.

20. Brubaker 2015b.

21. Zuberi 2001.

22. See Phelan, Link, and Feldman 2013; on claims about biological racial distinctions that everyday Americans encounter, see Roberts 2011.

23. Hattam 2004.

24. On semantic moves regarding race, see Bonilla-Silva 2002.

25. Brubaker 2015a; Morning 2017; Osuji 2017. It can be argued, however, that exceptions are made for some mixed-race people (though not those with some African ancestry) and for groups that have not yet been tightly linked to traditional American racial categories, like Latin American, Middle Eastern, or North African groups.

26. Bonilla-Silva 2002.

27. Curcio and Mellino 2010; Skarpelis 2021; Giuliani 2015, 1.

28. Petrovich Njegosh 2015, 84.

29. Picker 2017, 10.

30. Ibid., 142.

Chapter 4: Difference in Play: Sport and Descent

1. Apostle et al. 1983.

2. Kyeremeh 2017; Trimbur 2019; Woodward and Mindock 2020; on the United Kingdom, see Back, Crabbe, and Solomos 2001.

3. Azzarito and Harrison 2008; Burdsey 2020; Carrington 2010; Entine 2000; Foy and Ray 2019; Hartmann 2016; Hughey and Goss 2015; Shropshire 1996; Thangaraj 2015; Valeri 2010; Van Sterkenburg, Knoppers, and de Leeuw 2012; Williams 2001.

4. Morning 2011.

5. The sources for these data were Lapchick and Matthews 2001 and U.S. Census Bureau 2001.

6. Fuentes 2011; Grossi 2012; Marks 1995; Rutherford 2020.

7. The percentage in the Italian sample, moreover, is likely to be an underestimate. Ten respondents out of the total sample of 106 were not asked the sports question, because it was not included in the initial interviews. But because the missing ten individuals had all defined race as a matter of biology, we expect that they would also have embraced biological accounts of sports representation if asked about it.

8. For a detailed catalog of essential physical traits—and even psychological features like "inner strength"—attributed to black athletes by sports media coverage, see Hughey and Goss 2015.

9. A common variant was the tale of Africans running after lions and other large game as their prey. This image of the African as hunter may have reinforced the consistent masculinization of Africans in these accounts. See Gifford-Gonzales 1993.

10. Portelli 1989.

11. Ibid.

12. King, Lugo-Lugo, and Bloodsworth-Lugo 2010; Lutz and Collins 1993.

13. Wolf 2010[1982].

14. Barbujani 2005, 2006; Fuentes 2011; Marks 1995.

15. Rutherford 2020.

16. Ibid., 131.

17. Ibid., 143.

18. Alexander 2010; Thangaraj 2017.

19. United Nations 2019. "When successful Kenyan runners were actually asked if the story of running to school was true, most said no—they walked or took the bus like other kids" (Rutherford 2020, 149–50).

20. Alexander 2010.

21. Flavio may have confused *riserve* (reservations) with *risaie* (rice paddies).

22. See Thangaraj 2015 on the co-constitution of notions of whiteness, blackness, and East and South Asian-ness in the realm of sport.

23. Morning 2011.

24. Our Italian interviewees often used the expressions "central Africa" and "south Africa" to denote sub-Saharan Africa as a whole, rather than refer to particular countries like the Central African Republic or the Republic of South Africa.

25. Zerubavel 2018.

26. Bonilla-Silva 2002.

27. Ibid., 61; Cohen 2018; see also Stoler's (2011) "aphasia."

28. Many thanks to Stan Thangaraj for pointing out a related U.S. literature on the stereotyping of Asian Americans as "robotic, systematic, and without emotion," particularly in pursuits that are seen as cerebral, such as spelling bees (Dhingra 2020; Shankar 2019) and golf (Joo 2012; Thangaraj 2020).

29. Kim 1999.

30. Thangaraj 2017.

31. In the U.S. interviews, in contrast, Morning referred to the representation of "racial groups" in the National Football League.

32. Fanon 2008[1952].

33. Thanks to Dina Bader for two examples of such cartoons: see "Il leone si è addormentato" ("The lion is asleep," or as it is known in English, "The lion sleeps tonight") on La TV dei Bambini, "Canzoncine per Bambini"; and "I watussi" ("The Watusi") on "Canzoni per Bambini," both available on YouTube (accessed July 22, 2020). On these and other purveyors of classic racial stereotypes, see Gabrielli 2014; Gifford-Gonzales

1993, 1995; Hughey and Goss 2015; King, Lugo-Lugo, and Bloodsworth-Lugo 2010; Leoni and Tappi 2010; Lutz and Collins 1993; Miller 1998; Portelli 1989; and Van Sterkenburg, Knoppers, and de Leeuw 2010.

34. Thangaraj 2017; see also Rutherford 2020, 149.
35. Bonnet 2014, 1276.
36. Cerase 2014.
37. DiAngelo 2011, 66.
38. *Caffè macchiato* translates to "stained" or "spotted" coffee, a reference to the small amount of milk that is added to a cup of *espresso*. The combination of dark coffee and white milk has given rise to the racialized nicknames that Scacchi describes.
39. Ricci 2005.
40. Scacchi 2012, 267–68.
41. Bonilla-Silva 2002, 62.

Conclusion: Rethinking Race: A New Model of Descent-Based Difference

1. Barker 1981.
2. Taguieff 1988.
3. Hollinger 1998.
4. Morning 2009.
5. Marks 1995.
6. Panofsky 2014.
7. Fassin and Fassin 2006.
8. Bonilla-Silva 2002.
9. Brubaker 2015b.
10. Chandra 2012, 9.
11. Weber 1978[1956]; Clauss 1940; Takezawa 2011.
12. Devos and Banaji 2005.
13. De Genova 2006.
14. Waters 1990.
15. Our definition privileges the dimensions of essentialism that Haslam, Rothschild, and Ernst (2000, 118) call *inherence* (group members share "an underlying reality or sameness") and *necessity* (group membership requires a certain trait or traits).
16. Cornell and Hartmann 2007.
17. Morning 2017.
18. Haslam, Rothschild, and Ernst 2000.
19. Roth 2018.
20. Osuji 2017.
21. See also Wimmer 2012 on ethnic boundary-making.
22. Yzerbyt, Rogier, and Fiske 1998, 1089.
23. Silverman 2011; Taylor, Bogdan, and DeVault 2015.
24. Barker 1981.
25. For a detailed examination of the U.S. "one-drop rule," see Davis 1991.

26. Hancock 2002; Lucassen, Willems and Cottaar 1998.
27. Attributes of each concept of difference that correspond to the elements listed in our theoretical decomposition of conceptualization are italicized.
28. Hannaford 1996.
29. See Wikipedia, "Brown (racial classification)," https://en.wikipedia.org/wiki/Brown_ (racial_classification) (accessed December 22, 2020).
30. We are indebted to our NYU Department of Sociology colleague Linsey Edwards for this analogy.
31. Kim 1999.
32. Hattam 2004; Hannaford 1996.
33. See Hattam 2004 for a historical account of how Jewish thinkers in the United States in the early twentieth century promoted the notion of "ethnicity" as an alternative to the hierarchical "race" concept then applied to them and other Eastern or Southern European groups. Gans 1979 and Waters 1990 further describe how these European origins had lost their stigma in the United States by the late twentieth century.
34. See Jiménez 2010 on "ethnic affiliates" in the United States.
35. Guillaumin 2002[1972].
36. We thank Tommaso Vitale for this reminder; see, for example, Piasere 2015.
37. Perlmann and Waters 2002.
38. De Genova 2006.
39. Morning and Sabbagh 2005.
40. Fields and Fields 2012; but see also Barzun 1937 and Ludwig 2019.
41. Schiff 2015.

Appendix A: Interview Data and Methodology

1. The four exceptions to this age range were twenty-six, twenty-nine, thirty, and forty-one years old.
2. One respondent reported having a mother of partial African ancestry, but did not self-identify as black.
3. Morning used pseudonyms for the U.S. universities, because the faculty she interviewed there might have been identifiable had their institution's names been reported.
4. Morning 2011.
5. Bovenkerk, Miles, and Verbunt 1991, 386.
6. Elder 1976; Sica 2006.
7. Neuman 2006.
8. Hannaford 1996; Smedley and Smedley 2012; Bourdieu and Wacquant 1999, 43.
9. Bourdieu and Wacquant 1999, 54.
10. Hartigan 2013.
11. Armer 1973, 52.
12. Lamont 2000a. See Sniderman and Piazza 1993 for an example of an American researcher presuming that black-white difference would carry the same meanings in Italy as in the United States. And see the efforts of Lamont and her colleagues (2016, 27) to avoid

"the assumption that ethnoracial identity is most salient" and instead maintain "an open-ended perspective on groupness without obliterating the politics of categorization."

13. We also inquired about various topics that we do not cover in this volume—for example, potential sources of influence on the students' conceptualizations of difference, such as family, teachers, friends, or the media, the respondents' own identities, and their contacts with people of foreign origin. We also explored the potential impact of their notions of descent-based difference by eliciting their opinions on citizenship, education, and census policies.

14. Morning 2011.

15. Strauss 1987; Strauss and Corbin 1998.

16. Strauss 1987.

17. Bonnet 2014. For some examples of highly effective empirical explorations of social desirability in interviews on race in the United States and in France, see Bonilla-Silva 2002; Pierce 2012; Bonnet and Caillault 2015; and Cohen 2018.

18. Guillaumin 2002[1972].

19. Petrovich Njegosh 2015, 218; Bucholtz 2011, 387.

20. Lamont et al. 2016, 15.

21. Booth, Colomb, and Williams 2008.

22. Gabriel Abend's "Styles of Sociological Thought" (2006), though contrasting Mexican to U.S. academics, provides real insight into the challenges we faced as coauthors; see also Karen Bennett and Laura-Mihaela Muresan's "Rhetorical Incompatibilities in Academic Writing: English versus the Romance Cultures" (2016).

Appendix C: U.S. Interview Questionnaire

1. Results of the 1984–1985 study are reported in Lieberman 1997. Lieberman and his colleagues found that 74 percent of biologists, 49 percent of biological anthropologists, and 31 percent of cultural anthropologists agreed with this statement.

2. In 1997, babies identified as white had a median weight of 7 pounds, 7 ounces (3,360 grams), while Asian babies had a median weight of 7 pounds, 2 ounces (3,230 grams) and black newborns' median weight was 6 pounds, 15 ounces (3,170 grams). See National Center for Health Statistics 2003.

3. Lapchick and Matthews 2001; U.S. Census Bureau 2001.

REFERENCES

ABC News. 2013. "Italian MP Roberto Calderoli Compares Black Minister Cecile Kyenge to Orangutan." *ABC News*, July 14.

Abend, Gabriel. 2006. "Styles of Sociological Thought: Sociologies, Epistemologies, and the Mexican and U.S. Quests for Truth." *Sociological Theory* 24(1): 1–41.

AgenPress.it. 2018. "Liliana Segre. Togliere la parola 'razza' dalla Costituzione. Berlusconi d'accordo." *AgenPress.it*, February 5.

Alba, Richard. 2005. "Bright vs. Blurred Boundaries: Second-Generation Assimilation and Exclusion in France, Germany, and the United States." *Ethnic and Racial Studies* 28(1): 20–49.

Alba, Richard, and Nancy Foner. 2015. *Strangers No More: Immigration and the Challenges of Integration in North America and Western Europe.* Princeton, N.J.: Princeton University Press.

Alba, Richard, and Jennifer Holdaway, eds. 2014. *The Children of Immigrants at School: A Comparative Look at Integration in the United States and Western Europe.* New York: New York University Press.

Alba, Richard, and Mary Waters. 2011. "Dimensions of Second-Generation Incorporation: An Introduction to the Book." In *The Next Generation: Immigrant Youth in a Comparative Perspective*, edited by Richard Alba and Mary Waters. New York: New York University Press.

Alexander, Michelle. 2010. *The New Jim Crow: Mass Incarceration in the Age of Colorblindness.* New York: New Press.

Alim, H. Samy, and Angela Reyes. 2011. "Complicating Race: Articulating Race across Multiple Social Dimensions." *Discourse and Society* 22: 379–84.

Allievi, Stefano. 2002. "Muslims in Italy." In *New European Identity and Citizenship*, edited by Rémy Leveau, Khadija Mohsen-Finan, and Catherine Wihtol de Wenden. Aldershot: Ashgate.

Ambrosetti, Elena, and Eralba Cela. 2015. "Demography of Race and Ethnicity in Italy." In *The International Handbook of the Demography of Race and Ethnicity*, edited by Rogelio Sáenz, David G. Embrick, and Néstor P. Rodríguez. Dordrecht: Springer.

Ambrosini, Maurizio. 2013. "'We Are Against a Multi-Ethnic Society': Policies of Exclusion at the Urban Level in Italy." *Ethnic and Racial Studies* 36(1): 136–55.

Angel-Ajani, Asale. 2000. "Italy's Racial Cauldron: Immigration, Criminalization, and the Cultural Politics of Race." *Cultural Dynamics* 12(3): 331–52.

Antonsich, Marco. 2012. "Exploring the Demands of Assimilation among White Ethnic Majorities in Western Europe." *Journal of Ethnic and Migration Studies* 38(1): 59–76.

Apostle, Richard A., Charles Y. Glock, Thomas Piazza, and Marijean Suelzle. 1983. *The Anatomy of Racial Attitudes*. Berkeley: University of California Press.

Armer, Michael. 1973. "Methodological Problems and Possibilities in Comparative Research." In *Comparative Social Research*, edited by Michael Armer and A. D. Grimshaw. New York: John Wiley & Sons.

Arystanbek, Aizada. 2020. "Black Lives Matter and Kazakhstan: Interracial Solidarity and Where to Find It." *Lossi 36*, October 21.

Asmelash, Leah. 2021. "Idaho Moves to Ban Critical Race Theory Instruction in All Public Schools, Including Universities." CNN, April 27.

Azzarito, Laura, and Louis Harrison Jr. 2008. "'White Men Can't Jump': Race, Gender, and Natural Athleticism." *International Review for the Sociology of Sport* 43(4): 347–64.

Back, Les, Tim Crabbe, and John Solomos. 2001. *The Changing Face of Football: Racism, Identity, and Multiculture in the English Game*. Oxford: Berg.

Bail, Christopher A. 2008. "The Configuration of Symbolic Boundaries against Immigrants in Europe." *American Sociological Review* 73: 37–59.

Bailey, Stanley R., Fabrício M. Fialho, and Andrew M. Penner. 2016. "Interrogating Race: Color, Racial Categories, and Class across the Americas." *American Behavioral Scientist* 60(4): 538–55.

Balbo, Laura. 1989. "Oltre l'antirazzismo facile." *Democrazia e Diritto* (November/December): 11–22.

Balbo, Laura, and Luigi Manconi. 1990. *I razzismi possibili*. Milan: Giangiacomo Feltrinelli.

———. 1992. *I razzismi reali*. Milano: Feltrinelli.

———. 1993. *Razzismi: un vocabolario*. Milano: Feltrinelli.

Balibar, Étienne. 1991. "Is There a 'Neo-Racism'?" In *Race, Nation, Class: Ambiguous Identities*, edited by Étienne Balibar and Immanuel Wallerstein. London: Verso.

Balibar, Étienne, and Immanuel Wallerstein. 1991. *Race, Nation, Class: Ambiguous Identities*. London: Verso.

Banton, Michael. 1977. *The Idea of Race*. London: Tavistock Publications.

———. 2012. "The Colour Line and the Colour Scale in the Twentieth Century." *Ethnic and Racial Studies* 35(7): 1109–31.

Barbujani, Guido. 2005. "Human Races: Classifying People versus Understanding Diversity." *Current Genomics* 6: 1–12.

————. 2006. *L'invenzione delle razze*. Milan: Bompiani.

Barker, Martin. 1981. *The New Racism: Conservatives and the New Ideology of the Tribe*. Frederick, Md.: Aletheia Books.

Barzun, Jacques. 1937. *Race: A Study in Modern Superstition*. New York: Harcourt, Brace and Company.

Beaman, Jean M. 2017. *Citizen Outsider: Children of North African Immigrants in France*. Oakland: University of California Press.

Beauchemin, Cris, Christelle Hamel, and Patrick Simon, eds. 2015. *Trajectoires et origines, enquête sur la diversité des populations en France*. Paris: Institut national d'études démographiques (INED).

Beaud, Stéphane, and Gérard Noiriel. 2020. *Race et sciences sociales: Essai sur les usages publics d'une catégorie*. Paris: Agone.

Beltrán, Cristina. 2020. *Cruelty as Citizenship: How Migrant Suffering Sustains White Democracy*. Minneapolis: University of Minnesota Press.

Bennett, Karen, and Laura-Mihaela Muresan. 2016. "Rhetorical Incompatibilities in Academic Writing: English versus the Romance Cultures." *Synergy* 12(1): 95–119.

Bernhard, Patrick. 2019. "The Great Divide? Notions of Racism in Fascist Italy and Nazi Germany: New Answers to an Old Problem." *Journal of Modern Italian Studies* 24(1): 97–114.

Bessone, Magali. 2013. *Sans distinction de race? Une analyse critique du concept de race et de ses effets pratiques*. Paris: Vrin.

Bidussa, David. 1994. *Il mito del bravo italiano*. Milano: Il Saggiatore.

Binotto, Marco, Marco Bruno, and Valeria Lai. 2016. *Tracciare confini: L'immigrazione nei media italiani*. Milano: Franco Angeli.

Bird, Karen L. 2000. "Racist Speech or Free Speech? A Comparison of the Law in France and the United States." *Comparative Politics* 32: 399–418.

Blanchard, Pascal, and Nicolas Bancel. 1998. *De l'indigène à l'immigré*. Paris: Gallimard.

Bleich, Erik. 2011. *The Freedom to Be Racist? How the United States and Europe Struggle to Preserve Freedom and Combat Racism*. Oxford: Oxford University Press.

Bobo, Lawrence, James R. Kluegel, and Ryan A. Smith. 1997. "Laissez-Faire Racism: The Crystallization of a Kinder, Gentler, Antiblack Ideology." In *Racial Attitudes in the 1990s: Continuity and Change*, edited by Steven A. Tuch and Jack K. Martin. Westport, Conn.: Praeger.

Bonavita, Riccardo. 2009. *Spettri dell'altro: Letteratura e razzismo nell'Italia contemporanea*. Bologna: Il Mulino.

Bonilla-Silva, Eduardo. 1996. "Rethinking Racism: Toward a Structural Interpretation." *American Sociological Review* 62(3): 465–80.

————. 2000. "'This Is a White Country!': The Racial Ideology of the Western Nations of the World-System." *Sociological Inquiry* 70(2): 188–214.

————. 2002. "The Linguistics of Color Blind Racism: How to Talk Nasty about Blacks without Sounding 'Racist.'" *Critical Sociology* 28(1/2): 41–64.

————. 2003. *Racism without Racists: Color-Blind Racism and the Persistence of Racial Inequality in the United States*. Lanham, Md.: Rowman and Littlefield.

————. 2013. *Racism without Racists: Color-Blind Racism and the Persistence of Racial Inequality in the United States*. Lanham, Md.: Rowman and Littlefield.

Bonnet, François. 2014. "How to Perform Non-Racism? Colour-Blind Speech Norms and Race-Conscious Policies among French Security Personnel." *Journal of Ethnic and Migration Studies* 40(8): 1275–94.

Bonnet, François, and Clotilde Caillault. 2015. "The Invader, the Enemy within and They-Who-Must-Not-Be-Named: How Police Talk about Minorities in Italy, the Netherlands, and France." *Ethnic and Racial Studies* 38(7): 1185–1201.

Bontempelli, Sergio. 2015. "L'invenzione degli zingari: La questione rom tra antiziganismo, razzismo, ed etnicizzazione." *Iperstoria—Testi Letterature Linguaggi* 6: 43–56.

Booth, Wayne C., Gregory C. Colomb, and Joseph M. Williams. 2008. *The Craft of Research*, 3rd ed. Chicago: University of Chicago Press.

Boulila, Stefanie Claudine. 2018. "Race and Racial Denial in Switzerland." *Ethnic and Racial Studies* 42(9): 1401–18.

Bourdieu, Pierre, and Loïc Wacquant. 1999. "On the Cunning of Imperialist Reason." *Theory, Culture, and Society* 16(1): 41–58.

Bovenkerk, Frank, Robert Miles, and Gilles Verbunt. 1990. "Racism, Migration, and the State in Western Europe: A Case for Comparative Analysis." *International Sociology* 5(4): 475–90.

————. 1991. "Comparative Studies of Migration and Racism in Western Europe: A Critical Appraisal." *International Migration Review* 25(2): 375–91.

Breviglieri, Marc, and Tommaso Vitale. 2008. "Lutte anti-discriminatoire et politique de la mesure en Italie: Rapport de synthèse: Italie." Unpublished report. Brussels, Belgium: European Commission Directorate General for Employment, Social Affairs and Equal Opportunities.

Brubaker, Rogers. 1992. *Citizenship and Nationhood in France and Germany*. Cambridge, Mass.: Harvard University Press.

————. 2013. "Categories of Analysis and Categories of Practice: A Note on the Study of Muslims in European Countries of Immigration." *Ethnic and Racial Studies* 36(1): 1–8.

————. 2015a. "The Dolezal Affair: Race, Gender, and the Micropolitics of Identity." *Ethnic and Racial Studies* 39(3): 414–48.

————. 2015b. *Grounds for Difference*. Cambridge, Mass.: Harvard University Press.

Brubaker, Rogers, Mara Loveman, and Peter Stamatov. 2004. "Ethnicity as Cognition." *Theory and Society* 33(1): 31–64.

Bubola, Emma, and Gaia Pianigiani. 2020. "Italy Foreign Minister Shares Blackface Images of His Summer Tan." *New York Times*, August 27.

Bucholtz, Mary. 2011. "'It's Different for Guys': Gendered Narratives of Racial Conflict among White California Youth." *Discourse and Society* 22(4): 385–402.

Burdsey, Daniel. 2020. *Racism and English Football: For Club and Country*. London: Routledge.

Byron, Gay L. 2002. *Symbolic Blackness and Ethnic Difference in Early Christian Literature*. London: Routledge.

Calavita, Kitty. 2005. *Immigrants at the Margins: Law, Race, and Exclusion in Southern Europe.* New York: Cambridge University Press.

Capasso, Luigi, and Bernardino Fantini. 2016. "Mozione degli Antropologi italiani." Florence: Associazione Antropologica Italiana (AAI) e Istituto Italiano di Antropologia (IsIta).

Carr, Matthew. 2012. *Fortress Europe: Dispatches from a Gated Continent.* New York: New Press.

Carrington, Ben. 2010. *Race, Sport, and Politics: The Sporting Black Diaspora.* London: Sage Publications.

Carter, Donald Martin. 1997. *States of Grace: Senegalese in Italy and the New European Immigration.* Minneapolis: University of Minnesota Press.

Carter, J. Kameron. 2008. *Race: A Theological Account.* New York: Oxford University Press.

Castelli, Enrico, ed. 2000. *Immagini e colonie.* Rome: Museo Nazionale delle Arti e Tradizioni Popolari.

Castles, Stephen. 1993. "Migrations and Minorities in Europe: Perspectives for the 1990s: Eleven Hypotheses." In *Racism and Migration in Western Europe,* edited by John Wrench and John Solomos. Oxford: Berg.

Cerase, Andrea. 2014. "Disguising Online Racism in Italy: Symbols, Words, and Statements of 'New' Racist Discourse." VoxPol Inaugural Conference, King's College, London (September).

Chandra, Kanchan, ed. 2012. *Constructivist Theories of Ethnic Politics.* Oxford: Oxford University Press.

Clauss, Ludwig Ferdinand. 1940. *Die nordische Seele: Eine Einführung in die Rassenseelenkunde.* Munich: J. S. Lehmanns Verlag.

Clough Marinaro, Isabella, and Nando Sigona. 2011. "Introduction: Anti-Gypsyism and the Politics of Exclusion: Roma and Sinti in Contemporary Italy." *Journal of Modern Italian Studies* 16(5): 583–89.

Cohen, Mathilde. 2018. "Judicial Diversity in France: The Unspoken and the Unspeakable." *Law and Social Inquiry* 43(4): 1542–73.

Cole, Jeffrey. 1997. *The New Racism in Europe: A Sicilian Ethnography.* Cambridge: Cambridge University Press.

Coleman, David. 2006. "Immigration and Ethnic Change in Low-Fertility Countries: A Third Demographic Transition." *Population and Development Review* 32(3): 401–46.

Colombo, Asher, and Giuseppe Sciortino. 2004. "Italian Immigration: The Origins, Nature, and Evolution of Italy's Migratory Systems." *Journal of Modern Italian Studies* 9(1): 49–70.

Colombo, Enzo. 2010. "Changing Citizenship: Everyday Representations of Membership, Belonging, and Identification among Italian Senior Secondary School Students." *Italian Journal of Sociology of Education* 1: 129–53.

Cornell, Stephen, and Douglas Hartmann. 2007. *Ethnicity and Race: Making Identities in a Changing World.* Thousand Oaks, Calif.: Pine Forge Press.

Cousin, Bruno, and Tommaso Vitale. 2002. "Oriana Fallaci ou la rhétorique matamore." *Mouvements* 23 (September/October): 146–49.

————. 2006. "La question migratoire et l'idéologie occidentaliste de Forza Italia."
La Vie des Idées 11(January): 27–36.

————. 2014. "Le magistère intellectuel islamophobe d'Oriana Fallaci: Origines et
modalités du succès italien de la 'Trilogie sur l'Islam et sur l'Occident' (2001–2006)."
Sociologie 5(1): 61–79.

Cremonesi, Marco. 2018. "'La razza bianca rischia di sparire.'" *Corriere Della Sera*,
January 16.

Crowley, Michael, and Jennifer Schuessler. 2021. "Trump's 1776 Commission Critiques
Liberalism in Report Derided by Historians." *New York Times*, January 18.

Crul, Maurice, and John Mollenkopf, eds. 2012. *The Changing Face of World Cities:
Young Adult Children of Immigrants in Europe and the United States.* New York:
Russell Sage Foundation.

Crul, Maurice, and Hans Vermeulen. 2003. "The Second Generation in Europe."
International Migration Review 37(4): 965–86.

Curcio, Anna. 2011. "Il management della razza in Italia." *Mondi Migranti* 3: 91–120.

Curcio, Anna, and Miguel Mellino. 2010. "Editorial: Race at Work—The Rise and
Challenge of Italian Racism." *darkmatter*, October 10.

Dal Lago, Alessandro. 1999. *Non-persone: L'esclusione dei migranti in una società globale.*
Milano: Feltrinelli.

Daly, Faïçal. 1999. "Tunisian Migrants and Their Experience of Racism in Modena."
Modern Italy 4(2): 173–90.

Danewid, Ida, Giuseppe Grimaldi, Camilla Hawthorne, P. Khahlil Saucier, Gabriele
Proglio, Angelica Pesarini, and Timothy Raeymakers, eds. 2021. *The Black
Mediterranean: Bodies, Borders, and Citizenship.* London: London: Palgrave
MacMillan.

Davis, Floyd James. 1991. *Who Is Black? One Nation's Definition.* University Park:
Pennsylvania State University Press.

De Donno, Fabrizio. 2006. "La Razza Ario-Mediterranea: Ideas of Race and Citizenship
in Colonial and Fascist Italy, 1885–1941." *Interventions* 8(3): 394–412.

De Genova, Nicholas. 2006. "Introduction: Latino and Asian Racial Formations at the
Frontier of U.S. Nationalism." In *Racial Transformations: Latinos and Asians Remaking
the United States*, edited by Nicholas De Genova. Durham, N.C.: Duke University
Press.

————. 2013. "Spectacles of Migrant 'Illegality': The Scene of Exclusion, the Obscene of
Inclusion." *Ethnic and Racial Studies* 36(7): 1180–98.

————. 2018. "The "Migrant Crisis" as Racial Crisis: Do Black Lives Matter in Europe?"
Ethnic and Racial Studies 41(10): 1765–82.

Del Boca, Angelo. 1976–1984. *Gli italiani in Africa orientale.* Bari: Laterza.

————. 1986. *Gli italiani in Libia.* Bari: Laterza.

DeMillo, Andrew. 2021. "GOP States Weigh Limits on How Race and Slavery Are
Taught." Associated Press, February 3.

Deplano, Valeria. 2015. *L'Africa in casa: Propaganda e cultura coloniale nell'Italia fascista.*
Florence: Mondadori-Le Monnier.

Deplano, Valeria, and Alessandro Pes, ed. 2014. *Quel che resta dell'impero: La cultura coloniale degli italiani*. Milan: Mimesis.

De Schutter, Olivier, and Julie Ringelheim. 2010. *Ethnic Monitoring: The Processing of Racial and Ethnic Data in Anti-Discrimination Policies: Reconciling the Promotion of Equality with Privacy Rights*. Louvain, Belgium: Éditions Juridiques Bruylant.

Devos, Thierry, and Mahzarin R. Banaji. 2005. "American = White?" *Journal of Personality and Social Psychology* 88(3): 447–66.

Dhingra, Pawan. 2020. *Hyper Education: Why Good Schools, Good Grades, and Good Behavior Are Not Enough*. New York: New York University Press.

DiAngelo, Robin. 2011. "White Fragility." *International Journal of Critical Pedagogy* 3(3): 54–70.

Dikötter, Frank, ed. 1997. *The Construction of Racial Identities in China and Japan: Historical and Contemporary Perspectives*. Honolulu: University of Hawai'i Press.

Di Maio, Alessandra. 2009. "Black Italia: Contemporary Migrant Writers from Africa." In *Black Europe and the African Diaspora*, edited by Darlene Clark Hine, Trica Danielle Keaton, and Stephen Small. Urbana: University of Illinois Press.

Domingo, Andreu. 2008. "'Demodystopias': Prospects of Demographic Hell." *Population and Development Review* 34(4): 725–45.

Durupt, Frantz. 2017. "Blanquer porte plainte contre un syndicat qui a utilisé l'expression 'racisme d'Etat.'" *Libération*, November 21.

Duster, Troy. 1990. *Backdoor to Eugenics*. New York: Routledge.

Edmondson, Catie. 2021. "McConnell Attacks Biden Rule's Antiracism Focus, Calling It 'Divisive.'" *New York Times*, April 30.

El-Tayeb, Fatima. 2011a. *European Others: Queering Ethnicity in Postnational Europe*. Minneapolis: University of Minnesota Press.

———. 2011b. "'The Forces of Creolization': Colorblindness and Visible Minorities in the New Europe." In *The Creolization of Theory*, edited by Françoise Lionnet, Shu-mei Shih, and Étienne Balibar. Raleigh, N.C.: Duke University Press.

Elder, Joseph W. 1976. "Comparative Cross-National Methodology." *Annual Review of Sociology* 2: 209–230.

Entine, Jon. 2000. *Taboo: Why Black Athletes Dominate Sports and Why We're Afraid to Talk about It*. New York: Public Affairs.

Enwereuzor, Udo C., and Laura Di Pasquale. 2009. "RAXEN Thematic Study: Housing Conditions of Roma and Travellers: Italy." Florence: Cooperation for the Development of Emerging Countries (COSPE).

Essed, Philomena. 1990. *Everyday Racism: Reports from Women of Two Cultures*. Claremont, Calif.: Hunter House.

———. 1991. *Understanding Everyday Racism: An Interdisciplinary Theory*. Newbury Park, Calif.: Sage Publications.

European Commission. 2007. "Discrimination in the European Union." *Special Eurobarometer*. Brussels: European Commission. http://www.edrc.ro/docs/docs/cercetari/Special_Eurobarometer_Discrimination_2006.pdf. (accessed December 7, 2021).

————. 2012. "Discrimination in the European Union." *Special Eurobarometer.* Brussels: European Commission. https://europa.eu/eurobarometer/surveys/detail/1043. (accessed December 7, 2021).

Fallaci, Oriana. 2004. *The Trilogy of Oriana Fallaci.* New York: Rizzoli International.

Fanon, Frantz. 2008. *Black Skin, White Masks.* New York: Grove Press. (Originally published in 1952.)

Faso, Giuseppe. 2008. *Lessico del razzismo democratico: Le parole che escludono.* Rome: DeriveApprodi.

Fassin, Didier, and Éric Fassin, eds. 2006. *De la question sociale à la question raciale? Représenter la société française.* Paris: La Découverte.

Fassin, Éric. 2014. "(Sexual) Whiteness and National Identity: Race, Class, and Sexuality in Colour-Blind France." In *Theories of Race and Ethnicity: Contemporary Debates and Perspectives,* edited by Karim Murji and John Solomos. Cambridge: Cambridge University Press.

Favell, Adrian. 2016. "Just Like the USA? Critical Notes on Alba and Foner's Cross-Atlantic Research Agenda." *Ethnic and Racial Studies* 39(13): 2352–60.

Ferber, Abby L. 1999. *White Man Falling: Race, Gender, and White Supremacy.* Lanham, Md.: Rowman and Littlefield.

Fields, Karen E., and Barbara J. Fields. 2012. *Racecraft: The Soul of Inequality in American Life.* London: Verso.

Finaldi, Giuseppe Maria. 2009. *Italian National Identity in the Scramble for Africa: Italy's African Wars in the Era of Nation-Building, 1870–1900.* Bern: Peter Lang.

Fiske, Susan T. 2002. "What We Know Now about Bias and Intergroup Conflict, the Problem of the Century." *Current Directions in Psychological Science* 11(4): 123–28.

Fiske, Susan T., Amy J. C. Cuddy, and Peter Glick. 2007. "Universal Dimensions of Social Cognition: Warmth and Competence." *TRENDS in Cognitive Sciences* 11(2): 77–83.

Fleming, Crystal Marie. 2017. *Resurrecting Slavery: Racial Legacies and White Supremacy in France.* Philadelphia: Temple University Press.

Foldy, Erica Gabrielle, and Tamara R. Buckley. 2014. *The Color Bind: Talking (and Not Talking) about Race at Work.* New York: Russell Sage Foundation.

Fondazione ISMU. 2018. "XXIV Rapporto ISMU sulle Migrazioni 2018." Milano: FrancoAngeli.

Foner, Nancy. 2015. "Is Islam in Western Europe Like Race in the United States?" *Sociological Forum* 30(4): 885–99.

Foner, Nancy, and Patrick Simon, eds. 2015. *Fear, Anxiety, and National Identity: Immigration and Belonging in North America and Western Europe.* New York: Russell Sage Foundation.

Forgacs, David. 2014. *Italy's Margins: Social Exclusion and Nation Formation since 1861.* Cambridge: Cambridge University Press.

Foy, Steven L., and Rashawn Ray. 2019. "Skin in the Game: Colorism and the Subtle Operation of Stereotypes in Men's College Basketball." *American Journal of Sociology* 125(3): 730–85.

France 24. 2013. "No Such Thing as 'Race,' Say French Lawmakers." *France 24*, May 17.

———. 2018. "'Race' out, Gender Equality in as France Updates Constitution." *France 24*, June 28.

Franceinfo. 2020. "Le ministre de l'Education nationale, Jean-Michel Blanquer, dénonce 'l'islamo-gauchisme' qui 'fait des ravages à l'université.'" *Franceinfo*, October 22.

———. 2021. "Enseignement supérieur: On vous explique la polémique sur l'enquête visant l'"islamo-gauchisme' réclamée par le gouvernement." *Franceinfo*, February 17.

Frankenberg, Ruth. 1993. *White Women, Race Matters: The Social Construction of Whiteness*. Minneapolis: University of Minnesota Press.

Fredrickson, George M. 2002. *Racism: A Short History*. Princeton, N.J.: Princeton University Press.

Fuchs, Hailey. 2020. "Trump Attack on Diversity Training Has a Quick and Chilling Effect." *New York Times*, October 13.

Fuentes, Agustín. 2011. *Race, Monogamy, and Other Lies They Told You: Busting Myths about Human Nature*. Berkeley: University of California Press.

Gabrielli, Gianluca. 2014. "Insegnare le colonie: La costruzione dell'identità e dell'alterità coloniale nella scuola italiana (1860–1950)." In *Scienze della formazione, dei beni culturali e del turismo*. Macerata: Università degli studi di Macerata.

———. 2019. "Razzismo coloniale italiano: Dal madamato alla legge contro le unioni miste." *Novecento.org*, March 26.

Gaertner, Samuel L., and John F. Dovidio. 1986. "The Aversive Form of Racism." In *Prejudice, Discrimination, and Racism*, edited by John F. Dovidio and Samuel L. Gaertner. Orlando, Fla.: Academic Press.

Gallini, Clara. 1996. *Giochi pericolosi: Frammenti di un immaginario alquanto razzista*. Roma: Manifestolibri.

Gans, Herbert. 1979. "Symbolic Ethnicity: The Future of Ethnic Groups and Cultures in America." *Ethnic and Racial Studies* 2(1): 1–19.

Gariglio, Luigi, Andrea Pogliano, and Riccardo Zanini, eds. 2010. *Facce da straniero: 20 anni di fotografia e giornalismo sull'immigrazione in Italia*. Milan: Bruno Mondadori.

Gibson, Mary. 1998. "Biology or Environment? Race and Southern 'Deviancy' in the Writings of Italian Criminologists, 1880–1920." In *Italy's "Southern Question": Orientalism in One Country*, edited by Jane Schneider. Oxford: Berg.

———. 2002. *Born to Crime: Cesare Lombroso and the Origins of Biological Criminology*. Westport, Conn.: Praeger.

Gifford-Gonzales, Diane. 1993. "You Can Hide, but You Can't Run: Representation of Women's Work in Illustrations of Palaeolithic Life." *Visual Anthropology Review* 9(1): 23–41.

———. 1995. "The Real Flintstones? What Are Artists' Depictions of Human Ancestors Telling Us?" *Anthro Notes: National Museum of Natural History Bulletin for Teachers* 17(3): 1–5.

Gillette, Aaron. 2002. *Racial Theories in Fascist Italy*. New York: Routledge.

Gilroy, Paul. 1987. *"There Ain't No Black in the Union Jack": The Cultural Politics of Race and Nation*. London: Hutchinson.

Giuliani, Gaia, ed. 2015. *Il colore della nazione.* Milan: Mondadori Education.

———. 2019. *Race, Nation, and Gender in Modern Italy: Intersectional Representations in Visual Culture.* London: Palgrave MacMillan.

Giuliani, Gaia, and Cristina Lombardi-Diop. 2013. *Bianco e nero: Storia dell'identità razziale degli italiani.* Milan: Le Monnier.

Glassman, Jonathon 2011. *War of Words, War of Stones: Racial Thought and Violence in Colonial Zanzibar.* Bloomington: Indiana University Press.

Golash-Boza, Tanya Maria. 2011. *Yo Soy Negro: Blackness in Peru.* Gainesville: University Press of Florida.

Goldberg, David Theo. 1990. *Anatomy of Racism.* Minneapolis: University of Minnesota Press.

———. 2009. *The Threat of Race: Reflections on Racial Neoliberalism.* Oxford: Wiley-Blackwell.

Gonyea, Don. 2017. "Majority of White Americans Say They Believe Whites Face Discrimination." NPR, October 24.

Gonzalez-Barrera, Ana, and Phillip Connor. 2019. "Around the World, More Say Immigrants Are a Strength than a Burden." Washington, D.C.: Pew Research Center (March 14).

Gordon, Milton Myron. 1964. *Assimilation in American life: The Role of Race, Religion, and National Origins.* New York: Oxford University Press.

Green, Nancy L. 1999. "Le Melting-Pot: Made in America, Produced in France." *Journal of American History* 86(3): 1188–1208.

Grigolo, Michele, Costanza Hermanin, and Mathias Möschel. 2011. "Introduction: How Does Race 'Count' in Fighting Discrimination in Europe?" *Ethnic and Racial Studies* 34: 1635–47.

Grossi, Claudia. 2012. "Diversità genetica umana e sua percezione in tre categorie sociali." In *Quaternary, Prehistory, Archaeology.* Ferrara: Universita' degli studi di Ferrara.

Guglielmo, Jennifer, and Salvatore Salerno, eds. 2003. *Are Italians White? How Race Is Made in America.* New York: Routledge.

Guillaumin, Colette. 2002. *L'idéologie raciste.* Paris: Gallimard. (Originally published in 1972.)

Gullestad, Marianne. 2006. *Plausible Prejudice: Everyday Experiences and Social Images of Nation, Culture, and Race.* Oslo: Universitetsforlaget.

Hall, Bruce S. 2011. *A History of Race in Muslim West Africa, 1600–1960.* Cambridge: Cambridge University Press.

Hanchard, Michael. 1994. *Orpheus and Power: The Movimento Negro of Rio di Janeiro and São Paulo, 1945–1988.* Princeton, N.J.: Princeton University Press.

———. 2003. "Acts of Misrecognition: Transnormal Black Politics, Anti-imperialism, and the Ethnocentrisms of Pierre Bourdieu and Loïc Wacquant." *Theory, Culture, and Society* 20(4): 5–29.

Hancock, Ian F. 2002. *We Are the Romani People.* Hatfield: University of Hertfordshire Press.

Hannaford, Ivan. 1996. *Race: The History of an Idea in the West.* Washington, D.C.: Woodrow Wilson Center Press.

Hargreaves, Alec G. 1995. *Racism, Ethnicity, and Politics in Contemporary Europe.* Aldershot: Edward Elgar.

Hartigan, John. 2013. "Translating 'Race' and 'Raza' between the United States and Mexico." *North American Dialogue* 16(1): 29–41.

Hartmann, Douglas. 2016. *Midnight Basketball: Race, Sports, and Neoliberal Social Policy.* Chicago: University of Chicago Press.

Haslam, Nick, Louis Rothschild, and Donald Ernst. 2000. "Essentialist Beliefs about Social Categories." *British Journal of Social Psychology* 39(1): 113–27.

Hattam, Victoria. 2004. "Ethnicity: An American Genealogy." In *Not Just Black and White: Historical and Contemporary Perspectives on Immigration, Race, and Ethnicity in the United States*, edited by Nancy Foner and George M. Fredrickson. New York: Russell Sage Foundation.

Hawthorne, Camilla. 2017. "In Search of Black Italia: Notes on Race, Belonging, and Activism in the Black Mediterranean." *Jalada 05/Transition* 123: 152–74.

———. 2019. "Making Italy: Afro-Italian Entrepreneurs and the Racial Boundaries of Citizenship." *Social and Cultural Geography* 22(5): 704–24.

———. Forthcoming. *Contesting Race and Citizenship: Diasporic Politics in Italy and the Black Mediterranean.* Ithaca, N.Y.: Cornell University Press.

Hermanin, Costanza. 2011. "'Counts' in the Italian 'Nomad Camps': An Incautious Ethnic Census of Roma." *Ethnic and Racial Studies* 34(10): 1731–50.

Hochschild, Jennifer L. 1995. *Facing up to the American Dream: Race, Class, and the Soul of the Nation.* Princeton, N.J.: Princeton University Press.

Hochschild, Jennifer L., and John H. Mollenkopf, eds. 2009. *Bringing Outsiders In: Transatlantic Perspectives on Immigrant Political Incorporation.* Ithaca, N.Y.: Cornell University Press.

Hollinger, David A. 1998. "National Culture and Communities of Descent." *Reviews in American History* 26(1): 312–28.

Hopper, Matthew S. 2015. *Slaves of One Master: Globalization and Slavery in Arabia in the Age of Empire.* New Haven, Conn.: Yale University Press.

Hughey, Matthew W., and Devon R. Goss. 2015. "A Level Playing Field? Media Constructions of Athletics, Genetics, and Race." *Annals of the American Academy of Political and Social Science* 661(1): 182–211.

ImolaOggi. 2018. "Milano Bicocca: Convegno per eliminare la parola 'razza' dalla Costituzione." *ImolaOggi.it*, May 15.

Istituto Nazionale Previdenza Sociale (INPS). 2018. "Anno 2017: Lavoratori domestici." In *Statistiche in breve*. Rome: INPS, Coordinamento Generale Statistico Attuariale.

Jasanoff, Sheila, ed. 2004. *States of Knowledge: The Co-Production of Science and Social Order.* London: Routledge.

Jiménez, Tomás R. 2010. "Affiliative Ethnic Identity: A More Elastic Link between Ethnic Ancestry and Culture." *Ethnic and Racial Studies* 33(10): 1756–75.

Joo, Rachael Miyung. 2012. *Transnational Sport: Gender, Media, and Global Korea.* Durham, N.C.: Duke University Press.

Jordan, Winthrop D. 1968. *White over Black: American Attitudes toward the Negro, 1550–1812.* New York: W. W. Norton.

Kastoryano, Riva. 2002. *Negotiating Identities: States and Immigrants in France and Germany.* Princeton, N.J.: Princeton University Press.

———, ed. 2005. *Les codes de la différence: Race, origine, religion; France, Allemagne, États-Unis.* Paris: Presses de la Fondation Nationale des Sciences Politiques.

Katzew, Ilona. 2004. *Casta Painting: Images of Race in Eighteenth-Century Mexico.* New Haven, Conn.: Yale University Press.

Kendi, Ibram X. 2019. "The Day Shithole Entered the Presidential Lexicon." *Atlantic,* January 13.

Kevles, Daniel J. 1995. *In the Name of Eugenics: Genetics and the Uses of Human Heredity.* Cambridge, Mass.: Harvard University Press. (Originally published in 1985.)

Khouma, Pap. 2009. "Io, nero italiano e la mia vita ad ostacoli." *La Repubblica,* December 12.

———. 2010. *Noi italiani neri: Storie di ordinario razzismo.* Milan: Baldini Castoldi Dalai.

Kim, Claire Jean. 1999. "The Racial Triangulation of Asian Americans." *Politics and Society* 27(1): 105–38.

Kim, Gagyung. 2012. "Respect for Foreign Workers Starts with Not Labelling." *The National,* January 4.

Kim, Nadia Y. 2008. *Imperial Citizens: Koreans and Race from Seoul to L.A.* Stanford, Calif.: Stanford University Press.

King, C. Richard, Carmen R. Lugo-Lugo, and Mary K. Bloodsworth-Lugo. 2010. *Animating Difference: Race, Gender, and Sexuality in Contemporary Films for Children.* Lanham, Md.: Rowman and Littlefield.

Kohn, Hans. 1994. *The Idea of Nationalism: A Study in Its Origins and Background.* New York: MacMillan. (Originally published in 1944.)

Kuti, Tommy. 2019. *Ci rido sopra: Crescere con la pelle nera nell'Italia di Salvini.* Milan: Rizzoli.

Kyeremeh, Sandra Agyei 2017. "Corpi neri in spazi maschili bianchi: Le atlete italiane nere o di origini straniere nello sport italiano." *La camera blu: Rivista di studi di genere* 17: 183–208.

Labanca, Nicola. 1996. "L'Africa italiana." In *I luoghi della memoria,* edited by Mario Isnenghi. Roma-Bari: Laterza.

———. 2002. *Oltremare: Storia dell'espansione coloniale italiana.* Bologna: Il Mulino.

Lahiri, Jhumpa. 2016. *In Other Words.* New York: Alfred A. Knopf.

Lamont, Michèle. 2000a. *The Dignity of Working Men: Morality and the Boundaries of Race, Class, and Immigration.* Cambridge and New York: Harvard University Press and Russell Sage Foundation.

———. 2000b. "The Rhetorics of Racism and Anti-Racism in France and the United States." In *Rethinking Comparative Cultural Sociology: Repertoires of Evaluation in France and the United States,* edited by Michèle Lamont and Laurent Thévenot. Cambridge: Cambridge University Press.

Lamont, Michèle, and Virág Molnár. 2002. "The Study of Boundaries in the Social Sciences." *Annual Review of Sociology* 28(1): 167–95.

Lamont, Michèle, Graziella Moraes Silva, Jessica S. Welburn, Joshua Guetzkow, Nissim Mizrachi, Hanna Herzog, and Elisa Reis. 2016. *Getting Respect: Responding to Stigma and Discrimination in the United States, Brazil, and Israel.* Princeton, N.J.: Princeton University Press.

Lamont, Michèle, and Laurent Thévenot. 2000a. "Introduction: Toward a Renewed Comparative Cultural Sociology." In *Rethinking Comparative Cultural Sociology: Repertoires of Evaluation in France and the United States,* edited by Michèle Lamont and Laurent Thévenot. New York: Cambridge University Press.

———. 2000b. *Rethinking Comparative Cultural Sociology: Repertoires of Evaluation in France and the United States.* Cambridge: Cambridge University Press.

Lapchick, Richard E., and Kevin J. Matthews. 2001. *Racial and Gender Report Card.* Boston: Northeastern University, Center for the Study of Sport in Society. http://www.sportinsociety.org.

La Repubblica. 2013. "Borghezio: 'Kyenge ministro? E' governo del bonga bonga.'" *La Repubblica—Bologna,* January 16.

Lentin, Alana. 2014. "Post-Race, Post Politics: The Paradoxical Rise of Culture after Multiculturalism." *Ethnic and Racial Studies* 37(8): 1268–85.

Leoni, Giuliano, and Andrea Tappi. 2010. "Pagine perse: Il colonialismo nei manuali di storia dal dopoguerra a oggi." *Zapruder: Storie in Movimento: Rivista di storia della conflittualità sociale* 23: 154–67.

Lewis, David Levering. 2008. *God's Crucible: Islam and the Making of Europe.* New York: W. W. Norton.

Lieberman, Leonard. 1997. "Gender and the Deconstruction of the Race Concept." *American Anthropologist* 99(3): 545–58.

Lombardi-Diop, Cristina. 2012. "Postracial/Postcolonial Italy." In *Postcolonial Italy: Challenging National Homogeneity,* edited by Cristina Lombardi-Diop and Caterina Romeo. New York: Palgrave MacMillan.

Lombardi-Diop, Cristina, and Caterina Romeo. 2012. "Introductions: Paradigms of Postcoloniality in Contemporary Italy." In *Postcolonial Italy: Challenging National Homogeneity,* edited by Cristina Lombardi-Diop and Caterina Romeo. New York: Palgrave MacMillan.

Loveman, Mara. 1999. "Is 'Race' Essential?" *American Sociological Review* 64(6): 891–98.

———. 2014. *National Colors: Racial Classification and the State in Latin America.* Oxford: Oxford University Press.

Lucassen, Leo, Wim Willems, and Annemarie Cottaar. 1998. *Gypsies and Other Itinerant Groups: A Socio-Historical Approach.* Basingstoke: St. Martin's Press.

Ludwig, David. 2019. "How Race Travels: Relating Local and Global Ontologies of Race." *Philosophical Studies* 176: 2729–50.

Lutz, Catherine A., and Jane L. Collins. 1993. *Reading National Geographic.* Chicago: University of Chicago Press.

Mack, Rosamond E. 2001. *Bazaar to Piazza: Islamic Trade and Italian Art, 1300–1600.* Berkeley: University of California Press.

MacMaster, Neil. 2001. *Racism in Europe 1870–2000*. Basingstoke: Palgrave.

Maher, Vanessa. 1996a. "Immigration and Social Identities." In *Italian Cultural Studies: An Introduction*, edited by David Forgacs and Robert Lumley. Oxford: Oxford University Press.

———. 1996b. "Immigration and Social Identities." In *Italian Cultural Studies: An Introduction*, edited by David Forgacs and Robert Lumley. Oxford: Oxford University Press.

Maheshwari, Sapna. 2019. "Italian Airline Pulls Video with Actor in Blackface as Barack Obama." *New York Times*, July 3.

Maneri, Marcello. 1998a. "Immigrati e classi pericolose: Lo statuto dell'extracomunitario' nella stampa quotidiana." In *Relazioni etniche stereotipi e pregiudizi: Fenomeno immigratorio ed esclusione sociale*, edited by Marcella Delle Donne. Rome: EdUP.

———. 1998b. "Lo straniero consensuale: La devianza degli immigrati come circolarità di pratiche e discorsi." In *Lo straniero e il nemico: Materiali per l'etnografia contemporanea*, edited by Alessandro Dal Lago. Genova: Costa & Nolan.

———. 2003. "La construction d'un sens commun sur l'immigration en Italie: Les "gens" dans le discours médiatique et politique." *La Revue Internationale et Stratégique* 50: 95–104.

———. 2011. "Media Discourse on Immigration: The Translation of Control Practices into the Language We Live By." In *Racial Criminalization of Migrants in the 21st Century*, edited by Salvatore Palidda. Farnham: Ashgate.

———. 2018. "Media-Hypes, Moral Panics, and the Ambiguous Nature of Facts: Urban Security as Discursive Formation." In *From Media Hype to Twitter Storm: News Explosions and Their Impact on Issues, Crises, and Public Opinion*, edited by Peter Vasterman. Amsterdam: Amsterdam University Press.

Maneri, Marcello, and Fabio Quassoli, eds. 2020. *Un attentato "quasi terroristico": Macerata 2018, il razzismo e la sfera pubblica al tempo dei social media*. Rome: Carocci Editore.

Marks, Jonathan. 1995. *Human Biodiversity: Genes, Race, and History*. New York: Aldine de Gruyter.

Mattioli, Alberto. 2018. "'La razza bianca è a rischio.' Fontana choc, poi le scuse." *La Stampa*, January 16.

Mazouz, Sarah. 2020. *Race*. Paris: Anamosa.

Mellino, Miguel. 2011. "De-provincializzare l'Italia: Note su colonialità, razza e razzializzazione nel contesto italiano." *Mondi Migranti* 3: 59–90.

Merrill, Heather. 2006. *Alliance of Women: Immigration and the Politics of Race*. Minneapolis: University of Minnesota Press.

———. 2011. "Migration and Surplus Populations: Race and Deindustrialization in Northern Italy." *Antipode* 43(5): 1542–72.

———. 2013. "Who Gets to Be Italian? Black Life Worlds and White Spatial Imaginaries." In *Geographies of Privilege*, edited by France Winddance Twine and Bradley Gardener. New York: Routledge.

Miles, Robert. 1993. *Racism after "Race Relations."* New York: Routledge.

———. 1999. "Racism as a Concept." In *Racism*, edited by Martin Bulmer and John Solomos. Oxford: Oxford University Press.

Miller, Patrick. 1998. "The Anatomy of Scientific Racism: Racialist Responses to Black Athletic Achievement." *Journal of Sport History* 25(1): 119–51.

Ministero dell'Istruzione, dell'Università, della Ricerca. 2014. "Linee guida per l'accoglienza e l'integrazione degli alunni stranieri." Rome: Ministero dell'Istruzione.

Modood, Tariq. 2001. "'Difference,' Cultural Racism, and Anti-Racism." In *Race and Racism*, edited by Bernard Boxill. Oxford: Oxford University Press.

Montagu, M. F. Ashley. 1942. *Man's Most Dangerous Myth: The Fallacy of Race*. New York: Columbia University Press.

Morning, Ann. 2008. "Ethnic Classification in Global Perspective: A Cross-National Survey of the 2000 Census Round." *Population Research and Policy Review* 27(2): 239–72.

———. 2009. "Toward a Sociology of Racial Conceptualization for the 21st Century." *Social Forces* 87(3): 1167–92.

———. 2011. *The Nature of Race: How Scientists Think and Teach about Human Difference*. Berkeley: University of California Press.

———. 2017. "Kaleidoscope: Contested Identities and New Forms of Race Membership." *Ethnic and Racial Studies* 41(6): 1–19.

Morning, Ann, and Daniel Sabbagh. 2005. "From Sword to Plowshare: Using Race for Discrimination and Antidiscrimination in the United States." *International Social Science Journal* 57(183): 57–73.

Mosca, Giuditta. 2018. "C'è davvero chi vuole togliere (seriamente) la parola 'razza' dalla Costituzione." *Wired.it*, January 16.

Möschel, Mathias. 2007. "Color Blindness or Total Blindness? The Absence of Critical Race Theory in Europe." *Rutgers Race and Law Review* 9: 57–128.

———. 2011. "Race in Mainland European Legal Analysis: Towards a European Critical Race Theory." *Ethnic and Racial Studies* 34(10): 1648–64.

———. 2014. *Law, Lawyers, and Race: Critical Race Theory from the U.S. to Europe*. New York: Routledge.

National Center for Health Statistics (NCHS). 2003. "Table 1-27. Selected Birthweight Characteristics of Live Births by Educational Attainment, Age, and Race and Hispanic Origin of Mother: Total of 48 States and the District of Columbia, 2003." In *Vital Statistics of the United States, 2003*, vol. 1, *Natality*. Washington, D.C.: NCHS. https://www.cdc.gov/nchs/data/statab/natfinal2003.annvol1_27.pdf.

Ndiaye, Pap. 2009. *La condition noire: Essai sur une minorité française*. Paris: Folio.

Nelkin, Dorothy, and M. Susan Lindee. 1995. *The DNA Mystique: The Gene as Cultural Icon*. New York: Freeman.

Nelson, Shannon C. 2008. "Feeling Thermometer." In *Encyclopedia of Survey Research Methods*, edited by Paul J. Lavrakas. Thousand Oaks, Calif.: Sage Publications.

Neuman, W. Lawrence. 2006. *Social Research Methods: Qualitative and Quantitative Approaches*. Boston: Pearson Education.

Nobles, Melissa. 2000. *Shades of Citizenship: Race and the Census in Modern Politics*. Stanford, Calif.: Stanford University Press.

Noiriel, Gérard. 1988. *Le creuset français: Histoire de l'immigration (19ème–20ème siècles)*. Paris: Éditions du Seuil.

Obasogie, Osagie K. 2014. *Blinded by Sight: Seeing Race through the Eyes of the Blind*. Stanford, Calif.: Stanford University Press.

Observatoire du décolonialisme et des idéologies identitaires. 2021. "Qu'est-ce que le décolonialisme?" https://decolonialisme.fr/?page_id=73. (accessed December 7, 2021).

Olson, Joel. 2004. *The Abolition of White Democracy*. Minneapolis: University of Minnesota Press.

Omi, Michael, and Howard Winant. 2014. *Racial Formation in the United States*. New York: Routledge.

Onishi, Norimitsu. 2020. "A Racial Awakening in France, Where Race Is a Taboo Topic." *New York Times*, July 14.

———. 2021a. "Powerful Men Fall, One after Another, in France's Delayed #MeToo." *New York Times*, April 8.

———. 2021b. "Will American Ideas Tear France Apart? Some of Its Leaders Think So." *New York Times*, February 9.

Onishi, Norimitsu, and Constant Méheut. 2021. "Heating up Culture Wars, France to Scour Universities for Ideas That 'Corrupt Society.'" *New York Times*, February 18.

Organization for Economic Cooperation and Development (OECD). 2020. *International Migration Outlook 2020*. Paris: OECD.

Osuji, Chinyere. 2017. "Rachel Dolezal: 'Negra Frustrada' (Frustrated Black Woman)." Rutgers University–Camden, May 24. https://chinyereosuji.camden.rutgers.edu/2017/05/24/rachel-dolezal-negra-frustrada-frustrated-black-woman/comment-page-1/.

Palidda, Salvatore. 2000. *Polizia postmoderna: Etnografia del nuovo controllo sociale*. Milan: Feltrinelli.

Panofsky, Aaron. 2014. *Misbehaving Science: Controversy and the Development of Behavior Genetics*. Chicago: University of Chicago Press.

Patriarca, Silvana. 2015. "Fear of Small Numbers: 'Brown Babies' in Postwar Italy." *Contemporanea* 4(October–December): 537–68.

Perlmann, Joel, and Mary C. Waters, eds. 2002. *The New Race Question: How the Census Counts Multiracial Individuals*. New York and Annandale-on-Hudson, N.Y.: Russell Sage Foundation and Levy Economics Institute of Bard College.

Perry, Pamela. 2002. *Shades of White: White Kids and Racial Identities in High School*. Durham, N.C.: Duke University Press.

Pesarini, Angelica. 2014. "Madri nere figlie bianche: Forme disSubalternità femminile in Africa Orientale Italiana." In *Subalternità Italiane: Percorsi di ricerca tra storia e letteratura*, edited by Valeria Deplano, Lorenzo Mari, and Gabriele Proglio. Rome: Aracne.

———. 2020. "Questioni di privilegio. L'Italia e i suoi George Floyd." *Il lavoro culturale*, June 6.

Pesarini, Angelica, and Guido Tintori. 2020. "Mixed Identities in Italy: A Country in Denial." In *The Palgrave International Handbook of Mixed Racial and Ethnic Classification*, edited by Peter Aspinall and Zarine Rocha. London: Palgrave MacMillan.

Petrovich Njegosh, Tatiana. 2012. "Gli italiani sono bianchi? Per una storia culturale della linea del colore in Italia." In *Parlare di razza: La lingua del colore tra Italia e Stati Uniti*, edited by Tatiana Petrovich Njegosh and Anna Scacchi. Verona: Ombre Corte.

———. 2015. "La finzione della razza: La linea del colore el il meticciato." In *Il colore della nazione*, edited by Gaia Giuliani. Milan: Mondadori Education.

———. 2016. "Che cos'è la razza? Il caso dell'Italia." *From the European South* 1: 83–93.

Petrovich Njegosh, Tatiana, and Anna Scacchi, eds. 2012. *Parlare di razza: La lingua del colore tra Italia e Stati Uniti*. Verona: Ombre Corte.

Petruzzelli, Pietro. 2008. *Non chiamarmi zingaro*. Milano: Chiarelettere.

Pew Research Center. 2014. "A Fragile Rebound for EU Image on Eve of European Parliament Elections." Washington, D.C.: Pew Research Center (May 12).

———. 2018. "Being Christian in Western Europe." Washington, D.C.: Pew Research Center (May 29).

Phelan, Jo C., Bruce G. Link, and Naumi M. Feldman. 2013. "The Genomic Revolution and Beliefs about Essential Racial Differences: A Backdoor to Eugenics?" *American Sociological Review* 78(2): 167–91.

Phillips, Amber. 2017. "'They're Rapists': President Trump's Campaign Launch Speech Two Years Later, Annotated." *Washington Post*, June 16.

Piasere, Leonardo. 2015. *L'antiziganismo*. Macerata: Quodlibet.

Piccaluga, Maria Grazia. 2017. "La razza non esiste 'Via la parola dalla Costituzione.'" *La Provincia Pavese*, October 12.

Picker, Giovanni. 2017. *Racial Cities: Governance and the Segregation of Romani People in Urban Europe*. London: Routledge.

Pierce, Jennifer L. 2012. *Racing for Innocence: Whiteness, Gender, and the Backlash against Affirmative Action*. Stanford, Calif.: Stanford University Press.

Podestà, Gian Luca. 2014. "Imperio, racismo colonial y antisemitismo." *Pasajes de pensamiento contemporáneo* 44: 48–67.

Pollock, Mica. 2004. *Colormute: Race Talk Dilemmas in an American School*. Princeton, N.J.: Princeton University Press.

Portelli, Alessandro. 1989. "Su alcune forme e articolazioni del discorso razzista nella cultura di massa in Italia." *La Critica Sociologica* 89: 94–97.

Poushter, Jacob, and Janell Fetterolf. 2019. "A Changing World: Global Views on Diversity, Gender Equality, Family Life, and the Importance of Religion." Washington, D.C.: Pew Research Center (April 22).

Povoledo, Elisabetta. 2021. "Netflix to Debut Italy's First TV Show with a Majority Black Cast." *New York Times*, April 16.

Proglio, Gabriele, and Laura Odasso, eds. 2017. *Border Lampedusa: Subjectivity, Visibility, and Memory in Stories of Sea and Land*. London: Palgrave Macmillan.

Quassoli, Fabio. 1999. "Immigrazione uguale criminalità: Rappresentazioni di senso comune e pratiche organizzative degli operatori del diritto." *Rassegna Italiana di Sociologia* 40(1): 43–75.

Quillian, Lincoln. 1995. "Prejudice as a Response to Perceived Group Threat: Population Composition and Anti-immigrant and Racial Prejudice in Europe." *American Sociological Review* 60(4): 586–611.

———. 2006. "New Approaches to Understanding Racial Prejudice and Discrimination." *Annual Review of Sociology* 32: 299–328.

Re, Lucia. 2010. "Italians and the Invention of Race: The Poetics and Politics of Difference in the Struggle over Libya, 1890–1913." *California Italian Studies* 1(1): 1–58.

Reardon, Jenny. 2005. *Race to the Finish: Identity and Governance in an Age of Genomics.* Princeton, N.J.: Princeton University Press.

Reskin, Barbara. 2012. "The Race Discrimination System." *Annual Review of Sociology* 38: 17–35.

Ricci, Laura. 2005. *La lingua dell'impero: Comunicazione, letteratura, e propaganda nell'età del colonialismo italiano.* Rome: Carocci.

Rickards, Olga, and Gianfranco Biondi. 2014. "Un appello per l'abolizione del termine razza." *ScienzainRete*, October 14. https://www.scienzainrete.it/contenuto/articolo /olga-rickards-e-gianfranco-biondi/appello-labolizione-del-termine-razza/ottobre-2 (accessed April 19, 2021).

Rivera, Annamaria. 2014. "Una crisi anche politica e morale: L'Italia tra preferenza nazionale e ritorno della 'razza.'" In *Cronache di ordinario razzismo: Terzo Libro bianco sul razzismo in Italia.* Rome: Lunaria.

Rizzuti, Stefano. 2018. "È ora di togliere la parola razza dalla Costituzione." *Fanpage.it*, February 7.

Roberts, Dorothy. 2011. *Fatal Invention: How Science, Politics, and Big Business Re-Create Race in the Twenty-First Century.* New York: New Press.

Rodríguez-Muñiz, Michael. 2021. *Figures of the Future: Latino Civil Rights and the Politics of Demographic Change.* Princeton, N.J.: Princeton University Press.

Roth, Wendy D. 2018. "Unsettled Identities amid Settled Classifications? Toward a Sociology of Racial Appraisals." *Ethnic and Racial Studies* 41(6): 1093–1112.

Rutherford, Adam. 2020. *How to Argue with a Racist: What Our Genes Do (and Don't) Say about Human Difference.* New York: The Experiment.

Saada, Emmanuelle. 2007. *Les enfants de la colonie: Les métis de l'empire français entre sujétion et citoyenneté.* Paris: La Découverte.

———. 2012. *Empire's Children: Race, Filiation, and Citizenship in the French Colonies.* Chicago: University of Chicago Press.

Sabbagh, Daniel. 2003. *L'egalité par le droit.* Paris: Economica.

———. 2007. *Equality and Transparency: A Strategic Perspective on Affirmative Action in American Law.* New York: Palgrave Macmillan.

Saini, Angela. 2019. *Superior: The Return of Race Science.* Boston: Beacon Press.

Santerini, Milena. 2017. "È possibile eliminare la parola 'razza' dalla Costituzione?" *HuffPost Italia*, October 18.

Scacchi, Anna. 2012. "Negro, nero, di colore, o magari abbronzato: la razza in traduzione." In *Parlare di razza: La lingua del colore tra Italia e Stati Uniti*, edited by Tatiana Petrovich Njegosh and Anna Scacchi. Verona: Ombre Corte.

Scego, Igiaba, ed. 2020. *Future: Il domani narrato dalle voci di oggi.* Florence: Effequ.

Schaeffer, Merlin. 2013. "Which Groups Are Mostly Responsible for Problems in Your Neighbourhood? The Use of Ethnic Categories in Germany." *Ethnic and Racial Studies* 36(1): 156–78.

Schaub, Jean-Frédéric. 2015. *Pour une histoire politique de la race*. Paris: Éditions du Seuil.

Schiebinger, Londa. 1993. *Nature's Body: Gender in the Making of Modern Science*. Boston: Beacon Press.

Schiff, Stacy. 2015. *The Witches: Salem, 1692*. New York: Little, Brown & Co.

Schneider, Jens, Leo Chávez, Louis DeSipio, and Mary Waters. 2012. "Chapter 9: Belonging." In *The Changing Face of World Cities: Young Adult Children of Immigrants in Europe and the United States*, edited by Maurice Crul and John Mollenkopf. New York: Russell Sage Foundation.

Schofield, Janet Ward. 1986. "Causes and Consequences of the Colorblind Perspective." In *Prejudice, Discrimination, and Racism*, edited by John F. Dovidio and Samuel L. Gaertner. Orlando, Fla.: Academic Press.

Schor, Paul. 2009. *Compter et classer: Histoire des recensements américains*. Paris: Éditions de l'École des Hautes Études en Sciences Sociales.

———. 2017. *Counting Americans: How the U.S. Census Classified the Nation*. Oxford: Oxford University Press.

Sears, David O. 1988. "Symbolic Racism." In *Eliminating Racism: Profiles in Controversy*, edited by Phyllis A. Katz and Dalmas A. Taylor. New York: Plenum Press.

Sears, David O., Jim Sidanius, and Lawrence Bobo, eds. 2000. *Racialized Politics: The Debate about Racism in America*. Chicago: University of Chicago Press.

Semyonov, Moshe, Rebecca Raijman, and Anastasia Gorodzeisky. 2006. "The Rise in Anti-Foreigner Sentiment in Europe." *American Sociological Review* 71(3): 426–49.

Senato della Repubblica. Commissione straordinaria per la tutela e la promozione dei diritti umani. 2011. "Rapporto conclusivo dell'indagine sulla condizione di Rom, Sinti e Caminanti in Italia."

Shankar, Shalini. 2019. *Beeline: What Spelling Bees Reveal about Generation Z's New Path to Success*. New York: Basic Books.

Shropshire, Kenneth L. 1996. *In Black and White: Race and Sports in America*. New York: New York University Press.

Sica, Alan, ed. 2006. *Comparative Methods in the Social Sciences*. Thousand Oaks, Calif.: Sage Publications.

Sigona, Nando. 2011. "The Governance of Romani People in Italy: Discourse, Policy, and Practice." *Journal of Modern Italian Studies* 16(5): 590–606.

Silverman, David. 2011. *Interpreting Qualitative Data*. London: Sage Publications.

Silverman, Maxim. 1992. *Deconstructing the Nation: Immigration, Racism and Citizenship in Modern France*. London: Routledge.

Simon, Patrick. 2013. "Collecting Ethnic Statistics in Europe: A Review." In *Accounting for Ethnic and Racial Diversity: The Challenge of Enumeration*, edited by Patrick Simon and Victor Piché. New York: Routledge.

———. 2017. "The Failure of the Importation of Ethno-Racial Statistics in Europe: Debates and Controversies." *Ethnic and Racial Studies* 40(13): 2326–32.

Simon, Patrick, and Martin Clément. 2006. "How Should the Diverse Origins of People Living in France Be Described? AnEexploratory Survey of Employees' and Students' Perceptions." *Population and Societies* 425(July): 1–4.

Sivanandan, A. 1988. "The New Racism." *New Statesman and Society* 1: 8–9.

Skarpelis, Anna. 2021. "Race in Parentheses: Historical Legacies in the Production of Racial Absence." Unpublished manuscript.

Small, Stephen. 1993. "Unravelling Racialised Relations in the United States of America and the United States of Europe." In *Racism and Migration in Western Europe*, edited by John Wrench and John Solomos. Oxford: Berg.

Smedley, Audrey, and Brian Smedley. 2012. *Race in North America: Origin and Evolution of a Worldview.* Boulder, Colo.: Westview Press.

Smith, Anthony. 1991. *National Identity.* London: Penguin.

Sniderman, Paul M., Pierangelo Peri, Rui de Figueiredo, and Thomas Piazza. 2000. *The Outsider: Prejudice and Politics in Italy.* Princeton, N.J.: Princeton University Press.

Sniderman, Paul M., and Thomas Piazza. 1993. *The Scar of Race.* Cambridge, Mass.: Belknap Press of Harvard University Press.

Sniderman, Paul M., Thomas Piazza, Philip E. Tetlock, and Ann Kendrick. 1991. "The New Racism." *American Journal of Political Science* 35(2): 423–47.

Snyder, Timothy. 2021. "The War on History Is a War on Democracy." *New York Times*, June 29.

Soggia, Antonio. 2012. "Razza e politiche sociali negli Stati Uniti e in Italia, 1980–2010." In *Parlare di razza: La lingua del colore tra Italia e Stati Uniti*, edited by Tatiana Petrovich Njegosh and Anna Scacchi. Verona: Ombre Corte.

Solomos, John. 1991. "Political Language and Racial Discourse." *European Journal of Intercultural Studies* 2(1): 21–34.

Solomos, John, and John Wrench. 1993. "Race and Racism in Contemporary Europe." In *Racism and Migration in Western Europe*, edited by John Wrench and John Solomos. Oxford: Berg.

St. Louis, Brett. 2021. "Post-Millennial Local Whiteness: Racialism, White Dis/advantage, and the Denial of Racism." *Ethnic and Racial Studies* 44(3): 355–73.

Stolcke, Verena. 1995. "Talking Culture: New Boundaries, New Rhetorics of Exclusion in Europe." *Current Anthropology* 36(1): 1–24.

Stoler, Ann Laura. 1997. "Racial Histories and Their Regimes of Truth." *Political Power and Social Theory* (symposium on "Rethinking Race") 11: 183–206.

———. 2002. *Carnal Knowledge and Imperial Power: Race and the Intimate in Colonial Rule.* Berkeley: University of California Press.

———. 2011. "Colonial Aphasia: Race and Disabled Histories in France." *Public Culture* 23(1): 121–56.

Strauss, Anselm L. 1987. *Qualitative Analysis for Social Scientists.* Cambridge: Cambridge University Press.

Strauss, Anselm, and Juliet Corbin. 1998. *Basics of Qualitative Research: Techniques and Procedures for Developing Grounded Theory.* Thousand Oaks, Calif.: Sage Publications.

Suk, Julie Chi-hye. 2007. "Equal By Comparison: Unsettling Assumptions of Antidiscrimination Law." *American Journal of Comparative Law* 55(2): 295.

Sulmont, David, and Juan Carlos Callirgos. 2014. "¿El país de todas las sangres? Race and Ethnicity in Contemporary Peru." In *Pigmentocracies: Ethnicity, Race, and Color in Latin America*, edited by Edward Telles and Project on Ethnicity and Race in Latin America (PERLA). Chapel Hill: University of North Carolina Press.

Suzuki, Kazuko. 2017. "A Critical Assessment of Comparative Sociology of Race and Ethnicity." *Sociology of Race and Ethnicity* 3(3): 287–300.

Tabet, Paola. 1997. *La pelle giusta.* Torino: Einaudi.

Taguieff, Pierre-André. 1988. *La force du préjugé: Essai sur le racisme et ses doubles.* Paris: Éditions La Découverte.

Takezawa, Yasuko, ed. 2011. *Racial Representations in Asia.* Kyoto: Kyoto University Press and Trans Pacific Press.

Taylor, Charles. 1985. *Philosophy and the Human Sciences.* New York: Cambridge University Press.

Taylor, Steven J., Robert Bogdan, and Marjorie DeVault. 2015. *Introduction to Qualitative Research Methods: A Guidebook and Resource.* New York: John Wiley & Sons.

Telles, Edward E. 2004. *Race in Another America: The Significance of Skin Color in Brazil.* Princeton, N.J.: Princeton University Press.

Thangaraj, Stanley I. 2015. *Desi Hoop Dreams: Pickup Basketball and the Making of Asian American Masculinity.* New York: New York University Press.

———. 2017. "Danger and Desire: The Black Sporting Body." NYUPress, October 18. https://www.fromthesquare.org/take-a-knee/.

———. 2020. "'I Was Raised a Buddhist': Tiger Woods, Race, and Asian-ness." *Sociology of Sport Journal* 37(1): 27–35.

Timmermans, Stefan, and Iddo Tavory. 2020. "Racist Encounters: A Pragmatist Semiotic Analysis of Interaction." *Sociological Theory* 38(4): 295–317.

Todorov, Tzvetan. 1989. *Nous et les autres: La réflexion française sur la diversité humaine.* Paris: Éditions du Seuil.

Tosi-Cambini, Sabrina. 2008. *La zingara rapitrice: Racconti, denunce, sentenze (1986–2007).* Rome: Centro Informazione Stampa Universitaria (CISU).

Trimbur, Lucia. 2019. "Taking a Knee, Making a Stand: Social Justice, Trump America, and the Politics of Sport." *Quest* 71(2): 252–65.

Twine, France Winddance. 1997. *Racism in a Racial Democracy: The Maintenance of White Supremacy in Brazil.* New Brunswick, N.J.: Rutgers University Press.

United Nations. 2019. "World Urbanization Prospects: The 2018 Revision." New York: United Nations, Department of Economic and Social Affairs, Population Division.

United Nations High Commissioner for Refugees. 2019. "Desperate Journeys: Refugees and Migrants Arriving in Europe and at Europe's Borders (January–December 2018)." https://www.unhcr.org/desperatejourneys/.

U.S. Census Bureau. 2001. "Population by Race and Hispanic or Latino Origin for the United States: 1990 and 2000." PHC-T-1. Washington: U.S. Census Bureau. https://www.census.gov/data/tables/2000/dec/phc-t-01.html.

Valeri, Mauro. 2006. *Black Italians: Atleti neri in maglia azzurra.* Rome: Palombi.

———. 2010. *Che razza di tifo: Dieci anni di razzismo nel calcio italiano.* Rome: Donzelli.

Van den Berghe, Pierre L. 1970. *Race and Ethnicity: Essays in Comparative Sociology.* New York: Basic Books.

Van Sterkenburg, Jacco, Annelies Knoppers, and Sonja de Leeuw. 2010. "Race, Ethnicity, and Content Analysis of the Sports Media: A Critical Reflection." *Media Culture and Society* 32(5): 819–39.

———. 2012. "Constructing Racial/Ethnic Difference in and through Dutch Televised Soccer Commentary." *Journal of Sport and Social Issues* 36(4): 422–42.

Vasta, Ellie. 1993. "Rights and Racism in a New Country of Immigration: The Italian Case." In *Racism and Migration in Western Europe*, edited by John Solomos and John Wrench. Oxford: Berg.

Vertovec, Steven. 2021. "The Social Organization of Difference." *Ethnic and Racial Studies* 44(8): 1273–95.

Vimercati, Daniele. 1990. *I Lombardi alla nuova crociata*. Milan: Mursia.

Vincent, Elise. 2014. "Jeunes, apolitiques, entreprenants: La nouvelle élite noire." *Le Monde*, May 2.

Vitale, Tommaso. 2008. "Politiche locali per i rom e i sinti, fra dinamiche di consenso e effettività eugenetica." In *Biopolitica, bioeconomia, e processi di soggettivazione*, edited by Adalgiso Amendola, Laura Bazzicalupo, Federico Chicchi, and Antonio Tucci. Macerata: Quodlibet.

———. 2009. "Da sempre perseguitati? Effetti di irreversibilità della credenza nella continuità storica dell'antiziganismo." *Zapruder: Storie in Movimento: Rivista di storia della conflittualità sociale* 19: 46–61.

Wacquant, Loïc. 1997. "For an Analytic of Racial Domination." *Political Power and Social Theory* (symposium on "Rethinking Race") 11: 221–34.

Wagley, Charles. 1965. "On the Concept of Social Race in the Americas." In *Contemporary Cultures and Societies in Latin America*, edited by Dwight B. Heath and Richard N. Adams. New York: Random House.

Waters, Mary C. 1990. *Ethnic Options: Choosing Identities in America*. Berkeley: University of California Press.

Weber, Max. 1978. *Economy and Society: An Outline of Interpretive Sociology*. Berkeley: University of California Press. (Originally published in 1956.)

Welch, Rhiannon Noel. 2016. *Vital Subjects: Race and Biopolitics in Italy*. Liverpool: University of Liverpool Press.

White, Jeremy B. 2018. "Most Americans Believe Racism Is Still a Major Problem in Their Society, Survey Finds." *Independent*, May 30.

Whitman, James Q. 2017. *Hitler's American Model: The United States and the Making of Nazi Race Law*. Princeton, N.J.: Princeton University Press.

Wieviorka, Michel. 1992. *La France raciste*. Paris: Éditions du Seuil.

———. 1993. "Tendencies to Racism in Europe: Does France Represent a Unique Case, or Is It Representative of a Trend?" In *Racism and Migration in Western Europe*, edited by John Wrench and John Solomos. Oxford: Berg.

Wilder, Craig Steven. 2013. *Ebony and Ivy: Race, Slavery, and the Troubled History of America's Universities*. New York: Bloomsbury Press.

Wilkerson, Isabel. 2020. *Caste: The Origins of Our Discontents*. New York: Penguin Random House.

Williams, Jack. 2001. *Cricket and Race*. Oxford: Berg.

Wilson, William Julius. 1978. *The Declining Significance of Race: Blacks and Changing American Institutions*. Chicago: University of Chicago Press.

Wimmer, Andreas. 2012. *Ethnic Boundary Making: Institutions, Power, Networks.* Oxford: Oxford University Press.

———. 2015. "Race-centrism: A Critique and a Research Agenda." *Ethnic and Racial Studies* 38(13): 2186–2205.

Winant, Howard. 2007. "The Dark Side of the Force: One Hundred Years of the Sociology of Race." In *Sociology in America: A History,* edited by Craig Calhoun. Chicago: University of Chicago Press.

———. 2015. "Race, Ethnicity, and Social Science." *Ethnic and Racial Studies* 38(13): 2176–85.

Wolf, Eric R. 2010. *Europe and the People without History.* Berkeley: University of Berkeley Press. (Originally published in 1982.)

Wolfe, Patrick. 2001. "Land, Labor, and Difference: Elementary Structures of Race." *American Historical Review* 106(3): 866–905.

Woodward, Alex, and Clark Mindock. 2020. "Taking a Knee: Why Are NFL Players Protesting and When Did They Start to Kneel?" *Independent,* June 9.

Yzerbyt, Vincent Y., Anouk Rogier, and Susan T. Fiske. 1998. "Group Entitativity and Social Attribution: On Translating Situational Constraints into Stereotypes." *Personality and Social Psychology Bulletin* 24(10): 1089–1103.

Zerubavel, Eviatar. 2012. *Ancestors and Relatives: Genealogy, Identity, and Community.* Oxford: Oxford University Press.

———. 2018. *Taken for Granted: The Remarkable Power of the Unremarkable.* Princeton, N.J.: Princeton University Press.

Zhang, Gaoheng. 2013. "Contemporary Italian Novels on Chinese Immigration to Italy." *California Italian Studies* 4: 1–38.

Zuberi, Tukufu. 2001. *Thicker than Blood: How Racial Statistics Lie.* Minneapolis: University of Minnesota Press.

INDEX